Reaching Ou

Assertive outreach is a means of helping people with serious and persistent mental health difficulties who have not engaged with conventional mental health services. *Reaching Out* examines the application of psychological approaches in assertive outreach – a process which involves forming new relationships and offering hope to people who have been alienated from traditional methods.

Reaching Out begins with a discussion of topics including:

- engagement
- the team approach
- assessments
- team case formulation
- managing stress and burnout for staff.

The second half of the book focuses on the task of delivering psychological therapies and considers a range of models including psychodynamic therapy, family therapy, cognitive behaviour therapy and community approaches.

Reaching Out: the psychology of assertive outreach demonstrates that the relationship between staff and service users is essential to the process of recovery and personal growth. The approach will apply not only to assertive outreach teams, but also to clinical psychologists, counsellors and other mental health professionals who are interested in psychological approaches to outreach work.

Caroline Cupitt is a consultant clinical psychologist with Oxleas NHS Foundation Trust specialising in assertive outreach. She has worked in assertive outreach since 1996, in both statutory and non-statutory settings, and is particularly interested in fostering psychological approaches.

Reaching Out
The psychology of assertive outreach

Edited by Caroline Cupitt

Routledge
Taylor & Francis
LONDON AND NEW

First published 2010
by Routledge
27 Church Road, Hove, East Sussex BN3 2FA

Simultaneously published in the USA and Canada
by Routledge
270 Madison Avenue, New York, NY 10016

*Routledge is an imprint of the Taylor & Francis Group,
an Informa business*

© 2010 Selection and editorial matter, Caroline Cupitt;
individual chapters, the contributors.

Typeset in Times New Roman by
RefineCatch Limited, Bungay, Suffolk
Printed and bound in Great Britain by
TJ International Ltd, Padstow, Cornwall
Paperback cover design by Lisa Dynan

This publication has been produced with paper manufactured to strict
environmental standards and with pulp derived from sustainable
forests.

British Library Cataloguing in Publication Data
A catalogue record for this book is available from the British Library

Library of Congress Cataloging in Publication Data
A catalogue record for this book has been requested

ISBN 978–0–415–45406–3 (hbk)
ISBN 978–0–415–45407–0 (pbk)

Contents

Figures

Tables

Contributors

Caroline Cupitt is a Consultant Clinical Psychologist with Oxleas NHS Foundation Trust, specialising in assertive outreach. She has worked in assertive outreach since 1996, in both statutory and non-statutory settings, and is particularly interested in fostering psychological approaches.

Bob Diamond is a Clinical Psychologist working for Nottinghamshire Healthcare NHS Trust, interested in applying concepts and practice from critical and community psychology to services for people with enduring mental health difficulties.

Morna Gillespie has worked in assertive outreach since 2002 for Birmingham and Solihull Mental Health NHS Foundation Trust. She has a specific interest in engagement, both developing an evidence base through research and translating this into clinical practice through training of assertive outreach staff.

Alf Gillham is a Consultant Clinical Psychologist in psychiatric rehabilitation at Leverndale Hospital, South Glasgow. He previously worked in the Assertive Outreach Team for South Glasgow. He is also an Honorary Senior Lecturer at the Department of Psychological Medicine, Glasgow University.

Inger Gordon is a Systemic Psychotherapist and supervisor engaged in the public and private sectors. She works for Sussex Partnership NHS Foundation Trust in adult services as a couple/family therapist and teaches the MSc in systemic psychotherapy at Kensington Consultation Centre.

Abi Gray is a Clinical Psychologist with Sussex Partnership NHS Foundation Trust, working with Brighton and Hove Assertive Outreach Team. She has a particular interest in helping staff teams use psychological formulations to deliver interventions rooted in a psychosocial approach, in addition to working therapeutically with individuals with a diagnosis of schizophrenia.

Lucy Hickey is a Clinical Psychologist with Oxleas Foundation NHS Trust. She has worked in the Greenwich Assertive Outreach Team since 2003 and is particularly interested in applying systemic and psychodynamic ideas in this setting.

Paul Johanson is a Social Worker by background and was formerly team manager for Brighton and Hove Assertive Outreach Team. He is currently the Improving Access to Psychological Therapies (IAPT) Programme Manager for South East Coastal SHA.

Andrew Law is Operations Director at Tulip Mental Health Group and has over 20 years' experience in Health and Social Care. He has an MSc in psychodynamic practice from Middlesex University, Tavistock Clinic and from 1994 managed outreach services for Tulip Mental Health Group.

Alan Meaden is a Consultant Specialist Clinical Psychologist in rehabilitation working for Birmingham and Solihull Mental Health NHS Foundation Trust. He has worked in assertive outreach since 1996 and has a particular interest in assessment and engagement research and practice.

Sara Meddings is a Consultant Clinical Psychologist with Sussex Partnership NHS Foundation Trust. She has been working in assertive outreach since 1996 and is especially interested in developing user involvement and recovery oriented services. She is a family therapy practitioner and accredited cognitive behavioural therapist.

Alison Mulligan is a Clinical Psychologist with Oxleas NHS Foundation Trust. She has worked within assertive outreach in South East London since 2002 and has a particular interest in attachment theory, Cognitive Behaviour Therapy and psychosis.

Debbie Owen is a Community Mental Health Nurse with Sussex Partnership NHS Foundation Trust working in assertive outreach. She has worked in assertive outreach since 2000 and has developed a role specialising in work with families and carers.

Becky Shaw is a fellow of the Institute of Mental Health. She has used and worked voluntarily in the mental health services for 16 years. She teaches, researches and runs a self-help group. She is currently leading a project about crisis resolution and home treatment teams.

Stuart Whomsley is a Clinical Psychologist with Cambridgeshire and Peterborough NHS Foundation Trust who has worked in assertive outreach since 2002, in both city and rural areas. For five years he has been developing Team Case Formulations. He uses CBT, systemic and community psychology approaches in his work.

Acknowledgements

We would like to acknowledge the contribution of all those who have participated in meetings of the Network of Psychologists in Assertive Outreach over the last few years. The idea for this book and its development owes much to the lively discussions at these meetings.

As editor, I would like to thank David Hutchens for his help and support during the process of collating this book.

Introduction

Caroline Cupitt

Assertive outreach has become a common term within mental health services, used both to describe a specific team and a style of working. Dedicated Assertive Outreach Teams have been part of UK government policy since 1999, and during this time a distinctive British model of assertive outreach has begun to develop. One aspect of this is the integration of psychological approaches, resulting in more holistic services and new roles for psychological therapists. The application of psychological approaches to assertive outreach is the subject of this book.

What is assertive outreach?

Assertive outreach can go by a variety of synonyms, such as Assertive Community Treatment (ACT), Active Community Treatment or Intensive Support. However, a number of key features are required for these teams to meet the accepted definition (Department of Health, 2001). Using self-assessment, the Durham Mapping exercise of 2005 found there were 278 teams in the UK. This number has probably fallen slightly since that time, as the NHS financial crisis of 2006–7 forced some teams to close.

These teams serve a very specific population. Their clients are adults with severe and persistent mental health difficulties associated with a high level of disability. Characteristically they will also have frequently been admitted to hospital under the Mental Health Act, have multiple complex social problems, for example with street drugs, homelessness or the criminal justice system, and have a history of loss of contact with mental health services. They are the group of people staff worry most about, and yet also have the most difficulty maintaining contact with. They frequently dislike mental health services, are alienated from wider society and struggle on alone (Lukeman, 2003).

Reaching out and forming supportive relationships with this group of people is not easy. It requires a very different approach from what has gone before. To simply provide a conventional mental health service more assert-ively is unlikely to be very successful and could be thought to be unethical. So from its earliest beginnings, assertive outreach services have sought to provide something different: the sort of service which people would want and value (e.g. Sainsbury Centre for Mental Health, 1998). Early in the development of assertive outreach in the UK, several of the pioneers met to agree a shared definition of what they were trying to offer.

> Assertive outreach is a *flexible* and *creative* client-centred approach to engaging service users in a *practical* delivery of a wide range of services to meet complex health and social *needs and wants*. It is a strategy that requires the service providers to take an *active* role, working with service users, to secure resources and *choices* in treatment, rehabilitation, psychosocial support, functional and practical help, and advocacy . . . in equal priorities.
>
> (Joint Statement by SCMH, CMHSD, IMPACT, TULIP,
> North Birmingham AO Service, Kush Housing Association,
> The Working Together in London Initiative, 1999)

The psychology of assertive outreach

Assertive outreach was originally conceived of as a radical departure from conventional methods of providing mental health services, and psychosocial approaches have also always been part of the model (Stein and Santos, 1998). Over time the case for including psychological therapies has only got stronger, as the evidence base for psychological therapies for psychosis and complex mental health difficulties has increased (e.g. NICE, 2002). Psychological therapies are almost always highlighted in service user and carer surveys as the most wished for, but absent, aspect of treatment (Bird, 2006) so any service wishing to respond both to people's needs and wants must provide them.

Although a difficulty with engagement has not always been a key referral criterion for Assertive Outreach Teams, it has become so in the UK over the last ten years. For UK teams therefore the primary task is a psychological one: to build a supportive relationship through which all other interventions can be delivered. It is about offering hope to people who have often become alienated and disenfranchised. This is no easy task, and we will argue that considerable psychological expertise is needed within the team both to understand and to break through the isolation of people's lives.

Over the last 30 years, assertive outreach has continually developed in response to context, both of the different countries to which it has spread, and changes in policy within those countries. In the UK we have perhaps been particularly fortunate in experiencing a renaissance of interest in psychological therapies for psychosis and complex mental health difficulties over roughly the same time period.

The origins of assertive outreach

Assertive outreach is normally said to have begun in the 1970s when Leonard Stein and Ann Test created Training in Community Living (TCL) in

Madison, Wisconsin (Stein and Test, 1980). It is of course possible to find earlier examples of similar ideas, but TCL is of particular interest because it gained widespread recognition.

The deinstitutionalisation movement of the 1950s and 1960s in the USA had led to the development of community-based mental health services, but Stein and Test observed that people with severe and disabling mental health problems were finding the complex network of community care harder to access than the old institutions. Many did not seek out community care themselves and as a result ended up regularly admitted to hospital. They noted that there was a misconception about the kinds and extent of help people needed, and that many people rapidly dropped out of day care with no or few active attempts made to reinvolve them.

These two observations inspired them to create a very different kind of service, one which reconceptualised services and interventions, reorganised delivery of these services, and aimed to enable people commonly hospitalised to live in the community. This approach was originally offered to a relatively unselected, diagnostically mixed group of people as an alternative to hospital admission. They were not particularly difficult to engage, but had never before been offered a comprehensive community service.

It is easy with hindsight to overlook the radical nature of the TCL project. At that time in the US there were no integrated community mental health teams, such as we now take for granted in the UK. What is more, TCL dramatically raised the importance of practical and social support. As its name suggests, it sought to provide the kind of service people would want to engage with in order to live independently outside hospital and achieve their goals in life.

The key features of TCL were:

- multi-disciplinary: psychiatrist, nurses and social workers
- low client to staff ratio, normally 10:1
- offered to a broad group of clients who live independently
- support and education to others involved with clients
- services delivered in the community rather than office
- large amount of practical support in daily living
- assertive efforts to prevent clients dropping out of care
- caseload shared across the team
- 24-hour cover
- most services provided in-house, ensuring integrated clinical management (no separation between treatment and rehabilitation)
- service time unlimited (because effects cease when assertive outreach ceases)
- growth orientation, focusing on employment and psychological change.

The emphasis on growth and psychological change was in itself a radical step. One of the originators of the model, Ann Test, was a psychologist and her colleague, the psychiatrist Leonard Stein, had been influenced by radical anti-biological accounts of mental illness (Stein and Santos, 1998). They wanted TCL to have a psychosocial orientation that prioritised behaviour change, the formation of community relationships and vocational opportunity. This therapeutic approach was embedded in the team's overall philosophy. In Stein and Test (1980: 393) it is suggested that what people needed was 'freedom from pathologically dependent relationships', particularly with families and institutions. It is suggested that 'community programs must provide sufficient support to keep the patient involved in community life and encourage growth toward greater autonomy' (ibid.). To deliver the service, they retrained a typical mental hospital ward team, comprising a psychiatrist, psychologist, social worker, occupational therapist, nurses and aides (Stein and Test, 1979). They were able to use principles of behaviour modification, rehabilitation and social skills training, which were the accepted psychological approaches to psychosis and complex mental health problems of the time.

Ten years later, Test (1992: 157) describes TCL as offering 'direct assistance with symptom management' using psychological approaches. She notes that this includes 'enhancing their own coping strategies for dealing with serious symptoms'. She acknowledges that this intervention was not present in the original model, but by 1992 had become part of their ongoing program. It appears that this was being delivered by all staff, rather than a trained psychological therapist within the team. So we can assume that the team was offering people skills-based psychological interventions rather than formal psychological therapies. This approach continues to this day in many Assertive Outreach Teams.

Psychological skills, or psychological therapy?

To understand the development of psychological approaches in assertive outreach, it is helpful to make a clear distinction between skills-based psychological interventions and formal psychological therapies. This distinction has become increasingly important in recent years with the expansion of Cognitive Behaviour Therapy (CBT) into the field of psychosis and complex mental heath. We now have not just the possibility of a team taking a psychosocial approach, but of specialist staff who can offer formal psychotherapy based on an individual psychological formulation.

There continues to be a range of psychological skills which can be used by staff within community mental health teams. Team members often practise these skills after attending short training courses, supported by local supervision arrangements. Typically, this might include such interventions as coping strategy enhancement (Tarrier *et al.*, 1990). These CBT skills can be used to address someone's distress, in the absence of a psychological formulation. However, for people with very complex mental health difficulties, they may not work because of the interrelationships between symptoms, or deeper psychological needs. In these circumstances a psychological formulation is needed as part of a more formal therapeutic approach that seeks to understand the relationship between many different aspects of the person's life experience. Such a psychological formulation is always individual to the person concerned, and it may draw on a number of psychological theories. This is a more highly skilled task and staff need to have had substantial training, leading to accreditation as psychological therapists and to receive ongoing regular supervision (Grazebrook and Garland, 2005).

These two levels of skill are both needed within teams, and complement rather than compete with each other. However, the provision of formulation-based psychological therapies is only possible when teams have a trained psychological therapist on their staff, normally a clinical psychologist. Unfortunately, many services for people with psychosis, including many Assertive Outreach Teams, still have only skills-based interventions available to their clients.

Assertive Community Treatment

Over time TCL transformed into Assertive Community Treatment (ACT) and the Programme for Assertive Community Treatment (PACT) standards (Allness and Knoedler, 2003) have come to define ACT in the USA. These specify that teams must have a psychiatrist, nursing staff and a vocational specialist. However, staff with distinct psychological skills are considered desirable rather than essential, and include staff with a variety of qualifications in such areas as rehabilitation counselling, psychology and behavioural science. Thus, whilst the standards aim to promote a biopsychosocial approach, they do not require teams to have a member of staff whose clear remit is to promote psychological approaches. Staff with expertise in psychological therapies are viewed as non-essential and it is therefore unlikely that teams could routinely offer formal psychological therapies. This neglect of psychological therapies within ACT has caused the model to drift away from its original psychosocial philosophy of care, and, in the UK at least, it is now often perceived to promote a medical model. This was reflected in the Pan London Assertive Outreach Study (Wright *et al.*, 2003) which asked Assertive Outreach Teams in London to identify their team philosophy. Two-thirds described themselves as taking a largely medical approach and only one-third described taking a social inclusion approach. Thus only a minority of teams identified with Stein and Test's original philosophy of care. This shift has occurred despite the promotion of explicitly psychosocial models of assertive outreach, such as the Strengths Approach (Ryan and Morgan, 2004). These issues, however, are not new. Bond *et al.* (1991) describe four dimensions by which assertive outreach programmes often show variation: growth-orientation vs. survival orientation, population served, team vs. individual caseload approaches and short- vs. long-term approaches. They identify 'program drift' as a major cause of variation in assertive outreach, which may arise from either planned innovations or unplanned implementation problems.

Another influential publication has been the Dartmouth Assertive Community Treatment Scale (DACTS; Teague *et al.*, 1998), which sought to operationally define and measure the critical dimensions of ACT, drawing not just on the PACT standards, but a wide range of current literature and expert opinion. This also does not require teams to have a psychologist, and interestingly neither does the DACTS-UK (Freeman and Brooker, 2001), a version said to be specifically adapted for the UK.

Perhaps this failure to view psychological therapists as essential in ACT relates to the time and place of its origin. During the early years of ACT development, psychologists themselves did not demonstrate much interest in people with severe mental health difficulties (Stein and Test, 1979; Bond *et al.*, 1991). They were probably difficult to recruit and expensive to employ. In addition, perhaps the most relevant development in psychological therapies has been the application of Cognitive Behaviour Therapy to psychosis, which has largely occurred in the UK. Even in the UK, CBT has only recently been thought of as an essential part of community mental health services (NICE, 2002). The importance of psychological therapies in assertive outreach is perhaps only now becoming apparent.

UK assertive outreach policy

In the UK, assertive outreach services became widespread following their inclusion in *The National Service Framework for Mental Health* (Department of Health, 1999: 47).

> Assertive outreach or assertive community treatment is a form of intensive case management that provides a clinically effective approach to managing the care of severely mentally ill people in the community. Staff providing comprehensive assertive outreach care for clients will visit them at home, act as an advocate, and liaise with other services such as the GP or social services. Help is usually needed to find housing, secure an adequate income, and sustain basic daily living – shopping, cooking, and washing, for example. Opinion varies about the optimum staff–client ratio for assertive outreach. In some settings the ratio is a low as 1:12.
>
> Assertive outreach can establish a more stable community base, and reduce time spent in hospital. Of 23 controlled studies, 61 per cent reported significant reductions in hospital admissions. It is particularly useful for individuals with whom it is hard to sustain contact.

This was quickly followed by the more detailed *NHS Plan* (DoH, 2000). However, it wasn't until 2001 that the UK government clearly defined what they meant by assertive outreach, which appeared as a detailed service specification in *The Mental Health Policy Implementation Guide* (DoH, 2001). For the first time a psychologist was said to be an essential member of the team, and CBT was listed amongst the key interventions the team was to offer. This represented a major step forward, an incorporation into the UK model of the emerging and compelling evidence in favour of CBT approaches, which would later appear in many NICE guidelines (e.g. NICE, 2002). It was also a recognition that at least one member of staff should have high-level therapy skills, rather than relying on the generic psychological skills of all staff. Developing psychology posts in Assertive Outreach Teams finally had some impetus (Cupitt, 2001).

The promotion of psychological approaches by *The Mental Health Policy Implementation Guide* seems to be very much in the spirit of the original aims of TCL. It brings up to date a model that always sought to offer a psychotherapeutic approach. Unfortunately, however, the requirement on teams to have a psychology post has not always been adopted and the last survey, the National Study of Assertive Outreach, which looked at 233 teams nationally in 2004/5, found that only about a quarter of Assertive Outreach Teams actually had a psychology post, resulting in an estimated 70 UK assertive outreach clinical psychologists (Wright, 2005, 2006).

In part this deficit represents difficulties in recruitment. Psychology posts in Assertive Outreach Teams are certainly not always easy to fill. In 1999 most clinical psychology training courses did not teach or offer placements in assertive outreach and few psychologists wished to take posts in teams which they knew so little about. However, that can no longer be said to be the case. It is now quite possible to recruit a newly qualified psychologist who already has experience of assertive outreach, and consensus is emerging about the roles they should take (Young, 2008).

Another barrier has been the continuing assumption that staff with skills in psychosocial interventions, for example from Thorn courses, can meet all the psychological needs of Assertive Outreach Teams (e.g. Burns and Firn, 2002). Many teams continue to be influenced by the ACT standards, which give the impression that a psychologist is non-essential. They cite this model as the one supported by research evidence. However, the US studies certainly do not demonstrate that it is unnecessary to consider a psychologist to be an essential member of the team – they simply don't address the question at all. In fact the effectiveness of individual components of ACT services has rarely been investigated. As yet there is no evidence either way, to suggest whether psychological therapies are an effective or ineffective component of ACT. What we do know is that they are an effective intervention for people with psychosis, and since psychosis is the predominant mental health problem for clients of assertive outreach, it is logical to include them.

However, the provision of evidence-based psychological therapies within assertive outreach is still far from a reality. The National Study of Assertive Outreach found that although 80 per cent of teams said they could provide some psychological interventions, only 20 per cent could do so within a specified model (Wright, 2005, 2006). In other words, the vast majority of teams were not able to provide formal psychological therapies, by people familiar with their theoretical basis. Given the current push for evidence-based practice, this does not seem to be good enough.

Our collective experience, as clinical psychologists working in Assertive Outreach Teams, has taught us that the presence of a member of staff fully qualified to deliver formal psychological therapies is an essential prerequisite for a team to be able to provide high-quality psychological interventions at all levels. The presence of a psychology post within a team can profoundly influence the work of the whole team, as this book aims to demonstrate. For this reason we view a psychology post as an essential component of assertive outreach if it is to meet the original aspirations to provide a truly psycho-social approach to care. Many aspects of the original TCL model, such as the use of a team approach, have a psychological function which can be supported and developed when there is a psychologist working within the team.

What is more, we would assert that a wide range of psychological models and therapies are relevant to assertive outreach clients. If an Assertive Outreach Team aspires to respond to people's wants as well as their needs, a range of therapeutic approaches is required, to provide the necessary choice and flexibility. Whilst CBT currently stands in high favour, we have found other models can also be effective. We would like to introduce the reader to a range of psychological models and their application to assertive outreach services.

This book is the first of its kind to examine the psychological processes involved in assertive outreach. Previously some of us attempted to define and describe the role of psychologists in Assertive Outreach Teams in a briefing paper for the British Psychological Society (Cupitt *et al.*, 2006). However, this book goes much further, in trying to look both at the psychological processes involved in the overall service as well as how to deliver specific psychological therapies. In developing our ideas we have benefited from the regular meetings of the Network of Psychologists in Assertive Outreach, which has provided a forum for us to meet and exchange ideas. In fact, the idea for this book originated at one of these meetings. However, we hope that much of what we say will have relevance well beyond the scope of Assertive Outreach Teams per se, and influence the development of psychological approaches in many other kinds of teams.

The first half of the book outlines a psychological approach to the task of assertive outreach, beginning with the primary task of engaging service users. Despite the centrality of the concept of engagement to assertive outreach, its theorising and research has been neglected until very recently, and we consider this in chapter one. Engagement is generally achieved by use of a team approach in which every member of staff forms a relationship with each service user, as described in chapter two. This way of working provides a rich source of knowledge and the opportunity for the team as a whole to come to a psychological understanding of the person's difficulties. The use of such strategies can bring about a healing of their relationship with services, and indeed within their wider social network. To demonstrate this change, both to commissioners and service users, teams need to undertake careful assessment and outcome measurement. For this to be meaningful the tools must be carefully chosen and chapter three is devoted to exploring the different approaches available. In chapter four the way all this knowledge is brought together is described in terms of team case formulation, often facilitated by psychologists, but capable of drawing on many models of mental distress. Finally, in chapter five the issue of stress and burnout for staff is addressed, one which can be managed by effective and psychologically minded team working.

The second half of the book is devoted to the task of delivering psychological therapies. The main relevant models of psychological therapy are considered, beginning with chapter six, where insights from psycho-dynamic therapy about the process of forming therapeutic relationships with people experiencing psychosis are explored. Chapter seven considers the importance of working with families and the wider social system in which people live, often to support relationships that have been under great strain. The current enthusiasm to provide Cognitive Behavioural Therapies in assertive outreach can meet with many obstacles, and some of the practical implications for delivering Cognitive Behavioural Therapies are discussed in chapter eight. All forms of individual therapy, however, have their limits, and in chapter nine the alternative perspective of community psychology is explored, and some examples of its use in assertive outreach discussed.

Each chapter is written by a psychologist who has extensive experience of practising within an Assertive Outreach Team. Some have chosen to write in collaboration with colleagues from other perspectives to enrich the process, in rather the same way as they work within Assertive Outreach Teams themselves. They are familiar with the real-life adaptations required to make psychological therapies effective in an assertive outreach service. These may concern adopting a more informal therapeutic stance or setting, or they may mean that the process of therapy itself is less formally structured. In many cases these adaptations reflect the need to start from a different point. Our clients often do not seek out psychological therapies themselves and may need a lot of information and support to make an informed choice about their possible benefit. Many could be said to be within a pre-contemplative stage of change (Prochaska and DiClemente, 1982) requiring therapists to adapt their stance and methods. In making such adaptations therapists need to be very aware of the resulting ethical issues, and the implications for professional boundaries. These issues are discussed in depth in chapter ten.

References

Allness, D.J. and Knoedler, W.H. (2003) 'National Program Standards for ACT Teams', a companion document to *A Manual for ACT Start-Up*, Arlington, VA: The National Alliance for the Mentally Ill.

Bird, A. (2006) *We Need to Talk: the case for psychological therapies on the NHS*, London: The Mental Health Foundation.

Bond, G., Witheridge, T.F., Dincin, J. and Wasmer, D. (1991) 'Assertive Community Treatment: correcting some misconceptions', *American Journal of Community Psychology*, 19: 41–51.

Burns, T. and Firn, M. (2002) *Assertive Outreach in Mental Health: a manual for practitioners*, Oxford: Oxford University Press.

Cupitt, C. (2001) 'Developing psychology posts in Assertive Outreach', *Clinical Psychology Forum*, 5: 48–50.

Cupitt, C., Meddings, S., Amphlett, C. and Thomas, M. (2006) *Clinical Psychologists and Assertive Outreach*, Psychosis and Complex Mental Health Faculty Briefing Paper No. 21, Leicester: British Psychological Society.

Department of Health (1999) *The National Service Framework for Mental Health: modern standards and service models*, London: Department of Health.

Department of Health (2000) *The NHS Plan*, London: Department of Health.

Department of Health (2001) *The Mental Health Policy Implementation Guide*, London: Department of Health.

Freeman, J. and Brooker, C. (2001) *The Dartmouth Assertive Community Treatment Scale – UK adapted version*, Sheffield: The University of Sheffield.

Grazebrook, K. and Garland, A. (2005) 'What are Cognitive and/or Behavioural Psychotherapies?', paper prepared for a UKCP/BABCP mapping psychotherapy exercise, British Association for Behavioural and Cognitive Psychotherapies, July.

Lukeman, R. (2003) 'Service Users' experience of the process of being engaged by assertive outreach teams', unpublished thesis, Salomons, Canterbury Christ Church University.

National Institute for Clinical Excellence (2002) *Schizophrenia: core interventions in the treatment and management of schizophrenia in primary and secondary care*, London: NICE.

Prochaska, J.O. and DiClemente, C.C. (1982) 'Transtheoretical therapy: toward a more integrative model of change', *Psychotherapy: Theory Research and Practice*, 19: 276–288.

Ryan, P. and Morgan, S. (2004) *Assertive Outreach: a strengths approach to policy and practice*, Edinburgh: Churchill Livingstone.

Sainsbury Centre for Mental Health (1998) *Keys to Engagement: a review of care for people with severe mental illness who are hard to engage with services*, London: Sainsbury Centre for Mental Health.

Stein, L.I. and Santos, A.B. (1998) *Assertive Community Treatment of Persons with Severe Mental Illness*, New York: WW Norton and Company Inc.

Stein, L.I. and Test, M. (1979) 'From the hospital to the community: a shift in the primary locus of care', *New Directions for Mental Health Services*, 1: 15–32.

Stein, L.I. and Test, M. (1980) 'An alternative to mental hospital treatment: conceptual model, treatment model and clinical evaluation', *Archives of General Psychiatry*, 37: 392–397.

Tarrier, N., Harwood, S., Yusupoff, L., Beckett, R. and Baker, A. (1990) 'Coping strategy enhancement (CSE): a method of treating residual schizophrenic symptoms', *Behavioural Psychotherapy*, 18: 283–293.

Teague, G.B., Bond, G.R. and Drake, R.E. (1998) 'Program fidelity in Assertive Community Treatment: development and use of a measure', *American Journal of Orthopsychiatry*, 68: 216–232.

Test, M. (1992) 'Training in community living', in R. Liberman (ed.) *Handbook of Psychiatric Rehabilitation*, London: Macmillan.

Wright, C. (2005) 'Assertive Outreach – what's really going on in England?', workshop presented at the annual conference of the National Forum for Assertive Outreach, Keele University, April.

Wright, C. (2006) 'The National Assertive Outreach Study', presentation to the Network of Psychologists in Assertive Outreach meeting, London, December.

Wright, C., Burns, T., James, P., Billings, J., Johnson, S., Muijen, M,. Priebe, S., Ryrie, I., Watts, J. and White, I. (2003) 'Assertive outreach teams in London: models of operation', *British Journal of Psychiatry*, 183: 132–138.

Young, L. (2008) 'A multidisciplinary Delphi survey of clinical psychologists in assertive outreach teams: perceptions of their roles, contributions and clinical psychologists' experiences', unpublished thesis, Salomons, Canterbury Christ Church University.

Part I

Taking a psychological approach

1 Psychological processes in engagement

Morna Gillespie and Alan Meaden

Engagement can be seen as a stand-alone intervention as well as a central vehicle for the delivery of other interventions (McCabe and Priebe, 2004; The Sainsbury Centre for Mental Health, 1998). Placing engagement in such a prominent position necessitates first establishing a clear understanding of what we mean by the term, before examining the factors that affect it and the development of tools for measuring it.

Defining engagement: Alliance, Compliance or Participation?

Any definition of engagement must address how individuals view important relationships, how open they are to treatment and how useful they consider it to be. These three concepts are often referred to as Therapeutic Alliance, Compliance (usually with medication) and Participation; all of which are used synonymously with the term 'engagement'.

Within psychiatry, the term 'engagement' can mean medication compliance, attendance at appointments or a collaborative involvement in a therapeutic relationship (Catty, 2004). The latter most closely matches the concept of therapeutic alliance as defined by Bordin (1979). This theoretical perspective has the best fit with multi-disciplinary disciplinary team case management. Bordin's pan-theoretical model has three components: Goals (agreed-upon outcomes), Tasks (mutually accepted responsibilities of client and clinician to achieve goals) and Bonds (relationships between client and clinician, including trust, acceptance and confidence). Viewing engagement in this way clearly defines it as a process concerned with the individual and how they view their relationships with clinicians and important others.

This concept alone, however, is not adequate to capture fully all the processes involved in engaging service users in Assertive Outreach Teams. Catty (2004) notes the complexity of applying the construct of therapeutic alliance in a context where increased contact may not equate with a stronger alliance. In such circumstances the opposite may be true and service users may feel intruded upon by repeated attempts to make contact with them, weakening therapeutic alliance. Subsequent poor engagement may lead clinicians to increase their efforts to make contact, thus compromising therapeutic alliance still further. In order to be meaningful in assertive outreach settings, the concept of engagement may therefore need to be more broadly defined in order to encompass how the process relates to the service, its goals and ways of working.

The term 'compliance' has often been taken to mean engagement and is a well-established term within the treatment literature. May (1974) first described it as 'the extent to which a person's behaviour (in terms of taking medications, following diets, or executing lifestyle changes) coincides with medical or health advice' (as reported by Haynes (1979); cited in Blackwell, 1997: 5). McPhillips and Sensky (1998) perceive compliance to be the passive acceptance of clinician advice by the client, while adherence is characterised by clients having a more active, collaborative role. Although adherence through collaboration is more desirable, they acknowledge that to some extent compliance cannot be completely abandoned when working with clients with severe and enduring mental illness. Such approaches may be seen as closely allied with the supportive psychotherapy tradition with expected and pre-scribed roles for patient and clinician (Parsons, 1951).

Interestingly, Compliance Therapy (Kemp, Kirov, Everitt, Hayward and David, 1998) itself encourages a collaborative weighing up of the costs and benefits of taking medication and is only likely to be effective if the person themselves has a free and informed choice or is motivated to take their medication. Compliance can be seen as paternalistic and undermining of empowerment whilst informed choice embodies active participation (Fisher, 1997). A service where the emphasis is too focused upon compliance may create an imbalance in the power relationship between client and clinician, encouraging overly active, even aggressive interventions, coupled with pas-sive, submissive responses. Undoubtedly, however, the concept remains of importance to clinicians, and indeed policy makers, and features in many current measures of engagement as one or more items. We may usefully consider compliance as a core feature of engagement, reflecting service goals, but one that should be embedded within a broader collaborative process that promotes choice.

The concept of Participation attempts to provide an overarching frame-work, both encompassing broad service goals (attendance, engagement, termination of treatment, non-compliance and involvement in outpatient mental health settings), and a much more dynamic process, with clients actively involved in a treatment partnership, (Kazdin, Holland, and Crowley, 1997). This can best be seen in the two-dimensional model proposed by Littell, Alexander and Reynolds (2001) (see Figure 1.1).

This framework allows attitudes and behaviours to be perceived and cat-egorised differently by clients and clinicians. This is a dynamic process, influ-enced by client beliefs, goals, external constraints and experience of services. These in turn are influenced by clinicians, settings, and social and cultural factors. A relationship that is positive and collaborative is seen as the best way of managing these complex influences. The way in which individuals view

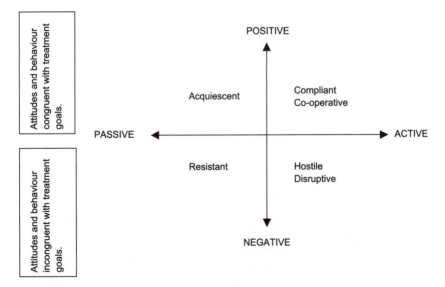

Figure 1.1 A framework for participation (adapted by permission from Littell, Alexander and Reynolds, 2001)

these relationships, in other words the therapeutic alliance, is fundamental and likely to facilitate the successful delivery of interventions. The participation framework is clearly helpful in emphasising both the dynamic aspects of engagement and the centrality of the therapeutic relationship.

The concepts of Therapeutic Alliance, Compliance and Participation all help us to define what we mean by the term 'engagement' and how it relates to individuals and services. However, most research in this area has focused on clinician- or researcher-defined perspectives regarding what is important and relevant. The perspectives of clients and carers, who may similarly be poorly engaged with services, are equally valid.

Service user and carer perspectives

Qualitative studies exploring service user experiences (e.g. Priebe, Watts, Chase and Matanov, 2005; Bradley, Meaden, Tudway, Earl-Gray, Jones, Giles and Wane, in submission; Lukeman, 2003) reveal the following themes as important determinants of how service users engage with services:

- feeling in control
- a sense of being autonomous
- feeling enabled
- active participation
- time and commitment
- social support without a focus on medication

- a partnership model of therapeutic relationships: feeling equal, valued and heard
- being listened to
- being treated as an individual
- staff being interested and respectful
- gradualness
- consistency
- practical help
- clinical help.

These themes suggest that good engagement is fostered when there is a respectful enabling partnership that offers time, understanding and support. These factors help clients move from viewing assertive outreach as a service which has been imposed on them, to one that they can work with collaboratively (Lukeman, 2003). Gillespie, Smith, Meaden, Jones and Wane (2004) found that clients and clinicians rated the importance of items on the Engagement Measure (Hall, Meaden, Smith and Jones, 2001) differently, although there was some overlap. For example, clients who perceived their treatment as useful were rated as well engaged by staff, but not necessarily by clients themselves. Clients and staff agreed more on items which measured discussing personal feelings, active involvement with treatment and attending appointments.

In attempting to resolve conceptual issues and apparent differences between clinicians and clients as to what factors should constitute engagement, engagement can best be seen as a multi-dimensional process:

> . . . not only referring to the initial stage of interest formation, but to the development of trust and rapport and ongoing involvement in interventions. It is more than attendance and retention, concerning not only the quantity but also the quality of interactions. Engagement is influenced by past experiences, current perceptions and future expectations. It is a process where clients are actively involved in collaboration and participation; it is not compliance and adherence to pre-determined service defined goals, or passive perfunctory pro-forma involvement.
>
> (Bradley *et al.*, submitted)

Example:
Michael is 29 years old and has been with the Assertive Outreach Team for two years. He is an active member of the Mental Health Trust's football team and has played with them abroad, saving and paying for this trip himself. He takes his medication sporadically as it makes him put on weight and affects his sexual performance. He also smokes cannabis on a regular basis, even though it can make him paranoid, as he sees it as a way of socialising. Michael is reluctant to attend appointments with his psychiatrist as the psychiatrist tries to persuade Michael to take his

medication regularly and to reduce his cannabis use. Michael, however, has engaged well with his care co-ordinator and openly discusses his mental health problems and any worries that he has. Michael is working with his care co-ordinator to secure some voluntary work in painting and decorating, as he is keen to get back to work.

Michael is a good example of how a person might not engage in certain aspects of their care plan (e.g. medication, decreasing drug use) but will engage in other aspects of it (e.g. sports, talking to care co-ordinator, seeking work). This person might be defined as 'non-compliant', as he is going against medical advice (a compliance definition), but could be considered well engaged (given the engagement definition by Bradley *et al.*, submitted) as he engages well with his care co-ordinator and is actively involved in the treatment goals he has defined collaboratively with his care co-ordinator.

Perhaps surprisingly there are currently no published empirical studies of carers' engagement with Assertive Outreach Teams. In an unpublished study, Rose, Amphlett and Larkin (in preparation) report findings from a qualitative analysis of seven carer interviews, exploring their concept of engagement with assertive outreach and factors which appeared to influence it. Their main findings were that a positive relationship between carer, client and team is held together by containment, continuity and collaboration.

Why measure engagement?

Developing engagement with service users is the primary focus of Assertive Outreach Teams (Department of Health, 2001). Indeed, the *Keys to Engagement* report (Sainsbury Centre for Mental Health, 1998a: 9) concluded that 'in areas where there are significant numbers of people from this client group, it will be difficult, if not impossible, to meet their needs through generic community mental health teams. Assertive outreach is required to engage and maintain engagement with clients'.

Teams need to ensure they are achieving what they were set up to do. In order to do this they need to measure the engagement of service users at regular intervals. There needs to be a more detailed examination of engagement than simply focusing on whether the person still has contact with the team or is taking their medication. A reliable, standardised measure of engagement is required to do this.

Since poor engagement is an essential criterion for entry into assertive outreach, engagement measures (e.g. Hall *et al.*, 2001a; Gillespie *et al.*, 2004; Tait, Birchwood and Trower, 2002; Wolfson and Cupitt, 2001) can be used as part of the assessment process to decide who is appropriate for the service. One Assertive Outreach Team in Birmingham routinely send the Hall *et al.* (2001a) engagement measure to referrers as part of their referral pack. If referrals score highly (33 and above) on this measure, indicating good engagement, their appropriateness would be questioned.

The quality or strength of relationships between clients and clinicians has long been thought to be predictive of outcome. Horvath and Symonds (1991) found that clients who have a good early alliance with their therapist are more likely to have a positive treatment outcome. In their seminal study, Frank and Gunderson (1990) clearly showed that clients with a diagnosis of schizophrenia who formed good alliances with their therapists within the first six months of treatment were significantly more likely to remain in psychotherapy, comply with medication and achieve better outcomes after two years, using less medication than clients who did not. A good therapeutic alliance has also been found to be associated with good outcomes in terms of fewer days in hospital, an increased ability to work (Priebe and Gruyters, 1993) and rehabilitation (Gehrs and Goering, 1994).

The assertive outreach model has been shown to have a positive impact on engagement and other outcomes. A review comparing Assertive Community Treatment with standard community care found that service users in Assertive Community Treatment were more likely to remain in contact with services, less likely to be admitted to hospital, spent less time in hospital, were more likely to be living independently, more likely to be employed and more satisfied with their care (Marshall and Lockwood, 1998). These studies, however, did not employ a standardised measure of engagement, relying instead upon proxy measures (e.g. drop-out from services). The more recent REACT study of Assertive Outreach Teams in North London found no significant difference in inpatient bed use or clinical or social outcomes. They did, however, find that service users were better engaged, as measured by the adapted Homeless Engagement Acceptance Schedule (Park, Tyrer, Elsworth, Fox and Ukoumunne, 2002), and were more satisfied with services (Killaspy, Bebbington, Blizard, Johnson, Nolan, Pilling and King, 2006).

Some studies have looked at the relationship between different aspects of engagement in relation to assertive outreach outcomes. Meaden *et al.* (2004) and Paget *et al.* (in press), in two studies of the same Assertive Outreach Team, report that some items on the Engagement Measure (Hall *et al.*, 2001a) were more related to outcome than others, in particular, those concerning the client–therapist interaction, the usefulness of treatment (as perceived by the client), openness and collaboration with treatment. The weakest predictors of outcome were compliance with medication and appointment keeping. In the second of these studies, engagement remained largely stable over a four-year period. Total engagement scores were not found to be predictive of future hospital usage. Collaboration with treatment was, however, associated with some reduced future bed use. Collaboration with treatment also increased over the four-year period, as did client–therapist interaction. In a similar, naturalistic study of a rural Assertive Outreach Team, Wane, Owen, Sood, Bradley and Jones (2007) found assertive outreach to be associated with significant reductions in hospital admissions, occupied bed days, improved engagement with services as measured by the Engagement Measure (Hall *et al.*, 2001a) and some aspects of health and social functioning, as measured by the Functional Analysis of Care Environments System (FACE; Clifford, 2000).

These findings clearly indicate that engagement serves as a platform for other activities, such as psychosocial interventions, which may themselves be more predictive of hospital usage (e.g. teaching effective coping skills).

Over-engagement and dependency

Much emphasis has been placed on engaging so-called 'hard-to-engage' service users, whilst very little has been written about the potential for over-engagement and creating dependency. Stein and Test (1980) have argued that the assertive outreach model should work against creating dependency by virtue of its having a team approach, whereby the team works with all service users and shares clinical responsibility for them, thus avoiding dependency on an individual keyworker (see chapter two).

Is it, however, possible that the assertive outreach model could lead to dependency? The strong emphasis on engaging people by creative and novel means, and through persistent social and practical support, may lead some service users to view clinicians and workers more as friends than health professionals (see chapter ten). Two participants in Priebe *et al.*'s (2005) study felt that this type of support encouraged dependency. Interestingly, when Minghella *et al.* (2002) asked service users how their Assertive Outreach Team could be improved, service users asked for more frequent visits, longer visits, weekend and evening work. It is clearly important that service users do not become overly dependent on the team and/or individual members of it. Assertive Outreach Teams should try to avoid dependency and disempowerment by assisting service users to develop skills which promote empowerment and personal growth (Lukeman, 2003).

Existing engagement measures do not appear to address this issue, equating instead high engagement scores with good engagement. Consequently, it is possible that someone who scores highly on an engagement measure could do so because they are engaged to an unhealthy degree, as illustrated below.

Example:
Anne is a 39-year-old woman who has been with the Assertive Outreach Team for five years and has a diagnosis of schizophrenia. Anne regularly calls the team on a daily basis to ask for support or when her next visit is. She attends all of her appointments as well as the team's women's group, drop-in and a large number of social activities. Anne is reluctant to attend activities which are not run by the team. She openly discusses her symptoms and feelings with staff and takes her medication as prescribed. Anne gets very distressed when staff discuss the possibility of her moving on from the team.

Such difficulties may be particularly evident in people with a diagnosis of co-morbid personality disorder. For example, 'frantic efforts to avoid real or imagined abandonment' is one of the DSM-IV (American Psychiatric Association, 1994) criteria for borderline personality disorder. Indeed, research has shown that there is a high prevalence of co-morbid personality disorders in the assertive outreach population (Ranger, Methuen, Rutter, Rao and Tyrer, 2004). The characteristics associated with co-morbid personality disorders could result in over-engagement and dependency. Research has also shown that the assertive outreach approach can increase behavioural disturbance in those who have a co-morbid or primary diagnosis of personality disorder (Tyrer and Simmonds, 2003), although there are some teams in the United States who report success with a dialectical behaviour therapy approach for people with personality disorder, using an adapted model of assertive outreach (Basevitz and Aubry, 2002).

Clearly it is important for engagement measures to adequately capture unhealthy engagement with Assertive Outreach Teams. The original version of the engagement measure (Hall *et al.*, 2001a) included an item which measured the appropriateness of the interaction between client and care co-ordinator. This item was later removed because it failed to discriminate statistically between clients who were poorly engaged and those who were well engaged. The issue of how to measure over-engagement needs to be given more consideration.

Methods of measurement

Naturalistic attempts to measure engagement have focused on attendance and retention as potential indices (Mowbray, Cohen and Bybee, 1993). Bond, McGrew and Fekete (1995) define the latter as 'uninterrupted reception of services'. These proxy measures have often been recorded as dichotomous variables (attendance or non-attendance), the number and duration of contacts, or the number of cancellations and failures to attend (e.g. Craig, Doherty, Jamieson-Craig, Boocock and Attafua, 2004). Others have measured engagement as the product of the average number of weekly sessions multiplied by the number of weeks spent in treatment (e.g. Fiorentine, Nakashima and Anglin, 1999). A number of reviews have used retention as a measure of engagement (e.g. Marshall and Lockwood, 1998) and, as previously described, have linked this to outcome (e.g. Bond, McGrew and Fekete, 1995).

Others have tried to obtain more qualitative information. Mowbray, Cohen and Bybee (1993), for instance, have developed an engagement status classification system based on weekly team consensus. 'Fully engaged' clients were those who completed assessments, negotiated plans and accepted services in the community. The 'limited engagement' group consisted of those classified as having accepted some assistance, but who were not fully completing assessments, formulating a plan or accepting community services. The 'not engaged' group clients refused all help. Having derived these weekly classifications, the authors then took the highest classification over the first four months of the study as the overall measure of client engagement. They found that this overall measure was related to number of contacts and duration of contacts.

These early attempts at measurement, with their emphasis on appointment keeping and compliance with expected service demands, tell us very little about the process of engagement, relationship aspects or what factors might be most useful in supporting clients or in developing services. Engagement measured in this way also assumes that all contact is good. High levels of contact may mean that a person is relapsing and that the team is providing additional services or the person is placing inappropriate demands on the team as a result of dependency. Such quantitative indices may be seen as too simplistic to measure engagement in a meaningful way. Indeed, Littell, Alexander and Reynolds (2001) argue that it is the quality, rather than the quantity of client participation, that is important.

Multi-dimensional measures of engagement

More recently, a number of scales have been developed by clinicians, largely working within Assertive Outreach Teams, to better capture the broad range of factors likely to be important. These have both drawn on the views of experienced clinicians and taken concepts from the psychiatric treatment and psychotherapy literature. Concepts such as co-operation, involvement in treatment, collaboration, participation, therapeutic alliance, medication compliance and service retention have been consistently adopted.

There are currently three clinician-rated measures (Hall, Meaden, Smith and Jones, 2001; Tait, Birchwood and Trower, 2002; Wolfson and Cupitt, 2001) and one self-report measure of engagement (Gillespie, Smith, Meaden, Jones and Wane, 2004) designed specifically for use with assertive outreach populations. One measure has also been developed for use with the homeless mentally ill: the Homeless Engagement and Acceptance Scale (Park, Tyrer, Elsworth, Fox, Ukoumunne and MacDonald, 2002). More recently a measure has been developed for use in residential rehabilitation settings, measuring engagement with the whole treatment team and process of rehabilitation itself (Meaden *et al.*, in preparation). A further measure exists within child protection services to assess family engagement (Yatchmenoff, 2005). A comparison of the adult measures is presented in Table 1.1.

These measures all assess a variety of factors identified by clinicians and taken from the relevant literature. These can be broadly categorised as:

- adherence to service goals (e.g. being available for appointments and taking medication);
- active involvement in treatment (e.g. collaboratively identifying treatment goals, collaboratively agreeing to interventions, carrying though agreed goals);
- communication and openness (e.g. discussing feelings, sharing problems).

Table 1.1 Comparison of engagement measures (adult populations)

Measure	Areas covered	No. items	Development	Rater	Rating	Psychometric properties
BEM[1] Wolfson & Cupitt (2001)	Contact Participation Collaboration Openness Help-seeking Treatment	6	Discussion amongst authors. Post development literature review & interviews with 5 clinicians. 8 expert reviewers. SEMI, UK Population	Clinician	4-point Likert Over the past month	Good test re-test reliability (client n = 38/clinician n = 4) (Pearson's R 0.86 total score; 0.68–0.84 item scores) Good face validity (experts'/clinicians' feedback)
EM[2] Hall, Meaden, Smith & Jones (2001)	Appointment keeping (2 items) Client–therapist interaction (1 item) Communication/openness (3 items) Client's perceived usefulness of treatment (1 item) Collaboration with treatment (3 items) Compliance with medication (1 item)	11	MDT discussions and based on previous measure used by AOT. SEMI, UK Population	Clinician	5-point Likert	Good internal reliability (n = 44) (Cronbach's alpha 0.89) Good test re-test reliability (n = 44) (Spearman's R 0.90 total score; 0.71–0.84 subscale scores) Good inter-rater reliability (client n = 22/clinician n = 2) (Spearman's R 0.95 total score; 0.86–1.00 subscale scores) Good face validity (feedback from clinicians) Good discriminatory capacity (>33 = good engagement)
SES[3] Tait, Birchwood & Trower (2002)	Client availability (3 items) Collaboration (3 items) Help-seeking (4 items) Treatment adherence (4 items)	14	Literature Review. Discussion amongst authors. SEMI, UK population	Clinician	4-point Likert	Good internal reliability (client n = 66/ clinician n = 5) (Cronbach's alpha 0.91) Good test re-test reliability (n = 15) (Spearman's R 0.90 total score; 0.80–0.97 subscale scores) Good criterion validity (reported by authors)

Measure	No. of items	Domains/Items	Source/Population	Respondent	Scale	Psychometric properties
EM[4] Gillespie, Smith, Meaden, Jones & Wane (2004)	11	Appointment keeping (2 items); Client–therapist interaction (1 item); Communication/openness (3 items); Client's perceived usefulness of treatment (1 item); Collaboration with treatment (3 items); Compliance with medication (1 item)	Authors rephrased Hall et al. (2001) measure. SEMI, UK Population	Client	5-point Likert	Good internal reliability (n = 25) (Cronbach's alpha 0.80); Good test re-test reliability (n = 12) (Pearson's R 0.85 total score); Concurrent validity with EM (Hall et al., 2001) (R = 0.49, p<0.05); Not predictive of engagement at 6 months
HEAS[5] Park, Tyrer, Elseworth, Fox, Ukoumunne & MacDonald (2002)	5	How the client feels about the worker; The degree to which the client can be engaged; The client's attitude to help; The client's attitude to housing; The way the client engages with others	Discussion with MDT to develop items. Pilot resulting in clarification of wording. Expert review of items by MDT and external reviewers. SEMI & Homeless, UK Population	Clinician	5- and 4-point Likert	Good internal reliability (n = 110) (Cronbach's alpha 0.85 total score); Good inter-rater reliability (n = 21) (Intra-Class Correlation Coefficient R = 0.77); Good face and content validity (as assessed by MDT); Good construct validity (Items 1, 2 & 5 significant relationships with items on a measure of social behaviour); Good predictive validity (accommodation and adequacy of support networks at 12 months predicted by score at 3 months)

(Continued overleaf)

Table 1.1 continued

Measure	Areas covered	No. items	Development	Rater	Rating	Psychometric properties
RRES[6] Meaden, Hacker, Paget, Jones and Thorne (in preparation)	Quality of relationship with staff team and different disciplines (3 items) Communication and openness about problems, symptoms, feelings and behaviours (4 items) Realistic rehabilitation goal setting (1 item) Perceived usefulness of rehabilitation goals (1 item) Degree of collaboration and active involvement in rehabilitation interventions (5 items) Appointment keeping (2 items) Compliance with medication (1 item)	17	Further development of Hall et al. Measure Interview with clinicians SEMI, UK Population	Clinician	5-point Likert	Good inter-rater reliability (n = 26) (Pearson's R 0.97 total score; from 0.72–0.94 item scores) Good test re-test reliability (n = 26) (Pearson's R 0.93 total score; 0.70–0.94 item scores) Good internal consistency (n = 49) (Cronbach's alpha = 0.93) Good face validity (feedback from clinicians) Cluster analysis (n = 49) revealed three independent clusters/potential sub-categories of engagement ('relationship and communication/openness', 'engagement with rehabilitation goals' and 'medication compliance').

1 = Bexley Engagement Measure; 2 = Engagement Measure; 3 = Service Engagement Scale
4 = Engagement Measure; 5 = Homeless Engagement and Acceptance Scale; 6 = Residential Rehabilitation Engagement Scale

These factors overlap with those identified by Meaden, Hacker, Paget, Jones and Thorne (in preparation) with regard to residential populations. Using cluster analysis these authors found that three independent clusters or potential sub-categories of engagement emerged:

- relationship and communication/openness
- engagement with rehabilitation goals
- medication compliance.

Each of the measures described gives different weightings to these broad factors and most attempt some categorisation of items. Whilst most ask about collaboration, openness and communication, others such as the Service Engagement Scale (SES) (Tait *et al.*, 2002) give more weight to compliance with medication and treatment. Items regarding medication compliance make the assumption that clients should be taking their medication (Cupitt, Wolfson and Gray, unpublished). Adaptations of the Engagement Measure (Hall *et al.*, 2001a), by contrast, all emphasise the perceived usefulness of treatment; whilst the Residential Rehabilitation Engagement Scale (Meaden *et al.*, in preparation) further assesses the quality of the relationship with different professionals and engagement with rehabilitation goals.

Each measure has different numbers of items, ranging from five (Homeless Engagement and Acceptance Scale) to 17 (Residential Rehabilitation Engagement Scale), with some scored on a four- and others on a five-point Likert scale, with potentially differing sensitivities to detect difference and change over time. Interestingly, only the Bexley Engagement Measure and Residential Rehabilitation Engagement Scale give a clear time frame over which ratings should be made.

Despite the differences in their development, all the above scales appear to have good reliability. However, in-depth assessments of the validity of these scales are lacking and it is unclear what each scale actually measures. Bradley, Jones, Meaden, Tudway and Wane (in preparation) have attempted to compare three of the main measures developed for assertive outreach populations (the Service Engagement Scale, Engagement Measure and Bexley Engagement Measure) using clinician raters from two Assertive Outreach Teams. These ratings were then compared against ratings on other known measures thought to tap into related processes and concepts. In a preliminary analysis, all of the measures studied were strongly associated with participation as assessed by the 'Involvement in treatment' item on the 'Response to care' subsection of the FACE, Health and Social Assessment Measure (Clifford, 2000). Subsequent regression analysis found that the measures differentially assessed satisfaction, therapeutic alliance, participation and insight. Participation was the only significant association for the Bexley Engagement Measure, whilst the Service Engagement Scale was found to be significantly associated with insight, as scored on the Insight Scale (Birchwood, Smith, Drury, Healy, MacMillan and Slade, 1994). The Engagement Measure was closely associated with both therapeutic alliance, as assessed by the Helping Alliance Questionnaire-II (Luborsky, Barber, Siqueland, Johnson, Najavits, Frank and Daley, 1996) and satisfaction, recorded using the Client Satis-faction Questionnaire (Larsen, Attkinson, Hargreaves and Nguyen, 1979). Interestingly, none of the measures were significantly associated with medica-tion compliance, as assessed by the 'Taking of medication' item in the 'Response to care' subsection of the FACE.

The psychology of engagement

A picture of which factors might be important in determining clients' engagement with Assertive Outreach Teams and workers is slowly emerging. These can be divided into factors associated with the service user and those associated with the service, as summarised in Table 1.2.

These studies reveal a wide range of clinical and demographic factors as well as client and service characteristics associated with engagement. Several of these studies, however, have small numbers of participants and remain unpublished. Subsequent larger scale studies may usefully wish to explore the validity of these findings and address the paucity of research regarding more disengaged clients. Despite these shortcomings, several studies have consist-ently highlighted similar factors relating to engagement. In particular a good therapeutic relationship and recovery style have been found to be important. Service users who want to make sense of their experiences, having an 'integrative recovery style', have been rated as better engaged with their care co-ordinators (Hall *et al.*, 2001b). Moreover, an integrative recovery style at three months following an acute episode has been shown to predict sub-sequent engagement at six months in non-assertive outreach populations (Tait *et al.*, 2003).

In the therapeutic alliance literature, the therapeutic relationship is central to good engagement. In their study, Hall, Smith and Meaden (2001b) found positive correlations between service users' engagement and both care co-ordinators' and clients' perception of the therapeutic relationship on the Helping Alliance Questionnaire-II (Luborsky *et al.*, 1996). Similarly, Priebe *et al.* (2005) interviewed 40 clients from nine Assertive Outreach Teams across London and found that clients valued staff who worked with them collabora-tively, in partnership. Gillespie *et al.* (2004) using staff- and service-user-rated engagement measures also found that service users who were rated as being actively involved in their care were more likely to be well engaged. Meaden *et al.* (2004) noted that assertive outreach service users who had a good relationship with their care co-ordinator, could discuss their feelings, prob-lems and symptoms with them and perceived their treatment as useful, spent less time in hospital. Increased openness about symptoms and active involvement with treatment were also identified by staff as related to good engagement in a qualitative study of 15 assertive outreach staff (Gray, 2001). A good therapeutic relationship, as rated by clinicians using the Helping

Table 1.2 Psychological factors/processes involved in engagement

Relationship to engagement	Factor	
Positive association	Service user	Service/staff
	• Experiences of paternal care[1]	• Assertive outreach model e.g. increased contacts, team approach[9, 10, 11, 15]
	• Integrative recovery style[1, 2]	• Social support[3, 5, 7, 12, 17]
	• Duration of illness[1]	• Practical support[3, 5, 7, 12, 17, 18]
	• Perceived usefulness of treatment[1, 6]	• Partnership/collaborative model of the therapeutic relationship[1, 3, 5, 6, 14, 17]
	• Reported guilt and humiliation[4]	• Time and commitment of staff[3, 13, 17]
	• Clients valuing their treatment and care[7]	• Take time to build a collaborative relationship[13, 16, 17]
	• Positive past experiences of services[8]	• Service users actively involved in their care[4, 19]
		• Give the client the opportunity to discuss symptoms, feelings and experiences[1, 5, 6, 19]
		• Engagement without focus on medication[3]
		• Treating clients as individuals and as adults[7]
Negative association	Service user	Service/staff
	• Alcohol and/or drug use[1]	• Focus on medication or immediate outcomes[8]
	• Desire to be independent[3]	• Compliance/medical model[1, 5, 6]
	• Poor therapeutic relationship[3]	• Treating clients as a group and like children[7]
	• Loss of control due to medication effects[3]	
	• Feels treated like a child[8]	
	• Negative past experiences of services[8, 19]	

(Continued overleaf)

Table 1.2 continued

Relationship to engagement	Factor
Not associated	Service user • Insight[1, 2, 4] • Symptoms[2, 4] • Illness appraisals (insight, health LoC, illness attributions)[4] • Compliance with treatment (i.e. taking medication, going along with treatment)[1, 5]

1 Hall, Smith & Meaden (2001)
2 Tait, Birchwood & Trower (2003)
3 Priebe, Watts, Chase & Matanov (2005)
4 Mayhew (2003)
5 Gillespie, Smith, Meaden, Jones & Wane (2004)
6 Meaden, Nithsdale, Rose, Smith & Jones (2004)
7 Bradley, Meaden, Tudway, Earl-Gray, Jones, Giles & Wane (submitted)
8 Sainsbury Centre for Mental Health (1998)
9 Klinkenberg, Calsyn & Morse (1998, 2002)

10 Henrinckx, Kinney, Clarke & Paulson (1997)
11 Burns & Santos (1995)
12 Minghella, Gauntlett & Ford (2002)
13 Addis & Gamble (2004)
14 Fakhoury, White & Priebe (2007)
15 Killaspy, Bebbington, Blizard, Johnson, Nolan, Pilling & King (2006)
16 Killaspy (2007)
17 Rose, Amphlett & Larkin (in preparation)
18 Lukeman (2003)
19 Gray (2001)

Alliance Scale, was found to predict fewer hospitalisations in new patients but not established ones (Fakhoury, White and Priebe, 2007).

Clearly a good collaborative therapeutic relationship helps clients to engage with services and results in positive outcomes in terms of reduced time in hospital. Similar findings have been reported for carers, who also felt that a collaborative approach, which was regular, continuous and consistent, in which staff took the time to listen to service users and built a trusting relationship with them, was an important element of engagement with assertive outreach (Rose, Amphlett and Larkin, in preparation).

Assertive Outreach Teams may be better at focusing on the collaborative nature of the therapeutic relationship and working towards agreed tasks than traditional community mental health teams (Killaspy, 2007). Killaspy further argues that this use of recovery-based practice may account for the increased engagement of service users when compared with community mental health teams (Killaspy *et al.*, 2006).

As well as working collaboratively, it is important to treat people as individuals. Bradley *et al.* (submitted) ran a focus group with five assertive outreach service users examining their experiences, thoughts and feelings about engaging with services. Service users were more likely to engage with assertive outreach if they felt they were treated as individuals, in a respectful and equal way. They were conversely less likely to engage if they felt they were being controlled, manipulated or staff were judgemental and/or disrespectful. Similar findings are reported by Ackerman and Hilsenroth (2003) who studied clinicians and looked at how their characteristics and style of intervention affected the therapeutic relationship. Clinicians who were perceived as experienced, understanding, supportive, warm and friendly, respectful and interested, flexible and active in their work were more likely to have a stronger therapeutic alliance with clients. Working collaboratively and facilitating talking about experiences were also found to be beneficial to the engagement process.

The assertive outreach model itself has been found to be associated with improved engagement of service users compared with standard services (e.g. Herinckx, Kinney, Clarke and Paulson, 1997; Burns and Santos, 1995). Service users are reported to be more satisfied with their care and less likely to drop out of treatment compared with those receiving standard case management (Herinckx *et al.*, 1997). Killaspy *et al.* (2006) compared outcomes for people within assertive outreach with those in community mental health teams. Although there was no difference in inpatient bed use, social or clinical outcomes, people within assertive outreach were better engaged and more satisfied with services. This suggests that characteristics of the model promote good engagement and satisfaction with services. These factors can be found in good Assertive Outreach Teams, but are not exclusive to them. Small caseloads, generally with a ratio of 1:10, are likely to be helpful, allowing staff to provide intensive social and practical support, which has been associated with good engagement (Priebe *et al.*, 2005; Gillespie *et al.*, 2004; Bradley *et al.*, submitted; Lukeman, 2003). The ability to respond flexibly and quickly in the event of crises is likely to be a further important factor.

Minghella, Gauntlett and Ford (2002) evaluated two London Assertive Outreach Teams on a variety of outcome measures. Although this study did not look at engagement directly, they did interview clients about what they liked or disliked about the team. Service users valued practical support, staff attitudes, help with accessing community resources and social activities. Interestingly, service users listed medication as one of the things they were least happy with. These findings are very similar to factors identified in engagement research. Clearly, things which people value are likely to encourage them to engage with the team (e.g. practical support) and things which they are unhappy with will not (e.g. medication).

People may not engage with assertive outreach due to negative past experiences of services, a feeling that services have little to offer (Sainsbury Centre for Mental Health, 1998) or because they are suspicious of them. They may feel that there is too much of a focus on medication and immediate outcomes. This may be especially true for people from black and ethnic minority backgrounds for a variety of reasons (Department of Health, 2003). There is a lack of research looking at the relationship between ethnicity and engagement, which is the focus of current research by our group.

Important factors in staff which help bring about engagement include 'having time' and the collaborative nature of the therapeutic relationship (Addis and Gamble, 2004). The increased number of contacts and the number of services provided by assertive outreach have also been associated with better engagement (Klinkenberg, Calsyn and Morse, 1998, 2002). Responding to needs in an honest, non-judgemental and open manner, which encourages self-determination and freedom of choice (Sainsbury Centre for Mental Health, 2001), are noted as important attributes which clinicians should possess. Staff should also be needs-led, able to work in informal settings, have realistic expectations, be committed to forming long-term therapeutic relationships, ideally be of a similar ethnic group and/or have experience of using mental health services (Sainsbury Centre for Mental Health, 2001). However, Solomon, Draine and Delaney (1995) found no difference in the therapeutic alliance between clients and case managers with or without experience of using mental health services.

Factors unrelated to engagement

A number of factors have been shown to be unrelated to engagement. Perhaps surprisingly, level of insight has not been shown to be associated with engagement (Hall *et al.*, 2001b; Tait *et al.*, 2003; Mayhew, 2003). These studies used the Insight Scale (Birchwood *et al.*, 1994) and staff-rated measures of engagement. Studies have also shown no relationship between psychotic symptoms and engagement (Tait *et al.*, 2003; Mayhew, 2003). Compliance has historically often been used synonymously with the term 'engagement with treatment', but studies have shown that items relating to compliance, e.g. 'How often do you take your medication as prescribed by your psychiatrist?', on engagement measures are not significantly correlated with overall engagement scores (Gillespie *et al.*, 2004; Meaden *et al.*, 2004).

Implications for clinical practice and service development

It is important to keep in mind that some of the above studies have small sample sizes. Replication using larger sample sizes and including less well-engaged participants is required to confirm these initial findings. A number of recommendations can be made, however, which may usefully inform both clinical practice and service development.

Research findings to date show that the assertive outreach model is the best existing approach, in terms of engaging clients. Care co-ordinators have the capacity to work more intensively than community mental health teams.

The emphasis should be on a collaborative relationship between the service user and team members. Service users need to feel actively involved in all aspects of their treatment and care and should be given time to put their viewpoint across and be involved in decision making. This means actively involving them in their care plan and not just ensuring that they have signed it. Relapse plans and advance directives are tools which can be used to enable clients to have more control and choice over their care. It is likely that the more involved a person is in this process, the more useful they will perceive their treatment, which in turn is associated with engagement (Meaden *et al.*, 2004).

Gray (2001) identified the following staff characteristics as helpful in engaging assertive outreach service users: optimism, perseverance, commitment, openness, empathy, understanding, friendliness, listening skills, supportiveness, low expressed emotion and patience. Service users value staff who are respectful, non-judgemental, treat them as individuals and do not try to control them. It is crucial to employ staff who have these characteristics and who will take time to build a therapeutic alliance with service users and this needs to be reflected in person specifications and staff personal development plans.

The evidence shows that engagement is not related to a person's level of symptoms or degree of insight. Therefore, a person should not be considered too unwell or lacking in insight to such a degree that it is not worth attempting to engage them.

Recovery style appears to play an important part in a person's degree of engagement. It is unclear, however, to what extent recovery style can be targeted successfully for intervention and further studies are needed to address this issue. Tait *et al.* (2003) suggest that with appropriate support at an early stage a person can be prevented from moving from an integrative style to a sealing-over style. However, Gillespie and Clarke (2007) found that a ten-week recovery group for people with severe and enduring mental health problems had little effect on their recovery style.

Addressing problematic substance use is important to promote better engagement (Hall *et al.*, 2001b). This is a critical area of work, given that 39 per cent of service users in assertive outreach in inner city areas have been found to use substances problematically (Graham *et al.*, 2001). Involving separate drug or alcohol teams may be useful but ideally this work should be carried out by the assertive outreach staff working with that person. The Department of Health's *Mental Health Policy Implementation Guide: dual diagnosis good practice guide* (2002) advocates an integrated treatment approach to substance use amongst people with severe and enduring mental health problems. This often means training staff to work with these co-occurring problems. One such approach is the model used by the Compass Programme in Birmingham, where assertive outreach staff are trained in a Cognitive-Behavioural Integrated Treatment (C-BIT) approach (Graham *et al.*, 2004) and are supported by a member of the Compass team to carry out the intervention.

Practical support is highly valued and vital to ensure that basic needs are being met. Maslow's (1943) hierarchy of needs suggests that lower-order needs such as food, water, shelter and warmth need to be met before a person can consider other areas of their life such as relationships and achievements. Margison (2005) describes a model of a hierarchy of needs adapted for use in working with people with psychosis (see Figure 1.2). Needs at the bottom of the hierarchy, such as food, shelter and physical security, are highlighted as priorities for targeting, before going on to address needs further up the hierarchy, such as physical health, relationships, sense of community, occupation,

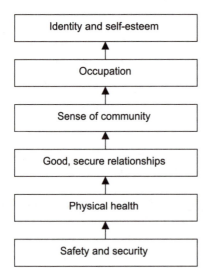

Figure 1.2 Hierarchy of needs (adapted by permission from Margison, 2005)

identity and self-esteem. Consequently, if an Assertive Outreach Team can assist someone to sort out their benefits or housing problems, the person will then be able to think about engaging in other activities, such as social, occupational and psychological interventions.

Having addressed basic needs, the focus may shift towards social activities. In order to engage service users, teams should look at organising social activities. This might involve setting up a sports group which accesses a local sports centre or one-to-one activities such as going to the gym. Group activities are especially beneficial in allowing people to meet others and build their own social networks, reducing dependency on services and professionals.

In line with recommendations from *Service User Involvement in Assertive Outreach and the Assertive Outreach Forum* (Gillespie and Amphlett, 2004), Birmingham and Solihull Mental Health NHS Trust have developed Assertive Outreach Service User Forums. At a recent forum, clients were asked how the team could be improved. A significant proportion (44 per cent) of the suggestions were related to wanting more social activities such as discos, holidays, day trips, bowling, etc., and having the opportunity to mix with others. One client stated they wanted 'more encouragement to build up social circles'.

Staff should also offer service users the opportunity to discuss how they are feeling as well as past experiences. This can be done during planned visits in a safe and containing way. This gives service users the feeling that they are being listened to and taken seriously, which can be a powerful and beneficial experience in itself (Department of Health, 2005).

Research suggests that there should be less focus on medication and compliance with treatment, as it does not help to engage service users. Indeed, medication side effects are one of the reasons why service users disengage from services (Priebe *et al.*, 2005; Gray, 2001). Instead of routinely asking people 'Are you taking your medication?', it may be more beneficial to ask 'What have you found helpful?' or 'How are you feeling?'. If medication is to be discussed, service users want more choice about which medication they take, information on its effects and side effects and to be given support if they choose to stop taking it (Sainsbury Centre for Mental Health, 2006).

Staging interventions

Clinical interventions should be determined by the client's stage or level of engagement and where they are in terms of their recovery journey (see Figure 1.3). For example, when someone is first referred to assertive outreach by a community mental health team, it may be helpful to try to engage with them by offering to go shopping together, if this is something that they would like help with. As they become more engaged, staff would work with the person towards shopping on their own. The same could be said for support with housing, benefits, accompanying a person to appointments, social activities, etc. As the person progresses and becomes more engaged, activities would be

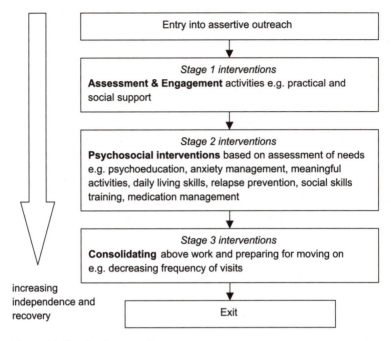

Figure 1.3 Staging interventions

based around developing skills to help them achieve more independence, based on the individual's needs. These could include things such as working on daily living skills, developing meaningful activities, psychoeducation, specific interventions such as relapse prevention, anxiety management, social skills training, medication management, etc. At the third stage, these skills are rehearsed and consolidated and preparation is made to move the person to a team offering a lower level of support such as a Community Mental Health Team. A person's stage of engagement and the interventions offered by the team can be reviewed at their Care Programme Approach review.

Example:
When Margaret first came to the Assertive Outreach Team she had been in hospital three times in the previous two years. She was very anxious and had paranoid thoughts about her neighbours. She was very reluctant to let staff into her flat to speak to her. Staff managed to build a relationship with Margaret by supporting her to sort out her benefits and reduce her debts. With the extra money, Margaret was able to decorate her flat and buy a washing machine. Margaret started attending the team's drop-in and made friends with other people from the team. Over time she engaged in psychological work on her anxiety and paranoia with the team's clinical psychologist and found better ways of coping. She built in these coping strategies to her Relapse Prevention Plan, which she

developed with her Community Psychiatric Nurse. Margaret's confidence improved, as did her ability to manage her mental health. She has started attending an art class at the local college. She has remained out of hospital for the last 18 months and Margaret and the team are thinking about her moving on to the local Community Mental Health Team.

This type of phasic model is used by Lincolnshire Partnership NHS Trust (2004) in their *Integrated Care Pathway for Assertive Outreach*. Hogarty (2002) also advocates therapy for people with a diagnosis of schizophrenia based on three stages: basic, intermediate and advanced. The basic phase is similar to the engagement phase, where a therapeutic alliance is formed and a treatment plan agreed collaboratively. The intermediate phase involves psychoeducation, medication management, increasing activities of daily living, relaxation techniques and social skills training. The advanced phase builds on skills learned in the intermediate phase and focuses on dealing with conflict as well as building up social and vocational activities.

Team supervision with an external facilitator can also help to identify team practices which may encourage dependency and try to address them. For example, which service users do we give lifts to? Should the team set up their own drop-in or encourage service users to attend mainstream activities? Individual supervision can also help clinicians identify practices or elements of the person's care plan which may foster dependency and look at ways to work with these.

When engagement fails

There are times when, despite offering a good service, it may not prove possible to improve someone's engagement, even after several years of assertive outreach (Paget *et al.*, in press). In this situation it is important to examine what has actually been offered to service users, together with whether clinicians involved have had the skills to deliver this in a sensitive, timely and collaborative way. However, even when appropriate and skilful attempts to engage have been made, some service users may still remain disengaged and have persistent difficulty maintaining a life in the community.

There is surprisingly little literature on the situations in which assertive outreach does not work. For example, the need to manage potential risk behaviours may dominate team thinking and clinical efforts, leading the team to slip into a more coercive, compliance-orientated relationship. Other service users may present with a very chaotic lifestyle characterised by transient relationships or involvement in criminal activities, such as prostitution or drug dealing, that may make attempts to develop a therapeutic relationship particularly difficult.

For some, the informed choice to refuse assertive outreach may need to be respected (see chapter ten). Where the ability to maintain community living and engage in community treatment is problematic, some form of supported residential service may be needed (Paget *et al.*, in press). Factors to consider here may be:

- persistent risk issues which cannot be managed in the community: risk of self-harm, violence, suicide, self-neglect, exploitation, abuse by others;
- excessive fragility or a lack of resilience in the face of stressors such that the person is likely to have severe problems regulating their behaviour and emotions and is unable to develop effective coping strategies for managing these.

Engagement, both as an intervention in its own right and as a platform for other approaches, may therefore not be possible for everyone. This high-lights the importance of measuring engagement systematically to assess both suitability for services and subsequent progress.

Conclusions

Engagement may best be seen as a dynamic, multi-dimensional process, with clinicians and clients viewing different aspects of the process as important. Service goals and ways of working are most reflected in the concepts of compliance and participation, whilst therapeutic alliance is perhaps most useful in understanding engagement in relation to individuals and is an important addition to the dynamic process of participation. A number of measures have been developed which are in routine use but further work needs to be done on refining their validity and relevance to client and carer perspectives. Further investigation is also needed of the factors that affect engagement. This has important implications for both training of profes-sionals and the way in which services are provided and interventions targeted. Maintaining good engagement is a platform for reaching out to service users who often have the highest levels of unmet need and distress.

References

Ackerman, S. and Hilsenroth, M. (2003) 'A review of therapist characteristics and techniques positively impacting the therapeutic alliance', *Clinical Psychology Review*, 23: 1–33.

Addis, J. and Gamble, C. (2004) 'Assertive outreach nurses' experience of engage-ment', *Journal of Psychiatric and Mental Health Nursing*, 11: 452–460.

American Psychiatric Association (1994) *Diagnostic and Statistical Manual of Mental Disorders* (4th edn), Washington, DC: APA.

Basevitz, P. and Aubry, T. (2002) *Providing Services to Individuals with Borderline Personality Disorder in the Context of ACT: research base and recommendations*, Ottawa: Centre for Research on Community Services, Faculty of Social Sciences, University of Ottawa. Available online at: http://www.sciencessociales.uottawa.ca/crecs/pdf/pinecrest.pdf

Birchwood, M., Mason, R., MacMillan, F. and Healy, J. (1993) 'Depression, demoralization and control over psychotic illness: a comparison of depressed and non-depressed patients with chronic psychosis', *Psychological Medicine*, 23: 387–395.

Birchwood, M., Smith, J., Drury, V., Healy, J., MacMillan, F. and Slade, M. (1994) 'A self-report Insight Scale for psychosis: reliability, validity and sensitivity to change', *Acta Psychiatrica Scandinavica*, 89: 62–67.

Blackwell, B. (1997) *Treatment Compliance and the Therapeutic Alliance*, Amsterdam: Harwood Academic Publishers.

Bond, G.R., McGrew, J.H. and Fekete, D.M. (1995) 'Assertive outreach for frequent users of psychiatric hospitals: a meta-analysis', *The Journal of Mental Health Administration*, 22: 4–16.

Bordin, E. (1979) 'The generalisability of the psychoanalytic concept of the working alliance', *Psychotherapy: Theory, Research and Practice*, 16: 252–260.

Bradley, S., Jones, C., Meaden, A., Tudway, J. and Wane, J. (in preparation) 'The psychometrics of measuring engagement in assertive outreach'.

Bradley, S., Meaden, A., Tudway, J., Earl-Gray, M., Jones C., Giles, D. and Wane, J. (submitted) 'What do service user views tell us about engagement?'.

Burns, B.J. and Santos, A.B. (1995) 'Assertive community treatment: an update of randomized trials', *Psychiatric Services*, 46: 669–675.

Catty, J. (2004) 'The vehicle of success: theoretical and empirical perspectives on the therapeutic alliance in psychotherapy and psychiatry', *Psychology and Psychotherapy*, 7: 255–272.

Clifford P. (2000) *The FACE Assessment and Outcome System: psychometrics*, FACE Recording and Measurement Systems, Nottingham and Kansas.

Craig, T., Doherty, I., Jamieson-Craig, R., Boocock, A. and Attafua, G. (2004) 'The consumer-employee as a member of a mental health assertive outreach team. I. Clinical and social outcomes', *Journal of Mental Health*, 13: 59–69.

Cupitt, C., Wolfson, P. and Gray, A. (unpublished) 'An investigation into the validity and reliability of the Bexley Engagement Measure (BEM)'.

Department of Health (2001) *The Mental Health Policy Implementation Guide*, London: Department of Health.

Department of Health (2002) *Mental Health Policy Implementation Guide: dual diagnosis good practice guide*, London: Department of Health.

Department of Health (2003) *Inside Outside: improving mental health services for black and ethnic minority communities in England*, London: Department of Health.

Department of Health (2005) *'Now I Feel Tall': what a patient-led NHS feels like*, London: Department of Health.

Fakhoury, W.K.H., White, I. and Priebe, S. (2007) 'Be good to your patient: how the therapeutic relationship in the treatment of patients admitted to assertive outreach affects rehospitalisation', *The Journal of Nervous and Mental Disease*, 195: 789–791.

Fiorentine, R., Nakashima, J. and Anglin, M. (1999) 'Client engagement in drug treatment', *Journal of Substance Abuse Treatment*, 17: 199–206.

Fisher, D. (1997) 'Informed choice: the importance of personal participation in the healing process', in B. Blackwell (ed.) *Treatment Compliance and the Therapeutic Alliance*, Amsterdam: Harwood Academic Publishers.

Frank, A. and Gunderson, J. (1990) 'The role of therapeutic alliance in the treatment of schizophrenia – relationship to course and outcome', *Archives of General Psychiatry*, 47: 228–236.

Gehrs, M. and Goering, M. (1994) 'The relationship between the working alliance and rehabilitation outcomes of schizophrenia', *Psychosocial Rehabilitation Journal*, 18: 43–54.

Gillespie, M. and Amphlett, C. (2004) *Service User Involvement in Assertive Outreach and the Assertive Outreach Forum*, Birmingham and Solihull Mental Health NHS Trust.

Gillespie, M. and Clarke, A. (2007) 'Recovery group for people with severe and enduring mental health problems', *Clinical Psychology Forum*, 172: 15–18.

Gillespie, M., Smith, J., Meaden, A., Jones, C. and Wane, J. (2004) 'Clients' engagement with assertive outreach services: a comparison of client and staff perceptions of engagement and its impact on later engagement', *Journal of Mental Health*, 13: 439–452.

Graham, H.L., Copello, A., Birchwood, M.J., Mueser, K., Orford, J., McGovern, D., Atkinson, E., Maslin, J., Preece, M., Tobin, D. and Georgiou, G. (2004) *Cognitive-Behavioural Integrated Treatment (C-BIT): a treatment manual for substance misuse in people with severe mental health problems*, Chichester: John Wiley and Sons Ltd.

Graham, H.L., Maslin, J., Copello, A., Birchwood, M., Mueser, K., McGovern, D. and Georgiou, G. (2001) 'Drug and alcohol problems amongst individuals with severe mental health problems in an inner city area of the UK', *Social Psychiatry and Psychiatric Epidemiology*, 36: 448–455.

Gray, A. (2001) 'How staff in assertive outreach teams experience and manage relationships with clients who find it "difficult to engage" ', unpublished thesis, Canterbury Christ Church University College.

Hall, M., Meaden, A., Smith, J. and Jones, C. (2001a) 'The development and psychometric properties of an observer-rated measure of engagement with mental health services', *Journal of Mental Health*, 10: 457–465.

Hall, M., Smith, J. and Meaden, A. (2001b) 'Engagement with assertive outreach services: the importance of early parental experiences, the therapeutic relationship and recovery style', unpublished paper.

Herinckx, H.A., Kinney, R.F., Clarke, G.N. and Paulson, R.I. (1997) 'Assertive community treatment versus usual care in engaging and retaining clients with severe mental illness', *Psychiatric Services*, 48: 1297–1306.

Hogarty, G.E. (2002) *Personal Therapy for Schizophrenia and Related Disorders: a guide to individualized treatment*, New York: The Guilford Press.

Horvath, A.O. and Symonds, B.D. (1991) 'Relation between working alliance and outcome in psychotherapy: a meta-analysis', *Journal of Counseling Psychology*, 38: 139–149.

Kazdin, A., Holland, L. and Crowley, M. (1997) 'Family experience of barriers to treatment and premature termination from child therapy', *Journal of Consulting and Clinical Psychology*, 65: 453–463.

Kemp, R., Kirov, G., Everitt, B., Hayward, P. and David, A. (1998) 'A randomised controlled trial of compliance therapy: 18-month follow-up', *British Journal of Psychiatry*, 172: 411–419.

Killaspy, H. (2007) 'Assertive community treatment in psychiatry', *British Medical Journal*, 335: 311–312.

Killaspy, H., Bebbington, P., Blizard, R, Johnson, S., Nolan, F., Pilling, S. and King, M. (2006) 'The REACT study: randomised evaluation of assertive community treatment in north London', *British Medical Journal*, 332: 815–818A.

Klinkenberg, W.D., Calsyn, R.J., and Morse, G.A. (1998) 'The helping alliance in case management for homeless persons with severe mental illness', *Community Mental Health Journal*, 34: 569–578.

Klinkenberg, W., Caslyn, R. and Morse, G. (2002) 'The case manager's view of the helping alliance', *Care Management Journals*, 3: 120–125.

Larsen, D.L., Attkinson, C.C., Hargreaves, W.A. and Nguyen, T.D. (1979) 'Assessment of client/patient satisfaction: development of a general scale', *Evaluation and Program Planning*, 2: 197–207.

Lincolnshire Partnership NHS Trust (2004) *Integrated Care Pathway for Assertive Outreach*, published in the National Library for Health. Available online at: http://www.library.nhs.uk/SpecialistLibraries/Download.aspx?resID=82401 [accessed 20 February 2008].

Littell, J., Alexander, L. and Reynolds, W. (2001) 'Client participation: central and underinvestigated elements of intervention', *Social Services Review*, 75: 1–28.

Luborsky, L., Barber, J., Siqueland, L., Johnson, S., Najavits, L., Frank, A. and Daley, D. (1996) 'The revised helping alliance questionnaire (HAQ-II)', *Journal of Psychotherapy Practice and Research*, 5: 260–269.

Lukeman, R. (2003) 'Service users' experience of the process of being engaged by assertive outreach teams', unpublished thesis, Salomons, Canterbury Christ Church University College.

McCabe, R. and Priebe, S. (2004) 'The therapeutic relationship in the treatment of severe mental illness: a review of methods and findings', *International Journal of Social Psychiatry*, 50: 115–128.

McPhillips, M. and Sensky, T. (1998) 'Coercion, adherence or collaboration? Influences on compliance with medication', in T. Wykes, N. Tarrier and S. Lewis (eds) *Outcome and Innovation in Psychological Treatment of Schizophrenia*, Chichester: John Wiley and Sons Ltd.

Margison, F. (2005) 'Integrating approaches to psychotherapy in psychosis', *Australian and New Zealand Journal of Psychiatry*, 39: 972–981.

Marshall, M. and Lockwood, A. (1998) *Assertive Community Treatment for People with Severe Mental Disorders*, The Cochrane Database of Systematic Reviews, Issue 2, Chichester: John Wiley and Sons Ltd.

Maslow, A.H. (1943) 'A theory of human motivation', *Psychology Review*, 50: 370–396.

Mayhew, S.L. (2003) 'Service engagement with assertive outreach and illness appraisals in individuals with psychotic illness', unpublished thesis, Birmingham University.

Meaden, A., Hacker., Paget, A., Jones, C. and Thorne, T. (in preparation) 'Developing a measurement of engagement: the Residential Engagement Scale for Psychosis'.

Meaden, A., Nithsdale, V., Rose, C., Smith, J. and Jones, C. (2004) 'Is engagement associated with outcome in assertive outreach?', *Journal of Mental Health*, 13: 415–424.

Minghella, E., Gauntlett, N. and Ford, R. (2002) 'Assertive outreach: does it reach expectations?' *Journal of Mental Health*, 11: 27–42.

Mowbray, C.T., Cohen, E. and Bybee, D. (1993) 'The challenge of outcome evaluation in homeless services: engagement as an intermediate outcome measure', *Evaluation and Program Planning*, 16: 337–346.

Paget, A.T., Meaden, A. and Amphlett, C.A. (in press) 'Engagement processes associated with outcome in assertive outreach: a follow up study', *Journal of Mental Health*.

Park, M.J., Tyrer, P., Elsworth, E., Fox, J., Ukoumunne, O.C. and MacDonald, A.

(2002) 'The measurement of engagement in the homeless mentally ill: the Homeless Engagement and Acceptance Scale – HEAS', *Psychological Medicine*, 32: 855–861.

Parsons, T. (1951) *The Social System*, Glencoe, IL: Free Press; as cited in D. Fisher (1997) 'Informed choice: the importance of personal participation in the healing process', in B. Blackwell (ed.) (1997) *Treatment Compliance and the Therapeutic Alliance*, Amsterdam: Harwood Academic Publishers.

Priebe, S. and Gruyters, T. (1993) 'The role of the helping alliance in psychiatric community care', *Journal of Nervous and Mental Disease*, 181: 552–557.

Priebe, S., Watts, J., Chase, M. and Matanov, A. (2005) 'Processes of disengagement and engagement in assertive outreach patients: qualitative study', *British Journal of Psychiatry*, 187: 438–443.

Ranger, M., Methuen, C., Rutter, D., Rao, B. and Tyrer, P. (2004) 'Prevalence of personality disorder in the case-load of an inner-city assertive outreach team', *Psychiatric Bulletin*, 28: 441–443.

Rose, C., Amphlett, C. and Larkin, M. (in preparation) 'An explorative study of carers' experiences of engaging with an Assertive Outreach Team'.

Sainsbury Centre for Mental Health (1998) *Keys to Engagement: review of care for people with severe mental illness who are hard to engage with services*, London: Sainsbury Centre for Mental Health.

Sainsbury Centre for Mental Health (2001) *The Capable Practitioner*, London: Sainsbury Centre for Mental Health.

Sainsbury Centre for Mental Health (2006) *Briefing 31: choice in mental health care*, London: Sainsbury Centre for Mental Health.

Solomon, P., Draine, J., and Delaney, M.A. (1995) 'The working alliance and consumer case management', *The Journal of Mental Health Administration*, 22: 126–134.

Stein, L. and Test, M. (1980) 'An alternative to mental hospital treatment 1: conceptual model, treatment program and clinical evaluation', *Archives of General Psychiatry*, 37: 392–397.

Tait, L., Birchwood, M., and Trower, P. (2002) 'A new (SES) to measure engagement with community mental health services', *Journal of Mental Health*, 11: 191–198.

Tait, L., Birchwood, M., and Trower, P. (2003) 'Predicting engagement with services for psychosis: insight, symptoms and recovery style', *British Journal of Psychiatry*, 182: 123–128.

Tyrer, P. and Simmonds, S. (2003) 'Treatment models for those with severe mental illness and comorbid personality disorder', *British Journal of Psychiatry*, 182 (suppl. 44), s15–s18.

Wane, J., Owen, A., Sood, L., Bradley, S., and Jones, C. (2007) 'The effectiveness of rural assertive outreach: a prospective cohort study in an English region', *Journal of Mental Health*, 16: 471–482.

Wolfson, P. and Cupitt, C. (2001) Bexley Engagement Measure, unpublished.

Yatchmenoff, D. (2005) 'Measuring client engagement from the client's perspective in nonvoluntary child protective services', *Research on Social Work Practice*, 15: 84–96.

2   The Whole Team Approach: containment or chaos?

Caroline Cupitt, Alf Gillham and Andrew Law

One of the most distinctive features of Assertive Outreach Teams is their approach to team working. Whereas community mental health teams tend to function as a collection of individuals who meet once a week to discuss a limited proportion of their work, staff in Assertive Outreach Teams work very closely together to provide a fully integrated service. There may be slight differences in exactly how this team working is done, but the effects of it are felt by both staff within the team and the people who receive a service from it. This gives a different flavour to the work and is one of the key factors in engaging people and encouraging them to remain engaged with the team. It is also an important tool in enabling the team to meet the very complex and enduring health and social difficulties of service users in a holistic way, whilst avoiding discontinuities caused by staff changes and absence. We would also like to argue that it provides a psychotherapeutic function for both staff and service users by allowing the team to contain and process difficult feelings and emotions.

Models of team working in assertive outreach

The effectiveness of teams has been shown to be enhanced when there are clear, shared objectives, differentiated roles and a need among members to work together to achieve team objectives (Carter and West, 1999). Two of these three aspects are very apparent in Assertive Outreach Teams, because they work with a well-defined population to achieve clear goals, and the complexity of the problems experienced by service users makes it easily apparent that team members must rely on each other to provide a comprehensive service. The area in which staff face potential difficulties is in role definition (see chapter five). For staff whose individual professional identity is very strongly held, it can be difficult to surrender to the degree of team working required, as we shall go on to discuss. Equally, staff without a clear professional identity can become mired in struggles to differentiate themselves within the team. Generally all teams foster a high degree of 'cross training' (Stein and Santos, 1998) in which team members equip each other with the basic skills of each speciality, whilst preserving the highly specialist skills of individuals where appropriate. In some teams, in order to promote core assertive outreach skills, staff have been encouraged to form a new professional identity, as an Assertive Outreach Worker (Witheridge, 1989).

In the UK, the assertive outreach service specification states that there should be a team approach (DoH, 2001), without ever defining what this might mean in practice. If one consults the literature, a range of models presents itself.

Keyworking

Sometimes Assertive Outreach Teams use a keyworker or case management model. This is more likely to occur in integrated than in stand-alone teams, in other words where assertive outreach workers are integrated into established locality Community Mental Health Teams. In these circumstances, the assertive outreach staff may meet only once a week. This approach is also sometimes used in rural areas where daily travelling distances would otherwise be very great.

This model of team working has been advocated by Burns and Firn (2002) as appropriate for stand-alone Assertive Outreach Teams. They argue that a primary keyworker, working alongside a secondary keyworker, can effectively meet the needs of service users and are sceptical about the necessity of further integration in team functioning. They go on to argue that many teams who say they use a team approach are in reality offering a keyworker model, albeit with some back-up from the wider team.

As a model of team working, the keyworker approach has the clear advantage of accountability, since a single worker is responsible for all the work with a particular service user. For service users there is also a single person to relate to in receiving the service. However, both of these features can easily become disadvantages. The responsibility that the worker bears can easily lead to stress and burnout, creating problems of staff retention and therefore discontinuity of care. The service offered is necessarily dominated and limited by the skills and point of view of the particular keyworker involved. Absences caused by sickness or leave can be highly disruptive to service users whose emotional difficulties require containment by a service which is both consistent and reliable. These disadvantages are great indeed when the service is being offered specifically to people with a history of difficulties with engagement.

The team approach

The term 'team approach' is used throughout the literature on assertive outreach, but is often poorly defined. It can mean either that the team operate as a whole with one caseload (see below as the Whole Team Approach) or that individual staff act as the primary contact point for their own caseload of approximately 10–12 people, with care being jointly provided with other members in a multi-disciplinary team. This latter model is advocated by the current *National Program Standards for ACT Teams* in the USA (Allness and Knoedler, 2003: 25), which state that, 'the service coordinator (case manager) is the first staff person called on when the client is in crisis and is the primary support person and educator to the individual client's family'. These tasks are also shared by other members of the team, who cover when the co-ordinator is absent. This model is widely used by Assertive Outreach Teams and appears to have become the dominant model within ACT (e.g. Stein and Santos, 1998). It neatly dovetails with the UK's Care Programme Approach (CPA), where the care co-ordinator is the primary contact point, simply extending the degree of shared work by the team as a whole, rather than changing the nature of team working itself.

The advantage of such a model is that accountability remains clear. If anything should go wrong, managers are comforted by the knowledge that the care co-ordinator remains primarily responsible. However, since this primary relationship is supplemented by other staff, holistic delivery of care is also possible. When it works well there is a 'team alliance approach' (Gold *et al.*, 2003: 293) whereby strong working alliances are formed between all members of the team and each individual service user, conferring many advantages. In particular Test (1979) emphasises the ability of the team to provide continuity so that care does not grind to a halt when the care co-ordinator is unavailable. She also suggests that a team approach allows many diverse points of view to be brought to bear on complex and difficult problems faced by service users, and that the ethos of shared responsibility helps to prevent staff stress and burnout.

Stein and Santos (1998) argue that the team should make clinical decisions according to a 'shared governance model'. In other words, when presented with a difficult and complex decision, the team put their heads together and discuss it until a consensus solution emerges. This may sound like a long and arduous process, but if the team's development has been values-based, very prolonged discussions are rare and valuable when they do occur. More recent support for such a model is found in Complexity Theory, which suggests that only a team approach can do justice to complex dilemmas (British Psychological Society, 2007).

The challenge of the team approach is to prevent slippage back into individual case management, such as observed by Burns and Firn (2002). The degree to which shared governance actually occurs varies greatly, depending on how well the team is functioning at any one time, the disposition of each care co-ordinator and the nature of the service users' difficulties. It remains possible for individual staff to resist team working and to function not very differently from keyworkers. People's contact with the team may be very much dominated by their care co-ordinator and this relationship can remain very stressful for both parties when crises happen.

The Whole Team Approach

We are referring to a particular model of team working as the Whole Team Approach to distinguish it from the Team Approach described above. The Whole Team Approach represents the greatest integration and co-operation possible within the team. Instead of promoting the idea that a single member of staff takes a primary role, people are encouraged to rely on the service, rather than on individual staff. There are no individual caseloads, but rather one team caseload. No relationship takes precedence over another, but rather the team as a whole functions as a network of supporters.

Whole team working was an early feature of assertive outreach in The Bridge Program at Thresholds in Illinois, established in 1978 (Witheridge and Dincin, 1985; Witheridge 1991). The Bridge Program sought to adapt Stein and Test's (1980) original model to a big city environment and the relatively homogeneous needs of frequent hospital users who were particularly difficult to engage (Witheridge, 1990). Its distinctive model of team working is sometimes known as the Bridge Model of assertive outreach (Bond *et al.*, 1995), the Total Treatment Approach (e.g. Engstrom *et al.*, 1990), the Total Team Approach (e.g. Witheridge *et al.*, 1982, Witheridge, 1991) or simply as the Team Approach (e.g. Navarro, 1995).

The Whole Team Approach was adopted by the Tulip Mental Health Group when they began offering one of the first UK assertive outreach services in 1990. Based on the original Bridge Model, this team was not multi-disciplinary and had only 4–6 staff, allowing staff members to develop a single shared identity. Tulip developed the model to incorporate more psychodynamic thinking (Navarro, 1995, 1998). The model has since been developed further to include multi-disciplinary working in larger teams, for example by IMPACT (Cupitt, 1997).

The Whole Team Approach has the same advantages as the Team Approach in that it can create a reliable and accessible service, in which truly holistic teamwork occurs and a sense of shared responsibility protects staff from stress and burnout. In fact, one can argue that these benefits are enhanced by the more collective nature of the support offered by the team. The approach naturally facilitates cross training between staff and this can lead not only to a more broadly skilled workforce but also a more culturally sensitive one. In addition, the highly visible nature of each staff member's work can facilitate effective team management and ensure that the team remains true to its core values. Because of the collective way responsibility is taken, the personal limits of individual staff members don't act to constrain the quality of care offered.

The Whole Team Approach changes the dynamic of the relationship between staff and service user in a very striking way, moving it away from the normal highly valued one-to-one relationship in favour of a network of supporters. Lowe (2003) describes the one-to-one relationship as like a lonely worker endlessly staggering, her arms embracing a restless person, in contrast to the team approach where the whole team are holding hands and surrounding the person, providing a strong and safe container. This metaphor suggests that assertive outreach services can be 'as strong and predictable as the bricks and mortar of the hospital used to be' (Lowe, 1999, cited in Lowe, 2003: 1).

Lowe (2003) talks of the Whole Team Approach as being the essential ingredient that is often missing in Assertive Outreach Teams, one that has the therapeutic power to sustain both service users and staff. For example, the experience of being held in mind by a whole team can help people to feel less overwhelmed by their difficulties by offering psychological containment (Navarro, 1998). Equally for staff, the experience of jointly holding responsibility can increase the team's capacity to think clearly in distressing and disturbing circumstances. This capacity is enhanced by the reflective space created by daily team meetings. As staff share their responses to service users, a deeper understanding is reached, both between staff and by the service user concerned. Because the approach offers a network of low-intensity relationships with staff, it is less likely to trigger negative transference experiences (Engstrom *et al.*, 1990) or Early Maladaptive Schema (Cupitt, 1999) than traditional one-to-one supportive relationships. When relationships do trigger difficult emotions, whole team working can make it easier to reflect on and tease out their meaning.

There are of course also disadvantages and challenges, particularly in marrying the approach to CPA requirements, which we shall discuss. Whole team working can descend into chaos if proper systems are not in place to co-ordinate the work. When members of the team do not share common values, there can be staff conflict. Many teams, such as Tulip, consider external consultancy an essential ingredient. Strong team management is equally important, and the Whole Team Approach is most likely to work well when these two features are combined.

Essential features of the Whole Team Approach

Working as a whole team confers many benefits, but these cannot be fully realised unless all the features of the Whole Team Approach are included. Most teams benefit from substantial training and visits to other services in order to fully grasp the model. It represents a radical departure from the usual keyworking model and it takes time for staff to adapt. Some staff may never enjoy the extent to which their personal autonomy is constrained, for example by not having control over their own diary of appointments. Anyone whose personal style is highly individualistic is going to find it difficult. For these reasons, it is essential that Assertive Outreach Teams using the Whole Team Approach include an explicit description of everyday working practices as part of their recruitment process.

We think there are four essential features for the Whole Team Approach to operate effectively.

1   The board
    This is a large white board, centrally placed in the team's main office. It
    has a permanent grid showing each day of the week, divided into one-
    hour slots, e.g. Figure 2.1. It is effectively the team's diary and principal
    planning tool. The board must be the largest size possible in order for
    these hourly slots to be large enough to contain all the appointments for
    that hour for the whole team. Some items like team meetings are fixed,
    others change according to need. There has to be an absolute rule that all
    work of the team is on the board, otherwise the team cannot function. It
    is created afresh each week by the whole team and updated daily in
    response to changing circumstances. It is the key reference point for the
    team and allows any member of the team to stand in for any other at a
    moment's notice. In some sense the board represents the team's ability to
    hold everyone in mind. It also creates a sense of shared identity and
    belonging.

2   Rotated visits
    The default assumption is that visits are rotated amongst team members,
    so that whilst an appointment may be fixed, say for 11 a.m. on a Tuesday,
    the particular member of staff who will visit changes every week, allow-
    ing all members of staff to remain in contact with all service users. There
    needs to be an express reason to deviate from this, based on someone's
    need and not simply for the convenience of the service. Such reasons need
    to be explored whenever they arise as they often reveal otherwise hidden
    aspects of the work. For example, a member of staff may repeatedly
    volunteer for a particular visit because of a strong identification. While
    this remains hidden it could become problematic for both parties, but
    once understood it can be used as a therapeutic tool. Over time, staff may
    come to play differing roles in someone's life and visits may not remain
    strictly rotated. However, whole team working should ensure reflection
    on the development of such roles so that they can remain truly help-
    ful. Staff in specialist roles may require some fixed appointments, for
    example when providing psychotherapy, but even where this is needed,
    the link to the rest of the team must not be lost.

3   Shared information systems
    When visits are rotated, it is rarely the case that the same member of staff
    sees someone twice in succession. To ensure continuity of care it is there-
    fore essential that all notes are kept in a single file, accessible to all team
    members. This also includes records of psychotherapy or other specialist
    interventions, since they do not occur in isolation from the rest of the
    person's life and therefore from the rest of their care. Similarly, tasks
    arising from contacts which cannot be completed within the same day
    need to be recorded in a shared system so that they can be picked up by
    any other member of staff on subsequent days, for example if the origin-
    ator is off sick. In the same way any post or telephone messages need to
    recorded in a shared book so that team members can respond for each

February 2008		1st Manager on-call: Andrew / 2nd Manager on-call: Kevin / Senior on-call: Lorraine						A/L: Mahesh all week / Days off			
Day	Date	On-call	9.00	10.00	11.00	12.00	1.00	2.00	3.00	4.00	Appointments
Mon	19	Marcia	Planning Mtg	M.K. / K.M. / K.W.	J.P. / M.Ka. / W.T. / D.R.	T.A. / J.G. / B.J.	Y.O. / C.K. / D.H.	A.L. / R.K. / R.L.	I.H. / D.J. / K.W.	Handover	10am S.M. CPA Mtg / 10am A.P. housing apt
Tues	20	Steven	Planning Mtg	A.Y. / K.W.	M.K. / M.C. / S.C.	M.A. / T.A. / O.B. / B.J.	S.B. / W.M. / D.W.	S.K. / B.M. / E.M.	I.L. / S.C. / K.W.	Handover	12.30 S.B. flat view / 2pm C.M. CPA Mtg
Wed	21	Alison	Planning Mtg	S.M. / N.N. / K.W.	L.C. / J.C. / M.R.	J.P. / J.R. / C.M. / R.C.	J.W. / M.M. / S.S.	S.F. / G.H. / J.G. / K.Me	P.McK. / T.W. / K.W.	Handover	11am S.M. Psych apt / 3pm R.C. dentist
Thurs	22	Brian	Planning Mtg	Referral Mtg	Admin	Clinical Review	Lunch	Clinical Superv.	Service Mtg	Service Mtg	
Fri	23	Paul	Board Planning	A.Y. / E.S. / K.W.	E.O. / A.W. / L.L	H.N. / F.R. / O.C.	C.T. / M.M. / R.B.	K.H. / L.L.	R.D. / A.G. / T.R. / K.W.	Handover	9.30 – 4.30 Substance Misuse training (Head Office) - Steven

Supervision:
Steven - Tues @ 10.00am
Paul – Fri @ 2.00pm

Hospital visits:
K.H.
M.R.
H.A.

Client Reviews:
K.W.
A.L.

Copyright: Tulip Mental Health Group 2001

Figure 2.1 The board

other. Although this can initially be confusing for other agencies, who persist in wishing to speak to the same member of staff, they quickly learn the advantages of always being able to speak to someone who knows the person concerned.

4   Daily meetings

The daily meeting is considered an essential component of both the Team Approach and the Whole Team Approach. However, when using the Whole Team Approach it is also the cornerstone of the care co-ordination system. The team meets for about an hour at the end of every day, to update each other, share concerns and make immediate plans. These end-of-day meetings also provide important emotional support for staff, and ensure that no one goes home at the end of the day feeling they have the sole responsibility for a difficult situation. As such they provide emotional containment for both staff and service users. Most teams also meet briefly at the beginning of the day to plan the day's work and update the board accordingly. In addition to the daily meetings, weekly meetings provide an opportunity to include sessional staff, review plans and address team business.

The experience of the Whole Team Approach

At its best such a model allows everyone to contain and work with very difficult problems, creating a therapeutic function of containment for the team. With adequate space and support for reflection, it allows staff to explore their own feelings about their work, which may range from unrealistic high hopes to extreme helplessness. It can be argued that the people referred to assertive outreach are by definition those whom services have not been able to think about, and so this process of team reflection is one of the critical ingredients in successful engagement. Hinshelwood (2004) argues that it is important to protect the attitude that forms the reflective stance, saying that the culture itself needs to be a 'culture of enquiry'. He feels that the therapeutic task is to keep things meaningful and suggests that an external consultant can help with this (e.g. Navarro, 1998). He also suggests that a team can develop a kind of internal consultancy within itself, but only if the individuals in the team feel understood. When the Whole Team Approach is working well, all this is possible in the daily round of team meetings (see also chapter six).

People who receive assertive outreach services often experience extremely complex health and social difficulties, which at times feel completely overwhelming. In turning to others for help, there is the fear that they too will become overwhelmed and thus the difficulties compounded. Such fears may often underlie people's reluctance to engage. Developing a relationship with a whole team, and being held in mind by that whole team, can help people to feel less overwhelmed by their difficulties and more confident about the likelihood of continuing support. Although many staff initially worry that it is confusing or overwhelming for people to meet routinely with all team members, in fact it very often promotes engagement.

Example:
When Michael was referred to the team, he had not only an enduring psychosis, but also a dependency on butane gas. He led an extremely chaotic lifestyle and the team found it very difficult to make regular contact. Members of the team visited in pairs several times a week, hoping to catch him in. Over time he gradually met everyone in the team and seemed to really appreciate the feeling of being cared about by so many people. He said with a smile, 'You're like the mafia with love.'

Very often, when sharing experiences in daily meetings, staff discover that they have formed quite different impressions of the same person. This allows for the reality testing that Hinshelwood (2004) refers to and enables staff to learn from their own differing experiences. On occasions this may reveal more about the staff than the service user, in particular in revealing belief systems and personal values. In conventional services these would remain hidden, and yet are often imposed on people or even used to pathologise them.

Example:
A nurse in the team visited Jerry at home and came back to the team with horror stories about the state of his flat. She described it as filthy and felt it was a high priority for the team to organise a clean-up. Whilst this was being arranged, the psychologist in the team visited and was surprised to find the flat looking OK. Jerry was unable to give much account of how this change had occurred and the team wondered if this was a reflection of his poor mental state. However, another visit by the nurse the following week revealed that in fact Jerry's flat had never changed. It was the very different hygiene standards of the staff which had influenced the assessment. In the handover meeting the nurse revealed that she cleaned every surface in her home weekly, whilst the psychologist couldn't remember the last time she'd washed her kitchen floor.

As staff share their responses to service users, they get to know each other in a much deeper way than ordinarily occurs in teams. Over time the team as a whole is more and more able to take into account the individual staff member's contribution to interactions and appreciate the different aspects of the person elicited by each member. Through this process, a truly balanced and holistic understanding of the person can be reached and then held, not just by an individual, but by the whole team itself.

Example:
We jointly visited Marilyn, whose children had been taken into care, on the birthday of one of her children, whom she hadn't been able to see,

even to give a present. Both workers returned from the visit giving radic-
ally different accounts of Marilyn. One thought she was deeply upset, the
other experienced her as fine and coping. The two workers were able to
represent the different experiences and ways of coping Marilyn was
using; one upset by the separation and loss and the other detached and
disengaged.

The experience of individual staff in the field is greatly enhanced by individual workers 'carrying their colleagues' views' in their minds when visiting
people on a one-to-one basis. Over time each worker can develop an internalised team, which they can use to check their assumptions and explore
neglected areas. This is similar to Hinshelwood's notion of an internalised
consultancy (Hinshelwood, 2004).

Example:
Before I went to see Alan, I would read through the last few contact
notes, noting who had visited and what had been discussed. When meeting with Alan and discussing in more detail issues that were current, I
would illustrate our discussions with references to what other staff had
said/thought, always naming them. I would say, 'Remember when you
spoke with Judy about this last week, you told her such and such and we
talked about this in one of our meetings and we wondered whether . . .'
In this way, not only would I be carrying my colleagues and their views
with me (it was like the whole team was sitting in the room), but Alan
knew that different individuals had different and complementary views
and cared enough to think and talk about him.

Incorporating specialist roles

When using the Whole Team Approach, specialist staff such as psychological
therapists are full members of the team. For this to be a reality, they need to
do a certain amount of generic work, alongside other team members (Cupitt
et al., 2006). The only exception to this might be if they were only funded to
work part time in the team and the team chose to prioritise their specialist
work over the generic team function. However, this has disadvantages and
in particular may undermine the therapeutic effectiveness of the Whole
Team Approach. Wherever possible, specialist staff should be employed full
time with the understanding that they perform their specialist function
part time.

For all specialist staff, their specialist role is to some extent shared. This
may occur through explicit 'cross training' or become a reality over time as a
result of close team working. So whilst a psychologist working within a team
could be conceived as carrying the torch of psychological therapies, she is not
the sole provider. Daily handover meetings allow a psychologist to share
emerging formulations and strategies, which other team members can then

debate, contribute to and take into their visits. In this way over time all staff develop their psychological skills and contribute to psychological interventions. This approach has the potential to allow a psychological formulation to reach all parts of the team's work, impacting on risk assessment, medication reviews, benefit applications, housing, etc. (see chapter four).

Some people will need periods of individual psychological therapy, provided from within the team. The boundaries of this need to be negotiated with both the service user and the team at an early stage. It is normally more appropriate to offer team confidentiality for such work, rather than agree to keep secrets from the rest of the team, which would seriously undermine the Whole Team Approach, and possibly work against the person's interests. It is also very important that, during periods when one member of staff is having more frequent contact with a person than the rest of the team, the person's connection to the rest of the team is not lost. Generally this can be achieved by planning two visits a week, the second visit rotating amongst the whole team. When engagement in psychotherapy is problematic this offers a helpful mechanism to re-engage when people drop out.

> **Example:**
> Devon had begun to meet the team psychologist weekly to explore interpersonal issues, stemming from his traumatic childhood experiences. He had never discussed these in detail before and, although ostensibly motivated to do so, often found the actual prospect so daunting that he would go out just before the psychologist's visit. Interestingly, he did not avoid other members of the team. During a period when he had missed appointments with the team psychologist for several weeks, other members of the team were able to gently encourage him to try again, whilst simultaneously alerting the psychologist to the need to slow the pace of her work. This achieved a re-engagement and a helpful piece of psychological therapy followed.

In the above example from Cupitt (1999), it appears that the introduction of a one-to-one relationship triggered an early maladaptive schema of mistrust in someone who had many reasons to mistrust close relationships. However, although this schema temporarily prevented the psychologist from having contact with Devon, whole team working was able to bring about a resolution of the therapeutic breach. When staff skilfully move between the foreground and background of the contact with someone in this way, people with profound interpersonal difficulties can be supported without discontinuities of care (see also chapter eight).

Attachment theory and the whole team

Assertive Outreach Teams by definition work with people who have very complex and long-standing mental health difficulties. Amongst such a group you would expect to find that many had experienced early trauma or neglect as children. When we also consider that Assertive Outreach Teams in the UK specifically target people who have difficulties sustaining contact with services, the proportion must be even higher. In fact, in our experience, it is nearly always the case that people's personal histories reveal extremely difficult early experiences and this is supported by the similar observations of others (e.g. Navarro, 1998).

The work of Bowlby (1969) has been very influential in understanding how the disrupted early attachments of children can lead to interpersonal difficulties for adults. He makes a fundamental distinction between secure and insecure attachments, the former arising out of parental–child interactions that are warm, consistent and predictable. People who are lucky enough to have such a start in life have found a secure base from which to go on to form adult relationships which are both satisfying and sustainable. Bowlby suggests that, in contrast, children whose parents are not able to provide optimal care will develop various types of insecure attachments.

Mary Main, amongst others, has studied the effects of such insecure early attachments on the interpersonal behaviour of adults (Main *et al.*, 1985). She suggests that there are three principal types of insecure attachment styles seen in adults: preoccupied/ambivalent, dismissing/avoidant and unresolved/ disorganised. Although the ambivalent attachment is generally considered the most common type of insecure attachment, because ambivalent people actively seek out supportive relationships, they do not necessarily become recipients of assertive outreach services. However, the avoidant and disorganised attachment styles appear to be very common amongst people referred to Assertive Outreach Teams. Bartholomew (1990) goes further in distinguishing two kinds of avoidant attachment styles, one dismissing and one fearful, the latter being associated with both a negative self-image as well as a negative view of others.

Berry *et al.*'s (2007) review of the role of adult attachment style in psychosis illustrates how important attachment style may be in understanding psychosis and in particular why some individuals do not easily engage with services. Studies have found significantly higher levels of insecure attachment in psychiatric groups than in controls, and, what is more, people with a diagnosis of schizophrenia have been found to have higher levels of insecurity than those diagnosed with an affective disorder such as depression (Dozier, 1990; Dozier *et al.*, 1991). Dozier (1990) also examined attachment organisation and the use of treatment. She found that more secure attachment ratings were associated with greater co-operation with treatment, whilst individuals with avoidant attachment strategies were more likely to reject treatment providers, disclose less and use treatment less. It would seem that it is this subgroup of people, with a history of psychosis and an avoidant attachment style, which is likely to form a large part of any Assertive Outreach Team's caseload.

Other research has shown that, by the time many people are referred to an

Assertive Outreach Team, they have become socially isolated, not just from services but also friends and family (Lukeman, 2003). There is a social poverty in people's lives that is often long-standing and profound. It is our impression that this reflects underlying avoidant or disorganised attachment styles, developed as an adaptive response to very difficult childhood experiences, and now functioning in adulthood to maintain social isolation. Gumley and Schwannauer (2006) go further to suggest that avoidance and resistance may in fact be seen as coping strategies for someone who has experienced psychosis, since they can be self-protective in intense interpersonal contexts. Typically people either avoid social situations entirely, or respond to them in such unusual ways that other people tend to back away.

The capacity to establish and organise collaborative bonds with others in adulthood is likely to be mediated by a person's attachment history and their internal working models of self and others. When working therapeutically with people with insecure attachments it is important to provide a secure base whilst disconfirming their problematic working models of relationships. This is something that people who come to assertive outreach have generally not found with their previous experiences of services. In many cases services have in fact repeated problematic relationship patterns whilst completely failing to provide a secure base (Seager, 2006).

In contrast, the assertive outreach service model has many features that make it therapeutic for people with a history of insecure attachment. It is said that people with an avoidant attachment style particularly welcome instrumental help, in other words exactly the kind of practical support that Assertive Outreach Teams emphasise in the early stages of engagement (Witheridge, 1989). In addition, the use of the Whole Team Approach means that no one relationship is likely to become intense or be experienced as intrusive. It is interesting that staff are very often concerned about the process of introducing more and more team members to service users in the first few months after referral, thinking that the person would prefer just to work with one or two. However, from a service user's perspective this appears to be less of a concern. In fact, some people say how much they like the feeling of being part of a network of support. One can speculate that those with avoidant attachment styles in particular would feel more comfortable with a network of low-intensity relationships than the traditional keyworker approach.

People with a disorganised attachment style are equally likely to present difficulties for a conventional keyworker relationship. Their changeable and unpredictable responses towards staff may be experienced as stressful or manipulative by team members who are trying to build up a consistent and warm rapport. Whole team working, where each member of staff contributes their own different attachment styles and personalities, can appear somewhat chaotic and disorganised to an outsider, but this may in fact mirror the service user's behaviour, and thus feel familiar to them. This suggests that the Whole Team Approach can be a good tool for initial engagement with this group. Over time, within the context of team working, it is then possible to gradually introduce a therapeutic approach in which attachment relationships become more organised. There is some debate about the extent to which adult attachment styles can change (Berry *et al.*, 2007), and it would appear to be a mistake to aim for a complete resolution of the disorganisation. Nevertheless, some movement seems to be possible, provided such a therapeutic endeavour proceeds very carefully and maintains a connection to the diversity of the whole team.

The extent to which teams are aware that they are working with attachment issues varies and many staff are unaware of the importance of the team as an attachment figure. Many staff feel frustrated by the sense of chaos that team working can bring, and one can hypothesise that this would be particularly keenly felt by staff who themselves have secure attachments and therefore value consistency and predictability. Gumley and Schwannauer (2006) describe a study by Dozier *et al.* (1994) which looked at the relationship between clinicians' attachment strategies and their ability to respond therapeutically. It was found that clinicians with secure attachment attend and respond to people's underlying needs, whereas clinicians who are more insecure respond to the most obvious presentation of needs. This suggests that engagement can be promoted by taking account of attachment issues.

Example:
Simon came to the team as a young man with a long history of disrupted attachments. His lifestyle was chaotic and he never stayed with anyone or in any place for long. Initial engagement focused on practical tasks associated with benefits and housing, and was mostly delivered by staff who themselves did not wish to seek confidences from him. At this stage both Simon and staff were displaying avoidant attachment styles. Simon welcomed this intervention and over time began to experience a little more stability in his life. The team then introduced the team psychologist, with the explicit aim of beginning to talk about his experience of trauma. The psychologist's more preoccupied attachment style was at first very difficult for Simon to tolerate, but over a long period of time and in several stages, he told his story.

For many people, particularly the young men who often form a large part of the team's caseload, there may be primary attachment figures still present in their lives. Teams often find themselves working with families, and in particular mothers, to support and develop these primary relationships (see chapter seven). Every team will also have service users who have lost all contact with their families of origin and live without any current close non-professional relationships. In our experience as many as 30 per cent of people will have no significant contact with anyone other than team members during an average week. In this situation, it is not uncommon for individual staff members or the team to become primary attachment figures for someone. This is not just a feature of assertive outreach, but has been observed to occur where staff in other health-care settings both provide a secure base and modulate anxiety for people (Adshead, 1998). This could potentially become overwhelming for individual staff members, and be traumatic for the person concerned, whenever the staff member is away or changes their job.

In the case of the Whole Team Approach, where people are encouraged to depend upon the service and not upon any individual, it is possible that the team itself may become an attachment figure. So although the individual team members may change, the service goes on and is truly capable of providing the security and consistency that is needed from a primary attachment figure. The caveat here is that any threat to the existence of the team will be experienced as catastrophic for such people, in ways that service managers are unlikely to appreciate fully. Given that as many as a third of users may have a deep attachment to the team in this way, it also becomes very challenging for teams to achieve the kind of discharge rate that managers often expect. If the team is truly functioning as a primary attachment, even where discharge is intellectually acceptable, the reality of separation might be emotionally experienced as catastrophic. All teams seem to have had experiences of 'failed discharges' which in this context could be more positively understood as successful attachments.

Evidence for whole team working

There is already good evidence favouring team working in mental health services. The British Psychological Society (2007) states that where the conditions for effective team working are in place, team working contributes to improved effectiveness (e.g. Cohen and Bailey, 1997; West and Markiewicz, 2004). However, it has also been found that working in 'pseudo teams' is worse than not working in inter-professional care teams at all (Carter and West, 1999; Yan et al., 2006). In Assertive Outreach Teams, where using a team approach has such importance, it would therefore appear likely to be one of the key factors in effectiveness.

Assertive outreach is often said to be the most researched model of community mental health care. However, most of the research has compared the model as a whole against other models such as case management (summarised by Marshall and Lockwood, 1998), rather than looking at individual components such as team working. A few researchers have boldly tried to determine which features of the model are really critical to success. McGrew and Bond (1995) surveyed the opinions of experts in the field and later of assertive outreach staff (McGrew et al., 2003), finding in both cases that a team approach is considered a critical ingredient. More recently, Burns et al. (2007) have attempted to deconstruct the components of the model through a systematic review and meta-regression of previous trials. They found that reductions in hospital admission achieved by ACT teams occur when rates of hospital admission are high in the first place. Teams with high fidelity to the

ACT model were more likely to reduce use of hospital care, and team organisation was critical, in other words the degree to which staff worked as a team rather than as independent practitioners. They conclude that there needs to be more research into team practices rather than team labels.

Perhaps more directly relevant to the Whole Team Approach is the much older meta-analysis by Bond *et al.* (1995). This looked at nine studies of Assertive Outreach Teams all using the Bridge Model. This analysis is of particular interest because it focuses on services using the Whole Team Approach to engage hard to reach individuals, a similar task to that given to current UK teams. They found that teams using the Bridge Model were able to achieve engagement which was exceptionally stable over time and substantially reduced rates of hospital admission.

Bond *et al.* (1991) have also reported a naturalistic study which compared, over a two-year period, the support offered to people with high inpatient bed use in Philadelphia. One group was supported by workers using a Whole Team Approach, the other was supported by individual case managers. They found that, although an individual case manager can have an enormous impact over the short term, many people receiving this approach continued to go through cycles of high hospital use; the authors identify discontinuities of care caused by staff turnover as a possible explanation for this. The Whole Team Approach, by contrast, took longer to have an impact, but the team became progressively more effective, achieving a greater reduction in admissions after two years. The authors suggest that teams take longer to become established when a Whole Team Approach is used and that such teams 'need a one-to-two-year grace period to get off the ground' (op. cit.: 96). Some UK evaluations of teams using a Whole Team Approach have failed to find reduced hospital admissions; this study implies that it could simply be the result of evaluating too soon.

The first Assertive Outreach Team to adopt the Bridge Model in the UK was Tulip, based in Haringey, London. In an early evlauation, Gauntlett *et al.* (1996) found that Tulip workers, using the Whole Team Approach, reported the highest levels of role clarity and team identification, the highest intrinsic and extrinsic job satisfaction and the lowest levels of burnout on nearly all dimensions, when compared with conventional Community Mental Health Teams.

Gauntlett *et al.* (1996) also interviewed people receiving services from the team, some of whom commented on the experience of receiving support from a whole team. For example:

'Every time someone came, it would be someone different. I've met a lot of people, and they have given me a lot of encouragement. Personally, I think it would have been a bit heavy for one person to come every week, for them, it would have been unfair for one person to take all that on, even though it's their job . . . I find that every one of them is different. They've all got their own way of approaching me and talking to me, but basically they're all saying something the same, especially when it's coming to give support.'

(op. cit.: 44)

Interestingly, Gauntlett *et al.* (1996) also note that, whilst people were generally pleased with the support they were receiving, most continued to express a preference for a single keyworker. Likewise staff, while recognising the advantages of a whole team approach, missed one-to-one therapeutic relationships. This supports the hypothesis that, while all parties wish for a secure one-to-one relationship, what works in practice is a more diverse network of support which can accommodate the challenges posed by a history of insecure attachments. This is further supported by Watts and Priebe (2002), who interviewed people receiving assertive outreach. Some of the participants in this study acknowledged that the Whole Team Approach had the advantage of protecting them against the pain of personal rejection when workers leave.

IMPACT and a new Tulip team, both using the Whole Team Approach, were formally evaluated in 1998 by Minghella *et al.* (2002). In line with expectations, they both demonstrated high rates of engagement and user satisfaction. These teams sought to target people who had histories of being difficult to engage, or being completely unengaged with services, so it is perhaps unsurprising that engagement was the primary outcome in the first year of operation. Outcomes such as reduced admission rates did not occur until later: a subsequent review of outcomes at the IMPACT team found substantial progress was made over the following year (Williamson, 1999) once engagement had been achieved and the team had become established.

Overcoming difficulties

Large Assertive Outreach Teams can have difficulties maintaining whole team working, and there is a tendency for smaller groups of staff to cluster around particular users in order to meet their needs coherently. In some instances this has been made into a more formal arrangement, by creating 'mini-teams' within the larger team (e.g. Dixon *et al.*, 1995). However, this approach needs caution as many of the advantages of whole team working can easily be lost. It is generally better for large teams to split into two smaller teams, as occurred in Tulip when they started to offer assertive outreach services in both the east and west of the London borough of Haringey.

Sometimes Assertive Outreach Teams encounter difficulties because of a tension between specialist roles and rotated visits. For the Whole Team Approach to function well, there needs to be some flexibility with visits, such that, although they generally rotate around staff members, particular relationships are allowed to develop as appropriate to meet particular needs. The most important thing is that such relationships are thought about carefully so that they can perform a therapeutic function, which is why a deviation from rotated visits must be agreed by the whole team. This does not mean that it is wrong, or against whole team working, for some relationships to be stronger than others, or to develop in special ways, provided the connection to the wider team is not lost.

When Assertive Outreach Teams adopt the Whole Team Approach, they still need to use the Care Programme Approach (CPA), which is a requirement of all statutory mental health services in the UK. For the purposes of CPA, a care co-ordinator must be named, but this can be done without undermining whole team working. The care co-ordinator need not have any more involvement in delivering care than any other member of the team and yet still co-ordinate care effectively. When using the Whole Team Approach care co-ordinators perform a solely administrative role in ensuring that the team has reviews and completes documentation as required (Witheridge, 1991).

In the early stages of establishing a new team, it is not uncommon for a lot of time to be spent in meetings. The team will need to spend time getting to know each other, establishing team values and developing effective communication systems. This can be perceived as a difficulty, and teams have often been criticised for spending too much time in meetings. However, it is our experience that over time the length and number of meetings reduce and eventually become no more than one would expect in any other Community Mental Health Team (CMHT). The IMPACT team was able to demonstrate this by doing an audit of time spent in meetings during the first and then the second year of operation. By the second year, the time spent in meetings was equivalent to that of a local CMHT.

Some staff find the reduced personal autonomy and interchangeable roles difficult to tolerate. There can be a longing for the familiar one-to-one relationship that many staff have been trained to expect and that may be a primary motivation for their work. When recruiting new staff this needs to be carefully explained and explored. For staff to enjoy this kind of work they need to be as interested in their relationships with colleagues as with service users, and in the process by which the team operates as a whole. For this to be effective the team needs to build a strong team identity based on shared values. The team also needs to explore differences actively, so that staff value each other's contributions to the work (Engstrom *et al.*, 1990). On an ongoing basis the team needs to be able to reflect on the work and its impact on the team, individually and collectively. This is best done by using skilled external facilitation, such as described by Navarro (1998).

There is always the possibility that, faced with a difficult task, the team will descend into chaos, leaving everyone feeling confused and unsupported. Using the Whole Team Approach is not a substitute for an active and effective team manager. In fact it requires strong and containing management from a hands-on team manager who also contributes to the daily work of the team. The manager is responsible for ensuring the team operates effectively, including commenting on team process. However, they are not a clinical lead, and the team as a whole must act collectively in clinical decision making. The manager needs to be able to identify line management issues, e.g. not following team decisions, and address them promptly. They need to ensure effective systems of communication exist within the team and are routinely used so that the team does not fragment into chaos.

Conclusions

A report on a Department of Health (2005) assertive outreach seminar asks 'Can we identify successful elements of assertive outreach?'. Many of those with experience in working in Assertive Outreach Teams feel that the use of a team approach is one of those key elements. However, it is often poorly defined and the psychological processes left unexamined. We hope that this chapter has begun to elucidate both the method and the processes involved, and that this will lead to further research.

References

Adshead, G. (1998) 'Psychiatric staff as attachment figures: understanding management problems in psychiatric services in the light of attachment theory', *British Journal of Psychiatry*, 172: 64–69.

Allness, D.J. and Knoedler, W.H. (2003) 'National Program Standards for ACT Teams', a companion document to *A Manual for ACT Start-Up*, Arlington, VA: The National Alliance for the Mentally Ill.

Bartholomew, K. (1990) 'Avoidance of intimacy: an attachment perspective', *Journal of Social and Personal Relationships*, 7: 147–178.

Berry. K., Barrowclough, C. and Wearden, A. (2007) 'A review of the role of adult attachment style in psychosis: unexplored issues and questions for further research', *Clinical Psychology Review*, 27: 458–475.

Bond, G.R., McGrew, J.H. and Fekete, D.M. (1995) 'Assertive outreach for frequent users of psychiatric hospitals: a meta-analysis', *The Journal of Mental Health Administration*, 22: 4–16.

Bond, G.R., Pensec, M., Dietzen, L., McCafferty, D., Giemza, R., Sipple, H.W. (1991) 'Intensive case management for frequent users of psychiatric hospitals in a large city: a comparison of team and individual caseloads', *Psychosocial Rehabilitation Journal*, 15: 90–98.

Bowlby, J. (1969) *The Making and Breaking of Affectional Bonds*, London: Tavistock.

British Psychological Society (2007) *New Ways of Working for Applied Psychologists in Health and Social Care: working psychologically in teams*, Leicester: British Psychological Society.

Burns, T., Catty, J., Dash, M., Roberts, C., Lockwood, A. and Marshall, M. (2007) 'Use of intensive case management to reduce time in hospital in people with severe mental illness: systematic review and meta-regression', *British Medical Journal*, 335: 336–340.

Burns, T. and Firn, M. (2002) *Assertive Outreach in Mental Health: a manual for practitioners*, Oxford: Oxford University Press.

Carter, A.J., and West, M.A. (1999) 'Sharing the burden – teamwork in health care settings', in R. Payne and J. Firth-Cozens (eds) *Stress in Health Professionals: psychological and organisational causes and Interventions*, Chichester: Wiley and Sons Ltd.

62 *Cupitt, Gillham and Law*

Cohen, S.G. and Bailey, D.E. (1997) 'What makes teams work: group effectiveness research from the shop floor to the executive suite', *Journal of Management*, 23: 239–290.

Cupitt, C. (1997) 'The assertive outreach psychologist', *Clinical Psychology Forum*, 103: 32–33.

Cupitt, C. (1999) 'Key factors in engaging with people with severe personality disorder', *Mental Health Care*, 2: 386–388.

Cupitt, C., Meddings, S., Amphlett, C. and Thomas, M. (2006) *Clinical Psychologists and Assertive Outreach:* Psychosis and Complex Mental Health Faculty Briefing Paper No. 21, Leicester: British Psychological Society.

Department of Health (2001) *The Mental Health Policy Implementation Guide*, London: Department of Health.

Department of Health (2005) 'Assertive outreach in mental health in England: report from a day seminar on research, policy and practice', 7th October.

Dixon, L.B., Krauss, N., Lehman, A.F. and DeForge, B.R. (1995) 'Modifying the PACT model to serve homeless persons with severe mental illness', *Psychiatric Services*, 46: 684–688.

Dozier, M. (1990) 'Attachment organisation and treatment use for adults with serious psychopathological disorders', *Development and Psychotherapy*, 2: 47–60.

Dozier, M., Cue, K.L. and Barnett, L. (1994) 'Clinicians as caregivers: role of attachment organisation in treatment', *Journal of Consulting and Clinical Psychology*, 62: 793–800.

Dozier, M., Stevenson, A.L., Lee, S.W. and Velligan, D.I. (1991) 'Attachment organisation and familial over-involvement for adults with serious psychopathological disorders', *Development and Psychopathology*, 3: 475–489.

Engstrom, K., Brooks, E.B., Jonikas, J.A., Cook, J.A. and Witheridge, T.F. (1990) *Creating Community Linkages: a guide to assertive outreach for homeless persons with severe mental illness*, Chicago: Thresholds.

Gauntlett, N., Ford, R. and Muijen, M. (1996) *Teamwork: models of outreach in an urban multi-cultural setting*, London: Sainsbury Centre for Mental Health.

Gold, P.B., Meisler, N., Santos, A.B., Keleher, J., Becker, D.R., Knoedler, W.H., Carnemolla, M.A, Williams, O.H., Toscano, R. and Stormer, G. (2003) 'The program of Assertive Community Treatment: implementation and dissemination of an evidence-based model of community-based care for persons with severe and persistent mental illness', *Cognitive and Behavioral Practice*, 10: 290–303.

Gumley, A. and Schwannauer, M. (2006) *Staying Well after Psychosis: a cognitive interpersonal approach to recovery and relapse prevention*, Hove: Wiley and Sons Ltd.

Hinshelwood, R.D. (2004) *Suffering Insanity: psychoanalytic essays on psychosis*, London: Bruner-Routledge.

Lowe, J. (1999) 'A new model for a new challenge – Tulip assertive outreach services', *Mental Health Review*, 4: 17–19.

Lowe, J. (2003) 'Progress of assertive outreach services: reflections and examples', *Mental Health Review*, 8: 31–34.

Lukeman, R. (2003) 'Service users' experience of the process of being engaged by assertive outreach teams', unpublished thesis, Salomons, Canterbury Christ Church University.

McGrew, J.H. and Bond G.R. (1995) 'Critical ingredients of assertive community treatment: judgements of the experts', *Journal of Mental Health Administration*, 22: 113–125.

McGrew, J.H., Pescosolido, B. and Wright, E. (2003) 'Case managers' perspectives on critical ingredients of Assertive Community Treatment and on its implementation', *Psychiatric Services*, 54: 370–376.

Main, M., Kaplan, N. and Cassidy, J. (1985) 'Security in infancy, childhood and adulthood: a move to the level of representation', in I. Bretherton and E. Waters (eds) *Growing Points of Attachment Therapy and Research*, Monographs of the Society for Research in Child Development, 50: 66–104.

Marshall, M. and Lockwood A. (1998) *Assertive Community Treatment for People with Severe Mental Disorders*, Cochrane Review.

Minghella, E., Gauntlett, N. and Ford R. (2002) 'Assertive outreach: does it reach expectations?', *Journal of Mental Health*, 11: 27–42.

Navarro, T. (1995) *Tulip Team Approach: a working paper*. London: Tulip.

Navarro, T. (1998) 'Beyond keyworking', in A. Foster and V. Zagier Roberts (eds) *Managing Mental Health in the Community: chaos and containment*, London: Routledge.

Seager, M. (2006) 'The concept of "psychological safety" – a psychoanalytically-informed contribution towards "safe, sound and supportive" mental health services', *Psychoanalytic Psychotherapy*, 20: 266–280.

Stein, L.I. and Santos, A.B. (1998) *Assertive Community Treatment of Persons with Severe Mental Illness*, New York: Norton.

Stein L.I. and Test, M.A. (1980) 'Alternatives to mental hospital treatment', *Archives of General Psychiatry*, 37: 392–397.

Test, A. (1979) 'Continuity of care in community treatment', *New Directions for Mental Health Services*, 2: 15–23.

Watts, J. and Priebe, S. (2002) 'A phenomenological account of users' experiences of Assertive Community Treatment', *Bioethics*, 16: 439–454.

West, M.A. and Markiewicz, L. (2004) *Building Team-Based Working: a practical guide to organizational transformation*, Oxford: Blackwell Publishing Inc.

Williamson, T. (1999) *Outcome Indicator Report*, London: IMPACT.

Witheridge, T.F. (1989) 'The Assertive Community Treatment worker: an emerging role and its implications for professional training', *Hospital and Community Psychiatry*, 40: 620–624.

Witheridge, T.F. (1990) 'Assertive Community Treatment: a strategy for helping persons with severe mental illness to avoid rehospitalisation', in N.L. Cohen (ed.) *Psychiatry Takes to the Streets*, New York: Guilford Press.

Witheridge, T.F. (1991) 'The "active ingredients" of assertive outreach', *New Directions for Mental Health*, 52: 47–64.

Witheridge, T.F. and Dincin, J. (1985) 'The Bridge: an assertive outreach program in an urban setting', *New Directions for Mental Health Services*, 26: 65–76.

Witheridge, T.F., Dincin, J. and Appleby, L. (1982) 'Working with the most frequent recidivists: a total team approach to assertive resource management', *Psychosocial Rehabilitation Journal*, 5: 9–11.

Yan, X., West, M.A. and Dawson, J.F. (2006) 'Good and bad teams: how do they affect individual well-being?' Aston Business School working paper.

3 Making assessment and outcomes meaningful

Alan Meaden

For many clients intensive specialist services such as assertive outreach lie at the end of a long care pathway that has often failed to meet their complex range of changing needs or to engage them in arriving at a collaborative understanding of these needs. Commonly a referral occurs during a lengthy stay on an acute psychiatric ward where people have received a limited range of treatments. They are likely to have experienced an impoverished social environment that has low expectations of them and led to poor social functioning, or alienated them and led to further disengagement from services and clinicians. On the other hand, some people may have received a comprehensive range of therapeutic interventions but without making progress on their recovery journey.

The aim of a good assessment process in assertive outreach is as much about determining how to offer help as it is about what can be offered to such individuals. Assertive Outreach Teams are generally better resourced than other Community Mental Health Teams, but have greater challenges engaging with their clients. Comprehensive assessment therefore remains important in order to make the most effective use of the specialist resources available. If a good-quality comprehensive assessment process is not in place then considerable time may be wasted attempting to work with clients who do not need assertive outreach or offering services in ways that are unacceptable to them.

Assessment may best be viewed as an ongoing process whereby consideration of a person's changing needs forms part of the process of negotiating therapeutic contact and the provision of services. Assessment should also lead into the measurement of outcome to inform service development and promote the evolution of innovative practice.

What constitutes meaningful assessment?

An assessment of needs requires careful consideration and care should be taken with definitions (Perkins and Repper, 1998). They must be relevant to the client's life and may include everything from basic human needs (for clothing, shelter, warmth) through to more complex needs (such as being connected to others, having religious and cultural affiliations). Assessment of needs should not be seen as an alternative to assessing symptoms and deficits. Whilst symptoms and deficits are less significant than functioning in planning for a person's future care, they continue to be important because they are strong determinates of long-term outcomes and care needs. Indeed, there is growing evidence that cognitive deficits in people diagnosed with schizophrenia are perhaps better predictors of longer-term functional outcomes than are symptoms (Wykes and Reeder, 2005).

It is also vital to ensure that assessment does not become a wholly negative process, focusing only on needs, deficits and problems. The strengths and assets of the person should be routinely considered along with broader factors that promote mental health (Margison, 2005). The Life Skills Profile (Rosen, Hadzi-Pavlovic and Parker, 1989) was developed as a clinician-rated measure of function and disability, or life skills, which affect how successfully people diagnosed with schizophrenia are able to live in the community or in hospital. It is the only measure endorsed by the *Mental Health Policy Implementation Guide* (Department of Health, 2001). The focus of the measure is on life skills in a positive way, emphasising what the person can do. This philosophy is expressed both in the way in which items are scored and how the subscales are labelled. The scale does, however, suffer from inter-rater reliability problems (Parker, Rosen, Emdur and Hadzi-Pavlov, 1991; Trauer, Duckmanton and Chiu, 1995). It can also be time consuming, but brief forms (LSP-20, LSP-16) are available (Rosen, Trauer, Hadzi-Pavlovic and Parker, 2001).

Example:

Bina is a young Asian woman with a ten-year history of receiving mental health services. She has a diagnosis of paranoid schizophrenia, a diagnosis which she rejects and feels stigmatised by. Her family has also rejected Bina since she divorced her husband because of domestic violence. In the past, assessment has focused on psychotic symptoms and her response to medication. Bina continues to experience persistent derogatory voices as well as significant negative symptoms. She leads a socially isolated life and spends much of her time watching television and sleeping.

Guided by careful persistent attempts to engage Bina in an ongoing dialogue about her broader needs, our assessment process has led to a better understanding of her cultural needs, her feelings of social isolation and lack of a meaningful valued role in her local community. This is in contrast to the previous symptom approach. We later share the findings of the team's FACE assessment with her, involving Bina in a dialogue, aimed at eliciting her views. Later, the idea of completing a quality-of-life measure (such as the WHOQOL) is introduced as a way of exploring her subjective quality of life and working towards supporting her in developing further meaningful and valued roles. Subsequent work focuses on understanding Bina's relationship with her voices and reducing the impact of negative symptoms.

In this example engagement was achieved during the assessment process by broadening its scope and actively involving the client. Thus, for the client, assessment becomes the first positive experience of the Assertive Outreach Team.

It is often useful to begin with a wide range of assessment areas. The National Institute of Clinical Excellence (NICE) Schizophrenia Guideline (2002) suggests a number of important domains that should be included in any assessment process:

1   Degree of symptomatic recovery.
2   Quality of life.
3   Degree of personal autonomy.
4   Ability and access to work.
5   Stability and quality of living accommodation.
6   Degree and quality of social integration.
7   Degree of financial independence.
8   Experience and impact of side effects of treatment.

A more general and extensive set of assessment areas for people with complex needs can be found in Meaden and Farmer (2006). A summary of these areas is provided in Table 3.1.

Table 3.1 Assessment areas

Current problems as defined by the service user

Current Mental State
Active/residual psychotic and non-psychotic symptoms
Severity of symptoms: their frequency, how intrusive, how preoccupied, how
distressing

Risk
Of and attitude towards relapse
To self (including accidental self-harm and neglect) and others
From others (exploitation)
Criminal convictions

Clinical History
History and pattern of illness
Duration of untreated psychosis (often an important predictor of longer-term
outcomes)
Previous treatments and treatment response
Premorbid functioning

Social Functioning
Longitudinal picture of family and social networks (including family dynamics)
Quality of life

Stigma and social isolation
Social isolation and inclusion

Lifestyle Assessments
Exercise
Healthy eating
Substance use
Cultural and spiritual needs
Gender and sexual needs

Engagement
Beliefs about and attitude to illness
Attitudes towards services
Attitudes towards treatment and treatment adherence
Side effects of medication

Personal Coping
Attempts to cope with difficulties
Coping style
Support systems
Early warning signs

Recovery Factors
Hopes and aspirations
Valued roles and goals
Personal strengths and preferences
Understanding of difficulties
Capacity for self-management
Recovery style

Carers' Assessment
Enmeshment/over-involvement
Criticism and hostility
Burden of care/quality of life
Psychiatric/psychological symptoms
Unmet needs
Personal strengths and preferences
Lack of non-carer valued roles and goals

Neurocognitive Assessment/Psychometric Assessment
Memory
Concentration
Attention
Executive functioning
Cognitive/information-processing biases
Assessments of personality

The assessment process must take into account individual factors such as:

- the current stage in an episode of psychosis (e.g. stability, relapse or residual difficulties);
- poor attention and concentration, requiring shorter meetings;
- social withdrawal or negative symptoms, requiring a slower pace and greater time to reply – such clients may benefit from a more supportive or gentle conversational style (Kingdom and Turkington, 2005);

- suggestibility, requiring the use of open questions;
- social anxiety or high levels of suspiciousness and mistrust, suggesting the involvement of fewer professionals;
- sensory impairment, requiring specialist advice;
- clients and/or their carers who have a limited understanding of English, requiring the use of interpreters, preferably with a knowledge of mental health issues.

Assessment may need to take place in a non-stigmatising setting away from mental health services, most likely in the person's own home, if this is their preference. Clients may find particular times of day difficult (e.g. due to the side effects of medication) and carers or family members may be working or have fixed commitments. Flexibility is therefore essential.

Assessment should always be seen in a multi-disciplinary team context, drawing on the different skills and knowledge of each professional. All members should agree on the assessment process and on which measures should be used at referral, care reviews and for service evaluation. In most cases the prioritisation of need should focus on whatever is considered to be most important and relevant by the client. However, in some circumstances the team may judge that there is a need to override clients' views: for example when a lifestyle choice of problematic substance use leads to objectively poor living conditions.

Specialist psychological assessments

Co-morbidities

Many service users experience a complex range of difficulties and suffer from more than one form of mental health problem. Historically, co-morbidity has been obscured by the single label of psychosis. Problems and distress related to depression, anxiety, obsessional symptoms, substance misuse, personality disorder, learning disability, acquired brain injury and autistic spectrum disorder need to be considered when planning care and may necessitate specific therapeutic interventions in their own right. Co-morbidity may not be readily apparent but when unrecognised can affect engagement and reduce empathy and care-giving on the part of clinicians and others. Interventions are also more likely to fail when co-morbidities are not included in a case formulation and translated into appropriate care plans.

Problematic substance use is associated with increased risk of relapse, medication non-compliance, aggression, depression, suicide, unstable housing and family burden (Drake and Mueser, 2001). It frequently goes unrecognised and unreported and requires routine assessment in order to ensure detection. Drake and Mueser (2001) offer a useful assessment approach consisting of several interlocking steps, beginning with detection (emphasising active use), long-term observation (relying on multiple data sources), proceeding to a more specialised assessment process (involving behavioural analysis to identify appropriate treatment goals). Assertive Outreach Teams have an advantage here since multiple data sources are available from within the team as a result of whole team working (see chapter two). However, this process may take a long time and require creative adaptations for very chaotic or poorly engaged clients. Good developmental histories are often hard to obtain and cognitive testing can be a challenge.

C-BIT (Graham *et al.*, 2004) emphasises a more flexible, client-centred and ongoing approach to assessment. This may focus initially upon a particular area of substance use (e.g. current pattern of use) with more details about the substance (e.g. amount and type) being collected at another time. Information on substance misuse may also be obtained informally, via proxy indices such as:

- current mood
- sleeping patterns
- appetite/eating patterns
- concentration
- general motivation
- physical health and withdrawal symptoms
- social networks (time spent with other known substance users)
- narrowing of the person's usual repertoire of behaviours.

Subsequently, it may prove possible to elicit the client's beliefs about their substance use and examine the pros and cons of such usage with them. In an Assertive Outreach Team these stages may be performed by different staff members, with the team then meeting to draw together an overall case formulation. Graham *et al.* (2004) suggest using the Substance Abuse Treatment Scale (McHugo, Drake, Burton and Akerson, 1995) as a clinician-rated measure to assess engagement problems, and the Readiness to Change (Treatment Version) Measure (Heather, Luce, Peck, Dunbar and James, 1999) to assess motivation to change and identify possible treatment goals. Ideally, these authors further recommend a urine analysis and blood test to provide some degree of objective assessment.

Impairments in social interaction and communication, commonly found in autistic spectrum disorders, may be misinterpreted as evidence of both positive and negative symptoms of schizophrenia spectrum disorders (Fitzgerald and Corvin, 2001). Individuals who present with both disorders often fall between services. It is important therefore to obtain a good developmental history whenever feasible and to assess as far as possible social interaction and communication difficulties. The involvement of assertive outreach staff in everyday activities with clients affords many opportunities for informally assessing such difficulties.

Clients presenting with personality difficulties often engender a degree of hostility and/or avoidance on the part of health-care staff. To a certain extent, pre-morbid personality characteristics influence the way in which all individuals cope with mental illness and how they respond to services and help-giving generally. For some, however, this influence may be more marked and can significantly impair engagement, care planning, intervention and subsequent recovery. It is important, therefore, when conducting an assessment, to give consideration to developmental history and actively seek informants when someone consents to this. However, it is not unusual to find that there is limited early history available and its accuracy is questionable. To the degree that personality difficulties can be understood, this is best expressed in terms of a Team Case Formulation (see chapter four) so that empathy and engagement can be promoted amongst all staff routinely involved in working with the person.

Assessment of negative symptoms and cognitive problems

It is important to assess neurocognitive functioning, which is generally, if subtly, compromised in people diagnosed with schizophrenia, and consider their relationship to negative symptoms (Meaden and Farmer, 2006). These are often associated with a poorer long-term prognosis (Andreason, 1982; Sharma and Harvey, 2002) and may limit the rate of clinical and personal recovery. Cognitive deficits highlighted in the literature include:

- verbal episodic memory
- semantic memory
- working memory
- attention
- executive function, including poor planning, cognitive preservation or disinhibition.

Fowler, Garety and Kuipers (1995) offer a useful brief test battery for assessing cognitive functioning in people with psychosis, including the National Adult Reading Test; Wechsler Adult Intelligence Scale (WAIS) III; Cognitive Estimation Test; and the Probabilistic Reasoning Task. However, such assessments are likely to be time consuming and it can be difficult to engage clients in the process.

Briefer assessments that can reliably identify the cognitive deficits reported in the literature are sorely needed. The Repeatable Battery for the Assessment of Neurological Status (Gold, Queern, Iannone and Buchanan, 1999) may prove to be one such measure. Any tools that are to be used regularly with assertive outreach clients need to be brief, flexible, engaging and have obvious relevance to everyday life. Tests from the Rivermead family of measures can be useful in this respect. They have been developed primarily for neurological rehabilitation purposes, and are less robust measures, but they can engage people's interest and have high face validity. Similarly, the Cognitive Estimates Test, which is short and can be administered in a conversational style, may be used to screen for difficulties with executive functioning. It is of great practical assistance if assessments can be staggered over a number of sessions. The Lura Nebraska Neuropsychological battery is well suited to this purpose, entailing a number of subtests which can be administered over several sessions. In contrast, such an approach invalidates the WAIS (though short forms are available). Special consideration should also be given to factors such as test effort, test anxiety, medication side effects and fluctuations in mental state (e.g. due to psychotic symptoms, substance use, chaotic lifestyle, etc.) when interpreting results.

The results and potential consequences of any testing need to be explored and communicated sensitively. Testing may trigger feelings of failure and hopelessness and may exacerbate psychotic symptoms such as derogatory voices. A more practical and more ecologically valid approach may involve carrying out cognitive assessments in the context of everyday or leisure activities. For instance, observing a client whilst engaged in a game of snooker or pool enables a range of cognitive functions to be informally assessed: visuo-spatial abilities, planning, mental arithmetic and concentration.

Example:

As Bina slowly began to engage in more activities, systematic observations were made of the possible impact of cognitive deficits and negative symptoms on her everyday life. Assessing real-world difficulties (e.g. problems remembering telephone numbers) was felt to be the approach most relevant to Bina. These were tabulated and the degree to which she needed promoting or structuring of activities was likewise recorded. As her engagement with the team developed, Bina began to enjoy shopping for clothes again. Her support worker accompanied Bina when shopping and using local community facilities, observing her use of lists, ability to plan ahead what she wanted, mental arithmetic, ability to handle money, etc. These observations were structured and recorded, for example in successfully recalling the telephone number of her local library in order to check on the opening times. These were all useful tests of Bina's short-term memory and executive functioning skills.

These structured observations led to an initial formulation that Bina did indeed have some problems planning complex tasks, as well as some concentration and short-term memory problems. Work was begun to support Bina in the use of memory and planning aids, such as electronic diaries.

When an assessment is being conducted, negative symptoms need to be distinguished from other factors such as depression or environmental under-stimulation, as may well be found in people who live in an environment which has low expectations of them. Poverty of speech and withdrawal may actually represent a coping strategy for dealing with positive symptoms such as paranoia, with the stigma of mental illness or even with the demands of others. As Kingdom and Turkington (2005) note, negative symptoms and associated cognitive deficits may induce negativity and burnout in clinicians and carers (see chapter five). The authors offer a useful set of cognitive therapy explanations for negative symptoms which can be used to reframe the person's experiences, both for the client and their carers. These highlight the sometimes protective nature of such symptoms and provide hope and optimism for change.

Risk assessment

The needs, hopes and aspirations of clients must be carefully balanced against the need to provide safe and effective services. A comprehensive risk assessment therefore remains important. A psychological perspective is invaluable here in order to avoid a mechanistic, actuarial or 'tick box' approach. Good risk assessment should lead to a sound shared risk formulation and promote therapeutic risk taking, enabling recovery as much as possible.

Risk behaviours need to be tightly and operationally defined. Each identified behaviour is likely to have its own risk trajectory and will therefore require separate assessment and formulation. Risk assessment is perhaps best seen as a process for arriving at a probabilistic judgement, leading to both false positives and false negatives. Any assessment of risk must therefore balance the interests and rights of the client against safety. Taking a full personal and clinical history is the best starting point to identifying which risk behaviours the person is likely to engage in (e.g. rape versus stalking; parasuicide involving overdose versus cutting) and who the likely victim may be (e.g. female staff). However, it can be difficult to elicit a full personal history from clients themselves. Relatives may be a useful source of early history, but there can be a lack of such informants for assertive outreach clients, where relationships with families have often broken down. The rich multiple observations of team members therefore become invaluable (see chapter two). Corroborative evidence may also be sought from clinical notes and, if relevant, from police and judicial records. Clinical notes are an important source of factual information and will often have detailed descriptions of critical incidents that have required acute intervention. Notes, however, are less useful in giving us a picture of change over time and may be incomplete and patchy as a result of periods of disengagement with services or the involvement of multiple professionals. Increasing the number of sources of information can lead to greater reliability in identifying the key concerns.

A number of methods exist for conducting risk assessments:

1   Clinical Judgement

    • Unstructured Professional Judgement: 'based on my clinical experience . . .'

- Structured Professional Judgement: 'based on what the literature says and my clinical experience, I think . . .'
- Anamnestic Assessment: 'based on what the person has done before and the circumstances involved . . .'

2   Actuarial Assessment

- Actuarial Risk Instruments: 'based on the person's score on this tool . . . they are this likely to engage in the same behaviour again . . .'

Each of these methods has its limitations and strengths. For instance, it is generally accepted that clinicians consistently overestimate risk and often pay attention to the wrong risk factors. Given the reliance on clinical judgement in most Assertive Outreach Teams, it is important to look for any opportunities to use actuarial methods. These are superior to predictions based on clinical judgement alone as they emphasise general factors identified as predictors of risk in empirical studies. Tools such as STATIC-99 (Hanson and Thornton, 2000) for sexual offending and the HCR-20 for risk of violence (Douglas and Webster, 1999) involve the consideration of empirically derived risk factors before arriving at a clinical judgement regarding the overall level of risk. There is increasing data on such risk tools, but much of the normative data remains confined to non-UK populations (e.g. Canadian studies) affecting their validity and generalisability. Recent Department of Health (2007) guidance provides a summary of the different risk tools available, who should use them and what training is required.

Whilst actuarial methods have better predictive value, they can be difficult to use with poorly engaged clients for whom a detailed history is not available. Most risk assessments therefore need to be multi-faceted, drawing on the team's gradually developing relationship with the client to identify areas of concern. The team is likely to find a dynamic view of risk most valuable which provides guidance on:

- treatment
- risk management strategies
- when the risk behaviour is most likely to occur
- under what circumstances the risk behaviour is likely to occur
- what the specific behaviour is likely to be and who are the likely victims.

Evidence needs to be gathered from a number of sources and incorporated into a shared formulation leading to a risk management plan (see chapter four). Consideration of three types of factors identified by Beech and Ward (2004) and Blumenthal and Lavender (2000) are useful here:

1   'Static/Historical Factors', which are, by nature, unchangeable through treatment (e.g. age at first offence, gender, number of convictions, number of previous suicide attempts, etc.). Attention should be paid to those

factors which have the highest predictive validity and specify the overall level of risk and likelihood of reoffending.

2   'Dynamic Stable Factors' are enduring, but may change over time or with intervention (e.g. command hallucinations commanding violence, trait anger, pro-offending attitudes, etc.). Assessment here involves understanding the factors which originally contributed to previous risk behaviours; for example, whether the behaviour was driven by delusional beliefs or depressed mood. It is at this level that a formulation of the offence will be most useful as it identifies areas for intervention.

3   'Dynamic Acute Factors' tend to be more rapidly changing factors (e.g. problematic substance use, social isolation, increase in voice-related distress, increased preoccupation with delusional beliefs). Their presence signifies an elevated likelihood and imminence of the risk behaviour occurring. Current risk assessment tools are of limited use here. Clinicians should consider likely triggering events to the behaviour, any early warning signs of risk noted previously and their frequency.

Example:

During an acute hospital stay David was initially willing to talk about his experiences and 'put my side of the story'. He saw engagement in this process as likely to improve his prospects for increased leave and eventual discharge. However, David was unwilling to engage in any discussion of his psychosexual functioning and only reluctantly discussed incidents of aggressive behaviour. He regarded assaults he had made on other people as entirely justified, and viewed sexual assaults either as mistakes or as the result of people not understanding his true motives.

David refused to complete any risk assessment tools or other formal measures. He agreed to complete a checklist of early warning signs of psychotic relapse (adapted from the Early Warning Sign Monitoring form developed by Birchwood *et al.*, 1989), because he was motivated to avoid future hospital admissions.

The team completed a timeline matching risk incidents and known relapses, through discussions with the ward team, criminal records, case notes and interviews with family members. This was used to help determine whether risk episodes occurred around the time of psychotic relapses and hence support a working hypothesis concerning the role of psychosis in risk behaviours.

Over time, as the team supported David through another relapse, the team's own observations were used to refine this assessment and develop a shared risk formulation plan. Clinician-rated actuarial measures (e.g. HCR-20, SVR-20 and Static 99) and team observations were used to complete an Early Warning Signs of Risk assessment to identify signs and symptoms thought to precede risk behaviours; these are in effect the idiosyncratic acute dynamic risk factors.

This idiosyncratic multi-disciplinary risk assessment process was used to develop an initial shared risk formulation and subsequently led to an agreed therapeutic treatment and management plan with the team.

David's Risk Assessment for Sexual Offending:

Historical/Static Factors
- Touching female ward staff inappropriately
- Touching a neighbour's daughter inappropriately (to give her protection from evil spirits)
- Sexual offence (three years imprisonment)

Dynamic Stable Factors
(Psychological Treatment Targets)
- Command hallucinations: Voice of Krishna
- Pro-offending attitudes: women should do what I want
- Grandiose beliefs: 'I am special and on a special mission'
- Interest in young (innocent) girls
- Social isolation and lack of a support network (family or friends)

Dynamic Acute Factors
(Early Warning Signs)
- Drinking red wine (bottles in his room)
- Reading and quoting religious texts
- Blessing staff
- Getting rid of possessions
- Use of over-familiar language with female staff
- Asking personal details of female staff
- Increased focus on young girls in the local neighbourhood

David's Risk Management Plan
1   Monitoring and supervision: frequent visits and observing any increase in Early Warning Signs of Risk.
2   Shared risk formulation with hostel staff and probation officer.
3   Ongoing efforts to improve social network and access to support for spiritual needs.
4   Ongoing efforts to address beliefs about voices and pro-offending attitudes.

Over time further informal structured observations were used to refine this plan. Therapeutic efforts focusing on dynamic stable factors were increasingly offered as engagement improved.

Useful assessment and outcome tools

Despite being strongly endorsed as a key component of mental health services (Department of Health, 1999) and the existence of powerful policies
aimed at improving care planning generally in the UK (Holloway, 2006),
there is not a well-established, nationally agreed set of assessment and outcome tools for use in Assertive Outreach Teams. The *Mental Health Policy
Implementation Guide* (Department of Health, 2001) makes some recommendations regarding assessment areas and processes but provides virtually
no guidance on suitable measures.

A variety of general assessment tools have been developed for psychosis,
that aim to standardise direct observations or interviews. The advantage of a
standardised method is that it allows comparisons between individuals and
in an individual over time. If assessment tools with good psychometric properties are chosen, different professionals should record similar findings. In
practice, clinicians will need to judge how helpful structured assessments are
likely to be, based on the person's engagement and stage of recovery. It may
be that more informal methods, as outlined in this chapter, are more feasible.

CUES-U and CUES-C have been developed as an approach to better
engage clients and their carers in the assessment process (Lelliott, Beevor,
Hogman, Hyslop, Lathlean and Ward, 2001) and as such are well suited to
assertive outreach. CUES-U is a brief self-report tool designed with and by
clients, to rate their experiences across a range of domains they consider to be
important. Sixteen items measure enduring states through the use of normative statements. Each statement is followed by two questions concerning the
extent to which this is similar to the client's own experience and to what
extent they are satisfied with this. Paying attention to what clients judge to be
important in their own lives is likely to promote engagement (Bowling, 1991).
CUES-U does not measure symptoms, though scores have been found to be
related to severity of HoNOS ratings (Lelliott *et al.*, 2001). CUES-U and
CUES-C can be completed by service users and their carers prior to care
reviews and brought to meetings to inform care planning. Information from
these tools may also usefully inform service evaluation and audit and
potentially inform service planning and commissioning (e.g. when planning
accommodation needs). McPherson, Summerfield, Haynes, Slade and Foy
(2005) have found CUES-U to be a valuable tool in both care planning and
benchmarking of services.

The Health of the Nation Outcome Scale or HoNOS (Wing, Cooper and
Beevor, 1996) is now part of the National Minimum Data Set (Fonagy,
Matthews, Pilling and Glover, 2005) for use across all mental health services.
HoNOS is predominantly a problem-focused measure and fails to fully capture the broad range of complex difficulties encountered by assertive outreach clients. Moreover, it offers little scope for service user involvement in its
completion, but may be complemented, as noted above, by CUES-U. Perhaps
most crucially, it is unclear to what extent scores on HoNOS, or changes

in them, are clinically meaningful or relevant to service users' lives and experiences.

The FACE system (FACE Recording and Measurement Systems) has been widely adopted by some 250 services nationally, including some Assertive Outreach Teams (Source: FACE Recording and Measurement Systems). The acronym originates from an earlier measure designed for the Functional Assessment of Care Environments. It has subsequently been developed over the last 15 years to encompass multiple areas of mental health assessment. The current Version 5 of the Core Assessment and Outcomes Package for Mental Health Services offers a fully integrated suite of documentation. All major domains of health and social functioning are included:

- psychological
- physical
- activities of daily living
- social and occupational functioning
- interpersonal relationships
- risk
- subjective quality of life.

FACE scores highlight key areas of need as well as possible client strengths and measures outcomes from the perspective of both the clinician and the client. FACE has been reported to capture change in some assertive outreach populations (Wane, Owen, Sood, Bradley and Jones, 2007).

The adult Camberwell Assessment of Need (CAN; Slade, Thornicroft, Loftus, Phelan and Wykes, 1999) is perhaps the most widely adopted needs-based assessment measure. The adult CAN covers 22 different areas of life, and can be used to assess the perceptions of the client, their carers and a mental health professional working with them. It assesses what sort of help is currently being received, how much help is needed and what help should be offered. The main aim is to identify serious needs and indicate where further specialist assessments are needed. A research version (CANR) and a short version (CANSAS) are also available.

Developments in policy and practice recognise the importance of a collaborative approach that includes service users and carers as partners in the planning and provision of treatment, and supports recovery (Roberts and Wolfson, 2004). All of these measures capture broad aspects of functioning and symptoms that may be relevant to understanding a client's needs, planning their care and measuring its effectiveness. None, however, fully capture the often highly complex range of unique difficulties, strengths and assets that may be relevant to providing high-quality comprehensive mental health care for a given individual. It is therefore likely that any Assertive Outreach Team will need to use more than one assessment tool.

Psychosocial assessments

A range of assessment tools for identifying and evaluating the usefulness of specific psychosocial interventions are now entering routine use. These assessments may be conceptualised as informing care planning and intervention at different levels. At the Symptom or Syndrome Level we might ask, 'Is the person hearing voices?'. At the Dimensions of Experience Level, 'How frequent and severe are they?'. At the Therapy Informing Level, 'What are the triggers, beliefs and consequences?' (Haddock and Tarrier, 1998).

Table 3.2 provides a useful summary of these assessment tools, when to use them and their pros and cons. Further details of useful measures are contained in Roberts, Davenport, Holloway and Tattan (2006).

If assessment tools are to be used routinely, team members will need to be trained and supervised in their administration and interpretation. Assessments of neurocognitive functioning and personality may require the specialised skills of a clinical psychologist. The team as a whole then needs to draw together all of the (often conflicting) information obtained, leading to a Team Case Formulation (see chapter four) that can be used for care planning purposes.

Establishing meaningful service outcomes

Assertive Outreach Teams have been established principally to engage clients with serious and enduring mental health needs, and high levels of acute service use, in effective treatment partnerships. Often implicit in this process is the assumption that adherence to medication will be promoted, to reduce the risk of relapse (and thereby hospital usage), improve management of symptoms and reduce risk behaviours. However, it is questionable whether such outcomes are really meaningful for services or their users. Evidence is emerging that medication compliance is not necessarily associated with reductions in hospital usage or overall engagement (see chapter one). More important, perhaps, is the fact that clients often see an emphasis on these outcomes as coercive and a continued focus on them is likely to bring about disengagement (Priebe, Watts, Chase and Matanov, 2005). Recovery principles, by contrast, emphasise the value of personal goals and values, aspirations and holding hope. These, by their very nature, will not readily translate into standardised national or local targets, although they are increasingly viewed as important by policy makers and commissioners.

We are now in an era of health service policy that demands the routine evaluation of care using standardised measures, targets and standards (Fonagy, Matthews and Pilling, 2004). This can also demonstrate to staff, clients and their carers that the careful persistent efforts of Assertive Outreach Teams result in sustained clinical improvement and recovery. Assertive Outreach Teams have until recently been largely inoculated against this trend, being already viewed as effective in reducing acute hospital use, promoting

Table 3.2 Summary table of useful assessment tools

Measure	Use	Considerations	When/How Often
Service Measures			
DACTS (Teague *et al.*, 1998)	The Dartmouth Assertive Community Treatment Fidelity Scale or DACTS contains 28 programme-specific items measuring the extent to which teams currently meet programme requirements: have fidelity to the Assertive Community Treatment model. The scale covers three key domains: human resources (structure and composition); organisational boundaries; and nature of services	Commissioner relevant Measured against service outcomes	Service Planning 12 monthly
DREEM (Ridgway & Press, 2004)	Has a service development focus and provides a collaborative user-led structure. Measures commitment of services to recovery-based care and their effectiveness in providing it.	Endorsed by the Care Services Improvement Partnership, Royal College of Psychiatrists and Social Care Institute for Excellence (2007). Useful in benchmarking services. Commissioner relevant	12 monthly
The Life Skills Profile (Rosen *et al.*, 1989)	Developed as a clinician-rated measure of function and disability. The focus of the measure (LSP-39) is on emphasising life skills in a positive way across five subscales: Self-care, Non-turbulence, Social Contact, Communication Bizarre, Responsibility. Each item has an individualised 4-point Likert rating scale	Inter-rater reliability is problematic Short forms are available Different versions have different subscales	6 monthly

(Continued overleaf)

Table 3.2 continued

Measure	Use	Considerations	When/How Often
FACE (www.facecode.com)	Several parts provide a broad assessment including social functioning and user views.	Useful in benchmarking services	6 monthly
Camberwell Assessment of Need (Slade *et al.*, 1999)	Needs-based assessment covers 22 different areas. Aims to identify serious needs and what sort of help is currently being received, how much help is needed and what help should be offered.	Well-established and widely adopted international measure with many versions available	3–6 monthly
Symptom/Syndrome/Diagnostic Measures			
Psychiatric Assessment Scale (Kraewiecka, Goldberg & Vaughan, 1977)	Presence & severity of positive, negative & disorganisation symptoms, depression & anxiety	Sensitive to change Specific training required Time consuming	3–6 monthly
Brief Psychiatric Rating Scale (Overall & Gorham, 1962)	Measures current psychiatric symptoms	Broad base snapshot of psychopathology	Weekly – monthly
Millon Clinical Multiaxial Inventory III (Millon, 1994)	175-item self-report inventory assesses clinical personality patterns, severe personality pathology and clinical syndromes	Designed only for people presenting with clinical symptoms. Maps onto DSM-IV but requires clinical validation Time consuming to score and interpret	Initial assessment
Dimensional Measures			
The Psychotic Symptom Rating Scales (Haddock, McCarron, Tarrier & Faragher, 1999)	Dimensions of psychotic experiences (e.g. frequency, severity)	Quick and relatively easy to use	Weekly

Measure	Description	Notes	Frequency
Beck Hopelessness Scale (Beck, Weissman, Lester & Trexler, 1974)	Hopelessness, suicidality	Easy and quick to administer and score	6 weekly
Beck Anxiety Inventory (Beck, Epstein, Brown & Steer, 1988)	General measure of anxiety	Easy and quick to administer and score	Monthly
Calgary Depression Scale (Addington, Addington & Maticka-Tyndale, 1993)	Depression	Measures depression independently of negative symptoms	6 weekly

Attitude towards/Awareness of Illness Measures

Measure	Description	Notes	Frequency
Engagement Scale (Hall, Meaden, Smith & Jones, 2001)	Dimensions of engagement: collaboration with treatment; appointment keeping; compliance with medication	Clinician and user versions Clinician version: observer rated – easy to administer	6 monthly
Insight Scale (Birchwood et al., 1994)	Awareness of illness, causes of illness, need for treatment	Psychiatric focus	Weekly
Scale to Assess Unawareness of Mental Disorder (Amador & David, 2004)	A multi-dimensional measure developed to assess insight across four subscales (17 items each): current awareness; current attribution; past awareness; past attribution. Includes items on medication, perception of symptoms and social factors	Broad focus with items designed to be adapted to individual views Need to complete a checklist before rating	Not specified – adapted to individual circumstances
Personal Beliefs About Illness Questionnaire (Birchwood, Mason, MacMillan & Healy, 1993)	Beliefs about psychosis, self in relation to psychosis, stigma, control	Psychiatric focus	3–6 monthly

(Continued overleaf)

Table 3.2 continued

Measure	Use	Considerations	When/How Often
Therapy Informing Measures			
Beliefs About Voices Questionnaire – Revised (Chadwick, Lees & Birchwood, 2000)	Identifying beliefs about voices: identity, purpose, power	Useful cognitive therapy and monitoring tool. Useful research tool	Baseline, post interventions
Cognitive Assessment of Voices (Chadwick & Birchwood, 1995)	Elicits antecedents, beliefs and cognitive/behavioural consequences of voice hearing	Use in conjunction with BAVQ-R	Engagement, post interventions
Beliefs & Convictions Scale (Brett-Jones, Garety & Hemsley, 1987)	Degree of conviction, preoccupation, intrusiveness and openness to disconfirmation of delusional beliefs	Useful cognitive therapy and monitoring tool Useful research tool	Weekly
Evaluative Beliefs Scale (Chadwick, Trower & Dagnan, 1999)	Identifies evaluative beliefs about self and others	May guide therapy and indicate core themes linked to psychotic concerns	Engagement, post interventions
Young Schema Questionnaires (Young & Brown, 1990)	Core schemas/personality styles	Use in combination with companion assessments. Young Parenting Inventory (Young, 1994), Young-Rygh Avoidance Inventory (Young & Rygh, 1994), Young Compensation Inventory (Young, 1995)	Engagement, post interventions
Antecedent & Coping Interview (Tarrier, 1992)	Identifies antecedents for psychotic symptoms and efficacy of coping strategies	Useful for guiding psychological interventions aimed at improving coping strategies	Engagement, post interventions

Relapse Monitoring

Measure	Description	Comments	Frequency
Early Signs Scale (Birchwood et al., 1994)	Early signs of relapse and incipient psychosis	User and carer versions available. Less useful if persistent high level of residual symptoms. Can been used to monitor recovery from acute psychosis	Weekly (depending on level at baseline)

Social Functioning/Inclusion/Quality of Life Measures

Measure	Description	Comments	Frequency
Social Functioning Scale (Birchwood, Smith, Cochrane, Wetton, Copestake, 1990)	Relationships, range of leisure activities	May lack relevance to user's needs in some areas	6 monthly
Lancashire Quality of Life Profile (Oliver, 1992)	An objective measure of quality of life. Provides an overall wellbeing score as well as scores across a range of dimensions: relationships, work, activity, home and finance	Sensitive to change. Provides an assessment of social functioning	6–12 monthly
Manchester Short Assessment of Quality of Life (MANSA) (Priebe, Huxley, Knight & Evans, 1999)	Short form of the Lancashire scale	Developed as part of the national minimum data set	6–12 monthly
WHOQOL (Skevington, 1999)	World Health Organisation of (subjective) Quality of Life. Assesses four domains of quality of life: physical, psychological, social and relationships and environment	Need to register as an official user and share data. Currently lacks UK norms. Many versions are available for different clinical populations and other countries	6–12 monthly

Personal Recovery

Measure	Description	Comments	Frequency
Recovery Style Questionnaire (Drayton, Birchwood & Trower, 1998)	Identifies recovery style: sealing, integrating or mixed	Identifying optimum time for interventions	Baseline & recovery

(Continued overleaf)

Table 3.2 continued

Measure	Use	Considerations	When/How Often
CUES-U (Lelliott *et al.*, 2001)	A 16-item brief assessment for clients to rate their experiences of domains they consider to be important (quality of interaction with mental health workers; sense of alienation and finance; daytime activities and social relationships), using normative statements	Use may promote engagement, inform care planning, service evaluation and planning, audit and commissioning. Scores are correlated with severity of HoNUS ratings	CPA Reviews
Carers (Burden, Needs Understanding) Measures			
Knowledge About Schizophrenia Interview (Barrowclough *et al.*, 1987)	Relative knowledge of schizophrenia, causes and treatments	Useful for planning and evaluating carer psychoeducation	Engagement phase and post intervention
Camberwell Family Interview (Leff & Vaughan, 1985)	Semi-structured interview examines expressed emotion, current family difficulties, knowledge of illness and family coping	Provides a good interview of family difficulties. Training required	Engagement phase and post intervention
General Health Questionnaire (Goldberg, 1972)	A general measure of psychological distress. Several versions available	Useful in eliciting and monitoring distress in relatives	Initial engagement phase and then monthly
CUES-C (Unattributed: DoH Outcomes Programme)	Carer version of the CUES-U designed to assess carers' needs across 14 items	Use may promote engagement, inform care planning, service evaluation and planning, audit and commissioning	CPA Reviews

independent living and employment, and increasing satisfaction with care, largely based on research done in the US (Marshall and Lockwood, 1998). A series of studies have, however, now highlighted the potential limitations of the model in the UK. The UK700 case management trial (Burns *et al.*, 1999), PRISM study (Thornicroft, Wykes, Holloway, Johnson and Szmukler, 1998) and the REACT study (Killaspy *et al.*, 2006) all show little clear advantage in outcomes over standard community care. With an increased emphasis on value for money these relatively expensive services have been more closely scrutinised, leading to their closure in some areas. Several reasons have been suggested for the poorer UK outcomes, in particular low fidelity to the original model (Marshall and Creed, 2000). However, some teams with high fidelity have also shown disappointing outcomes (Fiander *et al.*, 2003). An alternative explanation is that standard care has improved, making it difficult to produce the dramatic results of the early teams (Tyrer, 2000).

Where fidelity it thought to be an issue, it may be helpful to use the Dartmouth Assertive Community Treatment Fidelity Scale or DACTS, developed by Teague, Bond and Drake (1998). It assesses 28 programme-specific items measuring the extent to which teams currently meet programme requirements and therefore have fidelity to the Assertive Community Treatment model. Each item is rated on a 5-point scale ranging from 1 ('Not implemented') to 5 ('Fully implemented'). Anchors for these ratings were determined through a variety of expert sources as well as empirical research. The scale covers three key domains: human resources; organisational boundaries; and nature of services. Fidelity assessments enable measurement of how care is delivered against a specified standard and whether certain targets are being met (which are often linked to cost effectiveness, i.e. reduced hospital usage). A UK version has been developed: DACTS-UK (Freeman and Brooker, 2001).

Even when fidelity is high, it may still not be possible to reproduce in the UK earlier findings from the US. Nevertheless, measuring outcomes remains important. The REACT study (Killaspy *et al.*, 2006) attempted to capture a broader range of outcomes, including quality of life and social functioning, but arguably over too short a time period to show significant changes. Sadly, no attempt was made to assess recovery goals; indeed, the word recovery is not mentioned by these authors in their account of the study.

In trying to devise a set of relevant measures it must also be recognised that despite a well-established set of service principles and expectations, the clients of Assertive Outreach Teams are unlikely to be uniformly moving towards greater independence. There may be said to be a relatively small, but important, subgroup of clients who have ongoing or continuing care needs; indeed, early descriptions of assertive outreach describe it as a continuing care model (Lavender and Holloway, 1992). All these factors explain why it has been difficult to agree on a clear set of meaningful service outcomes.

As part of a national pilot of general outcome measures in mental health, Fonagy *et al.* (2004) found that no consensus emerged regarding which client or carer measures should be adopted within their reference group. However, a consensus did emerge regarding the principal domains that should be included within such a measure:

- symptom-related distress
- social functioning
- quality of life
- how well services met perceived needs
- whether the individual felt adequately informed about their care
- whether the individual felt engaged in care planning and was given choices about treatment
- how the individual felt about the nature of their relationship with key health-care professionals.

It has been suggested that quality of life, as perceived by the recipient of care, should be the final criterion by which the quality of that care should be judged (Wing, 1978).

Recovery outcomes

Recovery goals are frequently cited as an important component of modern mental health services but are rarely systematically assessed. Efforts to measure recovery have been surprisingly slow to develop. One difficulty has been arriving at a shared view of what recovery is that can be operationalised to produce reliable and valid measures. Good recovery measures need to be sensitive to multiple viewpoints, capture personal changes and produce meaningful service outcomes that relate to service aims, philosophy and interventions. These can in turn help to further our understanding of which factors best mediate recovery. Ralph, Kidder and Phillips (2000) and Campbell-Orde, Chamberlin, Carpenter and Leff (2005) provide a useful compendium of recovery measures developed in the US. Widely acknowledged as perhaps the most relevant and promising of these (Care Services Improvement Partnership, Royal College of Psychiatrists and Social Care Institute for Excellence, 2007) is the Developing Recovery-Enhancing Environments Measure (DREEM), developed by Ridgway and Press (2004). DREEM has a service development focus and provides a collaborative user-led structure that measures both the commitment of services to recovery-based care and their effectiveness in providing it. DREEM has mostly been developed in the context of residential and hospital-based care but has been adapted for use in other areas, for example in adolescent programmes. The items themselves are broadly applicable recovery questions and require only simple adaptations of terminology to become suitable for use in community services such as Assertive Outreach Teams.

Specific outcomes

Engagement can be seen as both a service aim and an outcome itself (Killaspy *et al.*, 2006; Meaden, Nithsdale, Rose, Smith and Jones, 2004). Through an emphasis on engagement and increased levels of contact, Assertive Outreach Teams provide a vehicle for the delivery of a broad range of therapeutic interventions (see chapter one). Improving access to psychosocial interventions is increasingly being seen as an important component of comprehensive mental health care. Developing a better understanding of clients' experience and perspectives on these interventions is also important (Macran, Ross, Hardy and Shapiro, 1999) and should be a focus of any service evaluation.

Satisfaction with assertive outreach services is a robust finding and needs to be routinely assessed using both quantitative (surveys) and qualitative measures (focus groups). Ideally service users themselves should be involved in developing this process, which itself should be externally facilitated and analysed.

Characteristics of non-responders are often difficult to define but remain crucial to improving the effectiveness of services. Not all clients respond successfully to assertive outreach and those who do not often have high levels of inpatient use. This group may go on to require some form of residential support or even forensic service.

Some studies have shown that hospital utilisation indices need to be carefully evaluated (Meaden *et al.*, 2004; Paget, Meaden and Amphlett, in press), with certain indices showing more change than others. It may prove worthwhile to measure hospital usage routinely in terms of both number of admissions and length of stay; especially for services where there are no effective alternatives to hospital-based care, such as respite. However, most Assertive Outreach Teams find that it takes some years to significantly reduce levels of hospitalisation, and indeed initially hospital usage can increase. If presented in context, this type of data can be helpful in supporting bids for service planning and commissioning.

Developing practice-based evidence: making assertive outreach work better

To ensure that assessments are routinely carried out they need to be fully integrated into team processes. A culture of routinely collating, analysing and feeding back information into a forum, which can translate them into service development plans, can provide a powerful process for designing and developing services in line with clients' needs. Stein and colleagues (as described by Dixon, 2000) most clearly demonstrate such a process in the development of the assertive outreach model itself. Begun in the late 1960s in Madison County in an era of institutionalisation, Test and Stein developed their service by routinely asking questions of themselves and their service:

- Who is benefiting and not benefiting?
- What are their needs?
- What combination of treatments might work best?
- What should be the aims of treatment?
- How long should treatment be offered for?

This process, prompted by clients who continued in their use of acute psychiatric hospital, led to four distinctive stages of service development and resulted in the model of assertive outreach we have become familiar with.

In Finland, researchers (Alanen, 1997; Alanen, Lehtinen, Lehtinen, Aaltonen and Rakkolainen, 2000) have adopted an Action Research methodology, in preference to randomised controlled trials, as being more relevant for service development purposes. Outcomes were compared following each introduction of new services or treatments. In a pioneering piece of work Alanen and colleagues (as described by Alanen, 1997) used this method to evaluate and develop their service and model at five different stages:

1   Single patients in individual therapy.
2   Family therapy and psychotherapeutic communities begun.
3   Open care initiated: improved access.
4   Need-adapted treatment approach begun.
5   Lowered barriers to open care: direct access and assertive outreach style working.

Meaningful outcomes (e.g. clients fully able to work) were then evaluated following each stage of development. Alanen (1997) reports some impressive outcomes in terms of those fully able to work and without symptoms. This approach has also been helpful in clarifying which psychological approaches benefit which groups, and at what stage of illness and recovery these are likely to be most effective (see Alanen *et al.*, 2000). The Need-Adapted Treatment model is now a national programme, adopted by several neighbouring countries.

Successfully adopting such a process requires establishing a culture of continually asking what works best for whom and at what stage of recovery different interventions are best introduced. This can be supported through a combination of:

- Relevant, structured, valid and reliable measures that all team members are signed up to and routinely complete.
- Agreeing sensible targets and service specification outcomes with commissioners that are meaningful to clients, carers and clinicians.
- Routine use of recovery measures.
- Qualitative measures to capture satisfaction and clients' experiences of interventions.

Assessment processes should not just be about fitting people into available resources. They should also be capable of identifying the need for real changes in the organisation and provision of services. One difficulty in the UK is that the way in which services are developed and delivered has tended to be driven by centralised processes in recent years. Producing local information on effective, innovative and efficient services and interventions that are inclusive of clients' and carers' views is one method of influencing this process.

Conclusions

A comprehensive assessment is a crucial first step in promoting meaningful and relevant outcomes for clients, carers, clinical staff and commissioners. Assessment should not been seen as a chore or an end in itself, but as an opportunity to identify unmet needs and difficulties and indeed as a therapeutic process in its own right.

Assessment processes in assertive outreach need to be flexibly and creatively undertaken and will depend in each case upon the person's stage of recovery and engagement. Appropriate training and ongoing support for staff to engage more actively in this process are vitally important.

References

Addington, D., Addington, J. and Maticka-Tyndale, E. (1993) 'Assessing depression in schizophrenia: the Calgary Depression Scale', *British Journal of Psychiatry*, 163 (suppl. 22): 39–44.

Alanen, Y.O. (1997) *Schizophrenia: its origins and need-adapted treatment*, London: Karnac.

Alanen, Y., Lehtinen, V., Lehtinen, K., Aaltonen, J. and Rakkolainen, V. (2000) 'The Finnish integrated model for early treatment of schizophrenia and related psychoses', in B. Martindale, A. Bateman, M. Crowe and F. Margison (eds) *Psychosis: psychological approaches and their effectiveness*, London: Gaskell.

Amador, X.F. and David, A.S. (2004) *Insight and Psychosis: awareness of illness in schizophrenia and related disorders*, 2nd edn, Oxford: Oxford University Press.

Andreason, N.C. (1982) 'Negative symptoms in schizophrenia: definition and reliability', *Archives of General Psychiatry*, 36: 1325–1330.

Barrowclough, C., Tarrier, N., Watts, S., Vaughan, C., Bamrah, J.S. and Freeman, H. (1987) 'Assessing the functional value of relatives' reported knowledge about schizophrenia', *British Journal of Psychiatry*, 151: 1–8.

Beck, A.T., Epstein, N., Brown, G. and Steer, R.A. (1988) 'An inventory for measuring clinical anxiety: psychometric properties', *Journal of Consulting and Clinical Psychology*, 56: 893–897.

Beck, A.T., Weissman, A.W., Lester, D. and Trexler, L. (1974) 'The assessment of pessimism: the hopelessness scale', *Journal of Counselling and Clinical Psychology*, 42: 861–865.

Beech, A.R. and Ward, T. (2004) 'The integration of aetiology and risk in sex offenders: a theoretical model', *Aggression and Violent Behaviour*, 10: 31–63.

Birchwood, M., Mason, R., MacMillan, F. and Healy, J. (1993) 'Depression, demoralization and control over psychotic illness: a comparison of depressed and non-depressed patients with chronic psychosis', *Psychological Medicine*, 23: 387–395.

Birchwood, M., Smith, J., Cochrane, R., Wetton, S. and Copestake, S. (1990) 'The Social Functioning Scale: the development and validation of a new scale of social adjustment for use in family intervention programmes with schizophrenic patients', *British Journal of Psychiatry*, 157: 853–859.

Birchwood, M., Smith, J., Drury, V., Healy, J., MacMillan, F. and Slade, M. (1994) 'A self-report insight scale for psychosis: reliability, validity and sensitivity to change', *Acta Psychiatrica Scandinavica*, 89: 62–67.

Birchwood, M.J., Smith, J., MacMillan, F., Hogg, B., Presad, R., Harvey, C. and Bering, S. (1989) 'Predicting relapse in schizophrenia: the development and implementation of an early signs monitoring system using patients and families as observers', *Psychological Medicine*, 19: 649–656.

Blumenthal, S. and Lavender, T. (2000) *Violence and Mental Disorder: a critical aid to the assessment and management of risk*, London: Jessica Kingsley Publishers.

Bowling, A. (1991) *Measuring Health: a review of quality of life measurement scales*, Milton Keynes: Open University Press.

Brett-Jones, J., Garety, P. and Hemsley, D. (1987) 'Measuring delusional experiences: a method and its application', *British Journal of Clinical Psychology*, 26: 257–265.

Burns, T., Creed, F., Fahy, T. *et al.* for the UK700 Group (1999) 'Intensive versus standard case management for severe psychotic illness trial. UK700 Group', *Lancet*, 353: 2185–2189.

Campbell-Orde, T., Chamberlin, J., Carpenter, J. and Leff, H.S. (2005) *Measuring the Promise: a compendium of recovery measures, Volume II: The Evaluation Centre at SRI*, available online at www.tecathsri.org/product_description.asp?pid=129

Care Services Improvement Partnership, Royal College of Psychiatrists and Social Care Institute for Excellence (2007) *A Common Purpose: recovery in mental health services*, London: Social Care Institute for Excellence.

Chadwick, P. and Birchwood, M. (1995) 'The omnipotence of voices II: the Beliefs About Voices Questionnaire', *British Journal of Psychiatry*, 166: 773–776.

Chadwick, P., Lees, S. and Birchwood, M. (2000) 'The revised Beliefs About Voices Questionnaire (BAVQ-R)', *British Journal of Psychiatry*, 177: 229–232.

Chadwick, P., Trower, P. and Dagnan, D. (1999) 'Measuring negative person evaluations: the evaluative belief scale', *Cognitive Therapy and Research*, 23: 549–559.

Department of Health (1999) *National Service Framework for Mental Health*, London: Department of Health.

Department of Health (2001) *Mental Health Policy Implementation Guide*, London: Department of Health.

Department of Health (2007) *Best Practice in Managing Risk*, London: Department of Health.

Dixon, L., (2000) 'Assertive community treatment: twenty-five years of gold', *Psychiatric Services*, 51: 759–765.

Douglas, K.S. and Webster, C.D. (1999) 'The HCR-20 violence risk assessment scheme: concurrent validity in a sample of incarcerated offenders', *Criminal Justice Behaviour*, 26: 3–19.

Drake, R.E. and Mueser, K.T. (2001) 'Substance abuse comorbidity', in J. Lieberman and R. M. Murray (eds) *Comprehensive Care of Schizophrenia*, London: Martin Dunitz.

Drayton, M., Birchwood, M. and Trower, P. (1998) 'Early attachment experience and recovery from psychosis', *British Journal of Clinical Psychology*, 37: 269–284.

FACE Recording and Measurement Systems, available online at http://www.facecode.com/

Fiander, M., Burns, T., McHugo, G.J. and Drake, R. (2003) 'Assertive community treatment across the Atlantic: comparison of model fidelity in the UK and USA', *British Journal of Psychiatry*, 182: 248–254.

Fitzgerald, M. and Corvin, A. (2001) 'Diagnosis and differential diagnosis of Asperger Syndrome', *Advances in Psychiatric Treatment*, 7: 310–318.

Fonagy, P., Matthews, R. and Pilling, S. (2004) *The Mental Health Outcomes Measurement Initiative: report from the chair of the outcomes reference group*, London: National Institute for Mental Health in England.

Fonagy, P., Matthews, R., Pilling, S. and Glover, G. (2005) *Outcomes Measures Implementation Best Practice Guidance*, London: National Institute for Mental Health in England.

Fowler D., Garety, P. and Kuipers, E. (1995) *Cognitive Behaviour Therapy for Psychosis: theory and practice*, Chichester: Wiley.

Freeman, J. and Brooker, C. (2001) *The Dartmouth Assertive Community Treatment Scale – UK adapted version*, Sheffield: The University of Sheffield.

Gold, J., Queern, C., Iannone, V. and Buchanan, R. (1999) 'Repeatable Battery for the Assessment of Neuropsychological Status as a screening test in schizophrenia. I: Sensitivity, reliability and validity', *American Journal of Psychiatry*, 156: 1944–1950.

Goldberg, D.P. (1972) *The Detection of Psychiatric Illness by Questionnaire (GHQ)*, Maudsley Monographs, no. 21, London: Oxford University Press.

Graham, H.L., Copello, A., Birchwood, M.J., Mueser, K., Orford, J., McGovern, D., Atkinson, E., Maslin, J., Preece, M., Tobin, D. and Georgiou, G. (2004) *Cognitive-Behavioural Integrated Treatment (C-BIT): a treatment manual for substance misuse in people with severe mental health problems*, Chichester: Wiley.

Haddock, G., McCarron, J., Tarrier, N. and Faragher, E.B. (1999) 'Scales to measure dimensions of hallucinations and delusions: the psychotic symptom rating scales (PSYRATS)', *Psychological Medicine*, 29: 879–889.

Haddock, G. and Tarrier, N. (1998) 'Assessment and formulation in the cognitive behavioural treatment of psychosis', in N. Tarrier and A. Wells (eds) *Treating Complex Cases: the cognitive behavioural therapy approach*, Chichester: Wiley.

Hall, M., Meaden, A., Smith, J. and Jones, C. (2001) 'The development of an observer-rated measure of engagement with mental health services', *Journal of Mental Health*, 10: 457–465.

Hanson, R.K. and Thornton, D. (2000) 'Improving risk assessment for sex offenders: a comparison of three actuarial scales', *Law and Human Behaviour*, 24: 119–136.

Heather, N., Luce, A., Peck, D., Dunbar, B. and James, I. (1999) 'Development of a treatment version of the Readiness to Change Questionnaire', *Addiction Research*, 7: 63–83.

Holloway, F. (2006) 'Pulling it all together: the care programme approach at its best', in G. Roberts, S. Davenport, F. Holloway and T. Tattan (eds) *Enabling Recovery: the principles and practice of rehabilitation psychiatry*, London: Gaskell.

Kingdom, D.G. and Turkington, D. (2005) *Cognitive Therapy of Schizophrenia: guides to individualised treatment*, New York: Guilford Press.

Killaspy, H., Bebbington, P., Blizard, R., Johnson, S., Nolan, F., Pilling, S. and

King, M. (2006) 'The REACT study: randomised evaluation of assertive community treatment in North London', *British Medical Journal*, 332: 815–820.

Kraewiecka, M., Goldberg, D. and Vaughan, M. (1977) 'A standard psychiatric assessment scale for rating chronic psychotic patients', *Acta Psychiatrica Scandinavia*, 55: 299–308.

Lavender, T. and Holloway, F. (1992) 'Models of continuing care', in M. Birchwood and N. Tarrier (eds) *Innovations in the Psychological Management of Schizophrenia*, London: Wiley.

Leff, J. and Vaughan, C. (1985) *Expressed Emotion in Families: its significance for mental illness*, New York: Guilford Press.

Lelliott, P., Beevor, A., Hogman, G., Hyslop, J., Lathlean, J. and Ward, M. (2001) 'Carers' and users' expectations of services – user version (CUES-U): a new instrument to measure the experience of users of mental health services', *British Journal of Psychiatry*, 179: 67–72.

McHugo, G.J., Drake, R.E., Burton, H.L. and Akerson, T.H. (1995) 'A scale for assessing the stage of substance abuse treatment in persons with severe mental illness', *The Journal of Nervous and Mental Disease*, 183: 762–767.

McPherson, R. Summerfield, L., Haynes, R., Slade, M. and Foy, C. (2005) 'The use of users' and carers' expectations of (CUES) in an epidemiological survey of need', *International Journal of Social Psychiatry*, 5: 34–43.

Macran, S., Ross, H., Hardy, G. E. and Shapiro, D. A. (1999) 'The importance of considering clients' perspectives in psychotherapy research', *Journal of Mental Health*, 8: 325–337.

Margison, F. (2005) 'Integrating approaches to psychotherapy in psychosis', *Australian and New Zealand Journal of Psychiatry*, 39: 972–981.

Marshall, M. and Creed, F. (2000) 'Assertive Community Treatment – is it the future of community care in the UK?', *International Review of Psychiatry*, 12: 191–196.

Marshall, M. and Lockwood, A. (1998) 'Assertive Community Treatment for people with severe mental disorders', *Cochrane Database of Systematic Reviews*, issue 2.

Meaden, A. and Farmer, A. (2006) 'A comprehensive approach to assessment in rehabilitation settings', in G. Roberts, S. Davenport, F. Holloway and T. Tattan (eds) *Enabling Recovery: the principles and practice of rehabilitation psychiatry*, London: Gaskell.

Meaden, A., Nithsdale, V., Rose, C., Smith, J. and Jones, C. (2004) 'Is engagement associated with outcome in assertive outreach?', *Journal of Mental Health*, 13: 415–424.

Millon, T. (1994) *Millon Clinical Multiaxial Inventory III*, Minneapolis, MN: Dicandrien Inc.

NICE (2002) *Schizophrenia: core interventions in the treatment and management of schizophrenia in primary and secondary care, Clinical Guideline 1*, London: National Institute for Clinical Excellence.

Oliver, J.P.J. (1992) 'The social care directive: development of a quality of life profile for use in community services for the mentally ill', *Social Work and Social Sciences Review*, 3: 5–45.

Overall, J.E. and Gorham, D.R. (1962) 'The Brief Psychiatric Rating Scale', *Psychological Reports*, 10: 799–812.

Paget, A.T., Meaden, A., and Amphlett, C. (in press) 'Can engagement predict outcome in assertive outreach?', *Journal of Mental Health*.

Parker, G., Rosen, A., Emdur, N. and Hadzi-Pavlov, D. (1991) 'The Life Skills Profile:

psychometric properties of a measure assessing function and disability in schizo-phrenia', *Acta Psychiatrica Scandinavia*, 83: 145–152.

Perkins, R.E., and Repper, J. (1998) 'Principles of working with people who experi-ence mental health problems', in C. Brooker and J. Repper (eds) *Serious Mental Health Problems in the Community: policy, practice and research*, London: Bailliere Tindall.

Priebe, S., Huxley, P., Knight, S. and Evans, S. (1999) 'Application and results of the Short Assessment of Quality of Life (MANSA)', *International Journal of Social Psychiatry*, 4: 7–12.

Priebe, S., Watts, J., Chase, M. and Matanov, A. (2005) 'Processes of disengagement and engagement in assertive outreach patients: qualitative study', *British Journal of Psychiatry*, 187: 438–443.

Ralph, R.O., Kidder, K. and Phillips, D. (2000) *Can We Measure Recovery? A com-pendium of recovery and recovery related instruments, Volume 1*, Cambridge, MA: The Evaluation Center @ Human Services Research Institute.

Ridgway, P.A. and Press, A. (2004) *Assessing the Recovery Commitment of Your Mental Health Services: a user's guide to the Developing Recovery Enhancing Environments Measure (DREEM)*, UK pilot version, P. Allott (ed.), email: Mentalhealthrecovery@blueyonder.co.uk

Roberts, G., Davenport, S., Holloway, F. and Tattan, T. (2006) *Enabling Recovery: the principles and practice of rehabilitation psychiatry*, London: Gaskell.

Roberts G. and Wolfson P. (2004) 'The rediscovery of recovery', *Advances in Psychi-atric Treatment*, 10: 37–49.

Rosen, A., Hadzi-Pavlovic, D. and Parker, G. (1989) 'The Life Skills Profile: a measure assessing function and disability in schizophrenia', *Schizophrenia Bulletin*, 15: 325–337.

Rosen, A., Trauer, T., Hadzi-Pavlovic, D. and Parker, G. (2001) 'Development of a brief form of the Life Skills Profile: the LSP-20', *Australian and New Zealand Journal of Psychiatry*, 35: 677–683.

Sharma, T. and Harvey, P.D. (2002) *Understanding and Treating Cognition in Schizo-phrenia*, London: Taylor & Francis.

Skevington, S.M. (1999) 'Measuring quality of life in Britain: an introduction to the WHOQOL-100', *Journal of Psychosomatic Research*, 47: 449–459.

Slade, M., Thornicroft, G., Loftus, L., Phelan, M. and Wykes, T. (1999) *The Camberwell Assessment of Need (CAN)*, London: Royal College of Psychiatrists.

Tarrier, N. (1992) 'Management and modification of residual posisitve symptoms', in M. Birchwood and N. Tarrier (eds) *Innovations in the Psychological Management of Schizophrenia*, Chichester: Wiley.

Teague, G.B., Bond, G.R. and Drake, R.E. (1998) 'Program fidelity in assertive com-munity treatment: development and use of a measure', *American Journal of Orthopsychiatry*, 68: 216–232.

Thornicroft, G., Wykes, T., Holloway, F., Johnson and Szmukler, G. (1998) 'From efficacy to effectiveness in community mental health services. PRiSM psychosis study 10', *British Journal of Psychiatry*, 173: 423–427.

Trauer, T., Duckmanton, R.A. and Chiu, E. (1995) 'The Life Skills Profile: a study of its psychometric properties', *Australian and New Zealand Journal of Psychiatry*, 29: 492–499.

Tyrer, P.J. (2000) 'Are small case-loads beautiful in severe mental illness?', *British Journal of Psychiatry*, 177: 386–387.

Wane, J., Owen, A., Sood, L., Bradley, S. and Jones, C. (2007) 'The effectiveness of rural assertive outreach: a prospective cohort study in an English region', *Journal of Mental Health*, 16: 471–482.

Wing, J.K. (1978) 'Planning and evaluating services for chronically handicapped psychiatric patients in the United Kingdom', in L.I. Stein and M.A. Test (eds) *Alternatives to Mental Hospital Treatment*, New York: Plenum.

Wing, J.K., Cooper, J.E. and Beevor, A. (1996) *The Health of the Nation Outcome Scale*, London: Royal College of Psychiatrists.

Wykes, T. and Reeder, C. (2005) *Cognitive Remediation Therapy for Schizophrenia*, New York: Brunner Routledge.

Young, J.E. (1994) *Young Parenting Inventory*, New York: Cognitive Therapy Center of New York.

Young, J.E. (1995) *Young Compensation Inventory*, New York: Cognitive Therapy Center of New York.

Young, J.E. and Brown, G. (1990) *Young Schema Questionnaire*, New York: Cognitive Therapy Center of New York.

Young, J.E. and Rygh, J. (1994) *Young-Rygh Avoidance Inventory*, New York: Cognitive Therapy Center of New York.

4 Team Case Formulation

Stuart Whomsley

In recent years clinical psychology has increasingly emphasised the use of psychological formulations as a basis for any intervention with people experiencing a mental health problem. Such a formulation is normally drawn up after a period of assessment and may be based on any number of different models of psychological functioning. Psychological formulations are of particular help when people have complex and long-standing difficulties, with many different factors involved. They can form the basis of a specific psychological intervention or of an entire care plan.

Most Assertive Outreach Teams work as a whole team and therefore need to adopt systems and practices which involve the whole team (see chapter two). In this context it can be useful to develop a shared formulation, to which every member of the team contributes, which can then guide the work of the whole team. Such a multi-disciplinary formulation is likely to incorporate a psychological approach, but also include ideas from other professional groups such as psychiatric nurses, social workers, occupational therapists and psychiatrists. As such it draws together the team's understanding of the client into one working document.

This chapter presents four different types of case formulation that have been used by UK Assertive Outreach Teams:

1   Engagement formulations, for beginning work with new referrals. These kinds of formulation tend to be psychologically orientated and focus on interpersonal issues.
2   A resources-model formulation, for ongoing work. These formulations seek to understand how the team can play a role in assisting someone's recovery journey.
3   A risk formulation, in order to keep the service user, staff teams and the community as safe as can be reasonably expected.
4   A moving-on formulation, for when the service user leaves the team. In this case particular attention needs to be paid to attachment issues and the factors involved in maintaining wellness.

This chapter will describe how to carry out each type of formulation as a whole team, giving examples of how they have shaped the work of the team that used them.

One of the challenges of bringing together a team understanding is that it frequently uncovers differences of opinion between staff. This can at times result in heated discussion, but such debate is ultimately healthy for the team if it leads to more consistent and appropriate support to service users.

Psychological formulations may have great therapeutic power when shared with service users. They can help someone to feel understood and cared for in a very personal way. However, some people will have developed strategies for coping with their distress that involve de-emphasising or denying aspects of their experience. For this group, who are often strongly represented in Assertive Outreach Teams, presenting a complete formulation can be distressing and caution is needed. It may only be possible to share the part of a formulation that is most relevant to the work of the team, or agree to do this at a suitable point in the future.

Formulation

> Formulation . . . is defined as a provisional explanation or hypotheses of how an individual comes to present with a certain disorder or circumstances at a particular point in time. A number of factors may be involved in understanding the aetiology of the disorder or condition. These include biological, psychological and systemic factors . . . All these variables interact under certain conditions to produce a specific condition or phenomenon . . . A comprehensive formulation then needs to examine all three models carefully.
>
> (Weersakera, 1996: 4, cited in Johnstone and Dallos, 2006: 6)

A good formulation will list and summarise a person's problems, specifying any interrelations between them. It draws upon psychological theory to explain why this person, at this time, is having these problems, in these circumstances. It helps to explain the processes and mechanisms, such as schemas or attachment style, which are helping to maintain the problems. Thus a good formulation theoretically informs which interventions are to be followed, helps to prioritise whenever a range of interventions is possible, and has treatment utility. Yet, because formulation is both a reflexive and scientific endeavour, a formulation as a whole and its component parts remain as hypotheses, open to revision and reformulation on the basis of new data.

Formulation is not an exact science. Because it involves one human trying to understand another, it is open to the biases to which we are all susceptible in our decision-making processes. Kuyken (2006) advises that clinicians should be:

> . . . generating formulations with attention to valid and weighted evidence (to minimise availability biases) with humility (to avoid dispositional

biases that can occur with overconfidence) and with openness to any change required by new data (to avoid anchoring biases). Although in practice formulation is not a rational and systematic process, the balanced synthesis of the intuitive and rational cognitive systems can probably enable 'good enough' formulation that does not deviate too far on the continuum from optimal to frankly dangerous formulations.

(Kuyken, 2006: 30)

The expanded use of formulation in mental health services has its political dimension. Case formulation can be either complementary or an alternative to traditional psychiatric diagnosis. Core to the practice of clinical psychology, it is increasingly attracting the attention of art therapists, occupational therapists, psychiatric nurses, psychiatrists and social workers, as a way to organise and enhance their clinical work. In addition to being open to all professions, case formulation can be practised by clinicians who follow a range of theoretical orientations that include cognitive-behavioural, psychodynamic and systemic.

The team context

Producing a client formulation as a team raises issues that do not arise when a clinician is working to formulate on their own, or directly with the client. Team Case Formulation needs to take account of a series of issues related to the facilitation of group discussions and decision making in groups. Factors that need to be considered include: the current stage in the life history of the team (i.e. whether the team is new or well established); the different professional backgrounds that the team members come from; and differences in 'vocalness' of team members (those who feel they always have, or should have, something to offer, and those who feel they never have anything to say). In addition, the facilitator needs to understand how the team normally communicates and talks about clients, to make it clear that Team Case Formulation is something different from supervision, Care Programming Approach (CPA) Reviews and professionals' meetings. To produce a good formulation, team dynamics need to be managed in order to guard against the biases that Kuyken (2006) warns against: a group, just like an individual, may weight information in a biased way, be overconfident in its decision-making and have an anchoring bias that leads it to favoured explanations and solutions.

The benefits of Team Case Formulation

Team Case Formulation can be a way to enhance the quality of care offered to clients of an Assertive Outreach Team. In addition, by creating a contained, creative, positive, and hopefully productive discussion space, it may also improve general team functioning. Some specific potential benefits of Team Case Formulation are as follows:

- It enables a gathering together of information that may otherwise become buried in the notes or remain part of oral culture.
- It is a forum where myths can be dispelled, through the uncovering of beliefs about a client that have no clear evidence base.
- It provides a forum for considering different ideas about how best to work with a client. Team members can share ideas about what has worked well in the past and what has not.
- Hypotheses can be generated by the formulation which can be tested out in future work.
- It introduces thinking psychologically about a client in a way that does not require a formal training in psychological approaches.

How to do Team Case Formulation

We need to take account of a number of issues when undertaking a Team Case Formulation. What follows is a series of good practice guidelines that have been found to enable effective Team Case Formulation:

Time and space

- Set aside a designated and protected time each week for Team Case Formulation. The forms of Team Case Formulation contained in this chapter take on average an hour each, apart from the Resources Formulation which takes 90 minutes.

Staff participation

- There is an expectation that all staff attend, and this may include secretarial staff.

Facilitation

- Use a template, such as those contained in this chapter.
- Rotate the role of facilitator. Initially it may be best for a psychologist to be the facilitator to help familiarise the team with the approach.
- The facilitator should ideally not be one of the people who knows the client best so that they can focus on the facilitation task.
- Carry out a different type of formulation each week to bring in variety, e.g. an Engagement Team Case Formulation one week, a Risk Team Case Formulation the next.
- The facilitator needs to ensure, and to actively encourage, all team members to express their views and ideas regardless of their position in the team hierarchy.

Scheduling clients

- Prioritise clients for Team Case Formulation. However, make sure that the less 'difficult' clients do not slip to the bottom of the list. If a team is using the four types of formulation contained in this chapter, it should have a prioritisation list for each.
- Ultimately all clients of the team should have all of the types of formulation that the team uses conducted for them.

Recording, sharing and reviewing

- Have the findings of the Team Case Formulation typed up straight after the session and placed on the client's file. They should be available to all team members for reflection.
- Where appropriate, identify who is going to discuss the Team Case Formulation with the client.
- Review how the Team Case Formulation has informed practice.

Four types of Team Case Formulation

As a means of demonstrating Team Case Formulation, the remainder of this chapter is based around the fictional case example of Patrick. It highlights many of the issues that assertive outreach clients present with. When Patrick first arrives in the team an Engagement Team Case Formulation is conducted. During his first year with the team Resources and Risk Team Case Formulations are conducted. Finally, after a period of successful work, the team reaches the conclusion of its work with Patrick and meets for the final time to produce a Moving-on Team Case Formulation.

Example:

Patrick was referred to the team when he was 32 years old. He has a history of polysubstance abuse and currently uses alcohol, cannabis and amphetamines. In the past he also used ecstasy and LSD. In his early twenties, he had a series of short periods in hospital where he was diagnosed with drug-induced psychosis. At 29 years of age he was admitted for a longer period under section three of the Mental Health Act and at this time received a diagnosis of schizophrenia. He had two further compulsory hospital admissions in his early thirties, the second of which followed an assault on his ex-wife's new partner over issues regarding access to his children.

Patrick was referred to the Assertive Outreach Team because of concern over the escalating number of hospital admissions, his poor engagement with services between admissions and the potential risk to his ex-wife's partner. Assessment showed that he had psychosis with a combination of paranoid and grandiose delusions. He hears voices that he believes to be

God. The voices give contradictory messages, alternating between suggestions that he is a bad and weak man and that he is in some way special and has been chosen for greatness. When using amphetamines, his thought is also disordered.

Although he has worked previously, he is currently unemployed. He lives in housing association property with his current partner, who is a service user with a diagnosis of bipolar disorder. He is in regular contact with his mother, brother and half-sister, who all live locally. He still has access to his two children although there are issues with his ex-wife's new partner.

Engagement Team Case Formulation

Patrick's initial referral to the team initiated a period of multi-disciplinary assessment. This included a review of his notes, a meeting with Patrick, and a meeting with the care co-ordinator from his previous mental health team. These provided sufficient information for the team to meet and conduct an Engagement Team Case Formulation.

The Engagement Team Case Formulation is based upon the overarching principle that a connection can be made between a client's past and present, in relation to psychological factors that include engagement, attachment, self-esteem and recovery-style. Furthermore, that an understanding of these connections can usefully inform future work with the client to bring about change.

Engagement Team Case Formulations are conducted using a simple but effective template developed by Cupitt (2005). This focuses the team on considering the client's past, present and future and subtly incorporates psychological concepts.

The engagement formulation for Patrick is as follows:

> *PAST: What is/are the most significant event/s in the person's past and how have these affected them? e.g. childhood in care, loss of intimate relationships, adult trauma.*

At seven years of age, Patrick lost his father, Duggie, an alcoholic who had committed suicide. He felt abandoned and this created a void in his life. His mother, Madge, remarried two years later. Although Patrick's younger brother, Declan, bonded well with their stepfather Bill, Patrick did not develop a close relationship with him. This confused Patrick and he felt isolated and rejected. His feelings of isolation intensified after the birth of his half-sister, Katie, when he was 12 years old, and his relationship with his stepfather deteriorated further. His mother remained loving and supportive. In his early teens, Patrick fell in with a bad crowd at school and began experimenting with drugs and alcohol. He started to perform poorly academically and his stepfather told him he was a failure. Despite this, he worked hard and achieved six GCSEs with good grades and made plans to stay in education. He started a course at the local college but was still taking drugs regularly. On finding pills in his room, his stepfather confronted him and, after a violent argument, threw him out of the house. Madge's attempts to reconcile the two of them failed and he moved to live in a shared house with friends from college.

Patrick dropped out of college and found work as a warehouseman in a local factory, the first of a series of such jobs. He started seeing Mary, whom he had first met at college. He was happy and felt needed for the first time since his father's death. They shared common interests, in particular music, and were regulars at raves where they both took drugs. They married when he was 19 years of age. Following Patrick's third hospitalisation, associated with drug use when he was 23 years old, Mary stopped using drugs. Patrick continued to use cannabis and amphetamines regularly.

After several years of trying to start a family, Patrick became the father of twins, Patrick and Rachel, when he was 25 years old. He decided to change his life and reduced his substance use and worked very hard; however, he found it hard to stay drug free. Finally, when he was 28 years old he split up with Mary due to conflicts over his continued drug use. He moved to live with friends he knew from his rave-going days. He continued to see his children regularly but feelings of isolation returned. About a year after he split up with Mary, he found out that she had started a relationship with someone new called Jason. When Jason moved in with Mary, Patrick's feelings of isolation intensified and his drug use increased. His mother remained supportive. Mary was persuaded by Jason that Patrick's drug use was a risk to the children. As a result, she would no longer let Patrick be alone with the children. The situation escalated and, when he was 31 years old, Patrick assaulted Jason during a psychotic episode after an argument over access to his children.

PRESENT: What is/are the most pressing issue/s in the person's present life? e.g. no trusting and open relationships, chaotic lifestyle, low self-esteem.

Patrick has ongoing issues when interacting with staff from mental health services. It was felt that staff tended to adopt the parental roles that he has previously experienced, thus mirroring his relationship with his stepfather, resulting in Patrick becoming aggressive with male authority figures. With female staff, he may bring out maternal and over-anxious behaviour. His general view is that services have nothing to offer him. Services receive a lot of calls from his current partner, mother and half-sister whenever they are concerned that his mental health is deteriorating.

His relationship with his new current partner, Sabrina, is a source of support and companionship; however, her mental health issues can be a source of stress for him and have the potential to affect his own mental health.

The ongoing problems over access to his children are a major issue for Patrick. Seeing his children boosts his self-esteem, and he has reported feeling suicidal when he has not had access to them. He is explicitly trying not to repeat for his children the experiences of the absent father he had.

Patrick still has substance abuse problems and there are clear links between this and his ongoing psychosis. He has a tendency to take anti-psychotic medication in the same way that he uses other drugs, which means that his medication is not always effective.

Although currently unemployed, Patrick wants to work; however, this is complicated by his belief that the dead-end jobs he has had are partly responsible for the deterioration in his mental health. Relative to his brother and half-sister, he feels a failure in this area of his life. Finding a job would increase his self-esteem. He has interests in gardening and cooking and, as his stepfather is now elderly, regularly helps his mother with household/garden jobs.

FUTURE: How are we working on these issues? What are we working towards? e.g. having a trusting open relationship, less chaotic lifestyle, self-management of symptoms, gaining self-esteem.

When interacting with Patrick team members need to be mindful not to replay the negative roles that he has experienced in the past. The team also need to show him that we have something to offer and can help him achieve his goals. There is also a need for the team to manage the anxieties in his relationships because high expressed emotion is likely to be detrimental to Patrick's psychological wellbeing and may lead to relapse. As Sabrina's problems impact upon him, the team consider that they have a duty of care to liaise closely with her team, but are aware that this must be done in an open way so as not to exacerbate his paranoia.

The team feel that they can help Patrick to achieve his goal of having more/better access to his children. To improve access to his children it is necessary to try to reduce the conflict with Jason. The risk of Patrick hitting Jason still remains and a repeat of the earlier assault would probably lead to his having no access to his children. This could give rise to feelings of anger, failure and low self-esteem, and might trigger increased persecutory voices. We know that Jason tries to provoke Patrick and, therefore, we need to help him to develop conflict resolution strategies.

A second goal that the team can help Patrick with is finding employment. This can be achieved by building on his strengths and interests which we can assess using a strengths model approach. The team can provide him with information on vocational training, for example, related to his interests in cooking and gardening, and can assist him in obtaining funding and accessing facilities. Helping Patrick to achieve his goals may also improve his engagement with the team.

Clearly, as a mental health team, one of our key roles is to help Patrick manage his psychosis. Our aim is to help improve his control over his own condition and to prevent further compulsory hospital admissions. Improving control can be achieved using a combination of antipsychotic medication and Cognitive Behaviour Therapy (CBT). For the CBT we will use formulation and case study approaches such as those of Morrison *et al.* (2004) and Kingdon and Turkington (2002). A specific factor that we need to address with Patrick is his tendency to take antipsychotic medication in the same way that he uses other drugs. The team will inform him about how his medication works through psycho-education. To help him have more control over the impact of his substance abuse on his life, we will adopt a harm-minimisation approach to his substance abuse and will use Miller and Rollnick's (2002) motivational interviewing approach.

After the Engagement Team Case Formulation had been conducted, the team felt more confident about working with Patrick. They had a better understanding of the reasons why he had posed challenges to his previous team and how they might address these in their future work. From the 'Future' section of the formulation they were able to produce a 'road map' of how they aimed to work with Patrick. This had specific goals that drew upon his positive strengths and went beyond how to engage with him, to include ideas for specific interventions. The team felt that this led nicely into the Care Programming Approach and it informed the first CPA Review.

The facilitator pointed out that, although the formulation was based upon a series of hypotheses based on the known facts, some of the hypotheses and even some of the facts could be inaccurate. The team were encouraged to test out these facts and hypotheses as they worked with Patrick. Some of the ideas from the formulation were shared with Patrick, as part of this process. This was done by his care co-ordinator. The outcome of this was mixed. Patrick appeared to appreciate that some of his concerns were understood, but he also became suspicious about how much was known about him and how this information had been obtained.

Understanding poor engagement

In considering how to engage with a client, it is worth spending some time exploring why they were thought to have had problems engaging with services in the past. If a client does not believe that they have a mental illness, for instance, they are unlikely to engage with services. After all, if you don't think that you have a mental illness, why would anyone engage with mental health services? In these instances creative means to engagement are needed. The team need to consider what it is that they could offer the client that they would find useful. As the Sainsbury Centre for Mental Health state:

> Successful therapeutic relationships very rarely just happen, but need to be carefully worked on from the first meeting. Assertive outreach workers should be prepared to spend a lot of time engaging service users and will need to be highly flexible and creative in their approach to this. It is particularly important to pay attention to the needs and priorities expressed by the user, rather than operating from a pre-set agenda. Getting involved in their daily living activities, such as shopping or cleaning, or sorting out problems with welfare benefits and utility payments can often be highly effective as a means of initial engagement.
>
> (The Sainsbury Centre for Mental Health, 2001: 11)

In addition, a shared language that does not include traditional psychiatric terminology could be useful.

A client may believe that they had a mental illness but that this is now a thing of the past. For some people this belief may be accurate; however, for others the 'it's all right now' attitude may indicate a 'sealing over' recovery style (Drayton *et al.*, 1998; Tait *et al.*, 2003) that is interspersed with episodes of psychosis. With such clients engagement may take a longer period of time and may involve hospital admission at times of relapse.

A client's experiences of psychosis may lead them to be wary of people in general, including mental health professionals. Paranoia is likely to make people suspicious of strangers knocking at their door offering them help and support. Munro (2008) succinctly summarises the relationship between persecutory delusions, engagement and risk management:

> The presence of persecutory delusions makes the sufferer pathologically wary: at the same time there is a total denial that psychiatric illness could possibly be at the root of the problems. Naturally this makes engagement with helping agencies very difficult and often means that no-one is truly aware of the severity of the illness or its degree of escalation.
>
> (Munro, 2008: 111)

In these circumstances a too 'assertive' approach may reinforce the paranoia. Therefore, a gentle approach that tentatively maintains contact and builds up trust is likely to be most effective. Alternatively, a hospital admission, that may unfortunately be compulsory, could still be an opportunity to build up trust and address some of their anxieties about mental health professionals. They may feel that they have been let down by mental health services in the past, following traumatic admissions and being forced to take medication that they felt that they did not need, or really did not help, or had unpleasant side effects.

A client's lifestyle may have made it difficult for services to engage with them, perhaps by living with a degree of chaos that frustrated the efforts of traditional services to gain or maintain contact with them. This chaos may be the result of psychosis, and/or personality and/or substance misuse. In addition, a client's lifestyle may also have brought them to the attention of members of the community whose interest in them may become a source of stress that they wish to avoid. An over-involved neighbour who wants to 'help'; a local community vigilante who sees the 'mad one' as a danger; or a drug dealer wanting to reclaim a debt; all these may lead to someone becoming reclusive. It is always useful to consider the real-world basis of a client's paranoia.

An appreciation of attachment theory in adults (Bartholomew and Horowitz, 1991; Hazan and Shaver, 1994) may also be beneficial in understanding engagement problems between a client and services. Obviously, dismissive-avoidant and anxious-avoidant attachment styles may be implicated in a client not wanting to engage with services. However, a client with an anxious-preoccupied style may also have had problems with engagement, perhaps by becoming dependent or demanding on services. Such a person may have engaged with services but have become over-demanding and caused the service to disengage. Attachment styles are enacted within relationships and therefore it is useful to consider the attachment style of the mental health worker as well as that of the client. Overall, the aim is for the team as a whole to become a secure attachment base for the client (see chapter two).

Resources Team Case Formulation

During his first year as a client the team gained a greater understanding of Patrick's life, enabling them to conduct a Resources Team Case Formulation. The Resources Team Case Formulation is an adaptation of a model developed by Hagan and Smail (1997) for individual work. Hagan and Smail developed an approach to formulation that supports their community psychology orientation (see chapter nine). Their model is focused upon the individual in their environment and places a strong emphasis on environmental factors as being key to psychological distress, specifically the person's access to power in their environment. As Hagan and Smail state: 'individual distress is the outcome of a social process whose origins – whether in time, space, or both – may lie far beyond the individual's ability to identify them' (1997: 261). To assist identification, Hagan and Smail developed a method called 'Power-mapping'. This they describe as:

> a flexible method for representing important aspects of his/her social environment, in terms of both the powers and resources available to

him/her (assets) and the extent to which s/he is subjected adversely to the proximal powers of other (liabilities).

(Hagan and Smail, 1997: 265)

This enables clinicians to map the clients' circumstances, target areas for action, monitor progress and measure outcomes in a way that provides a visual summary for the clinician and the client.

With the Resources Team Case Formulation the team considers a client's life under the following headings and associated subheadings.

A   *Home and family life*

    i   Parents
    ii   Relations
    iii Partner
    iv Children
    v   Love life

B   *Social life*

    i   Friends
    ii   Leisure
    iii Associations

C   *Personal resources*

    i   Intelligence
    ii   Embodiment
    iii Understanding of the past
    iv Confidence

D   *Material resources*

    i   Physical environment
    ii   Health
    iii Money
    iv Education
    v   Work

For each subheading, e.g. parents, the team considers and lists the positives and negatives. After discussion, a rating of both the positive and negative effects of this area on the person's life is decided upon and given a score between −3 and +3. This reflects the principle that an area can be both a resource and a liability in the person's life. On the basis of this appraisal, the team then considers how they might be able to intervene in this area of the client's life. There may be no intervention possible.

The 'Home and family life' section of the Resources Team Case Formulation for Patrick is as follows:

Home and family life

Parents:

+1 Madge, Patrick's mother, still provides support, and she attends CPA review meetings.

−3 Patrick's father, Duggie, was an alcoholic who killed himself when Patrick was seven.

Conflict with stepdad, Bill, has been ongoing; Patrick never felt accepted by him and this relationship was aggressive at times. Madge can some-times be needy and put pressure on Patrick when she is having problems with Bill. She can be over-anxious about Patrick, as she fears he will do what his father did; she rings services a lot and also encourages her daughter, Katie, to do likewise. Bill does not like Madge getting involved with Patrick's care.

Interventions:

Carer support for Madge could be offered. When the time is right, work with Patrick around the issues of loss and personal identity related to his father's death may be beneficial. The team should be mindful of the potential for further conflict between Patrick and Bill. The team should also be mindful of the dynamic between Madge and Bill in interventions that involve her. Family work may also be a possibility with different combinations of family members (see chapter seven).

Relations:

+1 Patrick's brother, Declan, and half-sister, Katie, still live locally and provide some support. Katie contacts services when she has concerns about Patrick and she can be easier to liaise with than their mother.

−1 Declan and Katie can be embarrassed about their brother as he has gained a reputation as a local 'nutter'. Patrick is very aware that he has achieved less than his siblings and feels bad about this.

Interventions:

The team need to find out how comfortable Patrick, Declan and Katie are about the team liaising with them. Psycho-educational work with the siblings may be possible and useful. The team could explore pos-sible ways for Patrick to feel closer to his siblings in terms of success. This could develop into family work.

Spouse/Partner:

+2 Patrick has been able to form and maintain relationships that have lasted; his marriage to Mary lasted nine years and she is still basic-ally positive about him. He currently has a partner, Sabrina, who provides love and support.

−2 Patrick's marriage breakdown was related to his substance misuse and mental health problems. Mary's new partner, Jason, is actively hostile to Patrick, and there has been a physical fight. Sabrina has a diagnosis of bipolar disorder and her mental health problems impact on Patrick.

Interventions:

Motivational interviewing for substance misuse may utilise Patrick's concern that his current relationship does not break down because of his substance misuse. The team need to be mindful of the risk issues related to Patrick and Jason, and to work with Mary to facilitate contact for Patrick with his children in a way that minimises risks in relation to Jason. Work is also needed to support Patrick and Sabrina as a couple and as carers for each other.

Children:

+3 Patrick's two children, little Patrick and Rachel, are a great source of pride to him, and Patrick has been a good father to them.

−2 There are difficulties with access to the children because of Jason. There are concerns that Patrick's children may become part of his delusional framework. There are likely to be issues with Child Protection if Patrick and Sabrina decide to have children.

Interventions:

The team can work with Mary to maintain Patrick's access to his children. CBT work with Patrick around delusions may prevent real-world events becoming incorporated into his delusional framework. The team would support Patrick and Sabrina should they decide to start a family. Family work may be beneficial.

Love life:

+1 He has a love life.

−1 Sabrina has been unfaithful to him during a manic episode.

Intervention:

No intervention indicated at the moment.

These findings can be presented graphically, as in Figure 4.1, which enables a rapid appraisal of where the resources and liabilities are in the person's life. The team went on to complete the other three sections – social life, personal resources and material resources – in the same way.

When the time came for the care co-ordinator to share parts of the Resources Team Case Formulation with Patrick, they were mindful of how Patrick had previously been both welcoming and suspicious when the Engagement Team Case Formulation had been shared with him. They were also aware that sharing the whole of the Resources Team Case Formulation could be overwhelming for Patrick. Therefore, they proceeded with care. However, Patrick welcomed what was shared with him, without reservation. Perhaps this was due to the careful approach taken by the care co-ordinator.

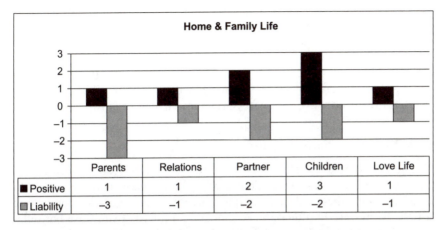

Figure 4.1 A graphical representation of the Home and Family Life section of the Resources Team Case Formulation

It may also be a reflection of the trust that had been built between Patrick and the team since the Engagement Team Case Formulation had been conducted.

Additional guidance for Resources Team Case Formulation

The following guidelines explain how to use the categories of the Resources formulation that may be open to differing interpretations:

- 'Parents', 'Relations' and 'Spouse/partner' include both past and present issues. For example, the parenting that the person received as a child and its ongoing impact on attachment, in addition to the ways in which living parents may be a positive resource or a liability in the present.
- 'Children' includes both any children the person may have and also any issues that they may have about not having any children.
- 'Associations' include formal clubs and societies in addition to informal ones such as being part of a group of clients who are often inpatients and know each other.
- 'Intelligence' includes an estimation of the client's intelligence and in addition how it may have been affected by psychosis and medication.
- 'Embodiment' includes the person's actual physical self, in addition to how they feel about it. So they may have a very physically fit body, but feel bad about it, or they may be a happy 'couch potato'. Both scenarios contain both negative and positive scores for the person's actual physical self and how they appraise it.
- 'Understanding of the past' may include a delusional understanding that the person has formed as a negative score because it has become a liability for them.

- 'Confidence' may include a consideration of both genuine confidence as a positive, and delusional or drug-induced confidence as a negative.
- 'Physical environment' includes both the client's home and the general area in which they live.
- 'Health' includes both physical and mental health. If the person's psychosis is controlled, then having a diagnosis of schizophrenia or bipolar disorder does not necessarily mean a high negative score.

Risk Team Case Formulation

People are sometimes referred to Assertive Outreach Teams because they engage in risky behaviours. Consequently, it is necessary for teams to carefully assess these risks (see chapter three) in preparation for conducting a Risk Team Case Formulation. A template for a Risk Team Case Formulation is presented in Figure 4.2. The formulation appreciates that risk is dynamic. As Morgan (2007: 8) states: 'Risk is not fixed, but is also often treated as such. Within a single individual, risk will vary with time, context and intervention.' The Risk Team Case Formulation may initially be conducted at a time of relative stability, but can then act as a guide for the team to consider risk in an ongoing manner. This can be particularly useful at times of potential crisis, when previously devised short-term interventions can be implemented to reduce risk. After the crisis, the effectiveness of the formulation, accuracy of warning signs and utility of interventions can be evaluated.

The first part of the Risk Team Case Formulation assesses the client's risk factors: what they are, how they may vary, and how the team, or the client, may affect them. The team then considers protective factors in the same way. Next the team considers the balance of risk against protective factors at that time. The team now takes some time to consider empathetically how they would feel if they were in the client's position. In addition, the team considers the short-term indicators that may suggest that risk has increased. If there is no crisis, then the team continues with ongoing longer-term work to reduce risk factors and maintain or increase protective factors. At the time of formulation the team also devises a short-term interventions plan to be implemented at times of crisis.

At times of potential crisis, the Risk Team Case Formulation is revisited. There is a reappraisal of the balance between risk and protective factors, a further period of empathetic reasoning, and a consideration of the risk indicators. If there is cause for concern, then the Risk Team Case Formulation can be used to guide short-term interventions. After a crisis there is an evaluation of how well the short-term interventions worked in reducing the risk and how useful the early indicators were in predicting it. There is then a return to the long-term work of reducing risk factors and maintaining or increasing protective factors.

RISK　　　　　　　　　　　　　　　**PROTECTIVE**

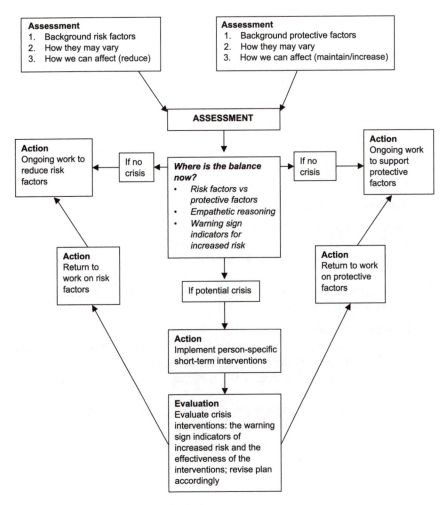

Figure 4.2 Risk Team Case Formulation

The Risk Team Case Formulation for Patrick is as follows:

Assessment-risk

Background risk factors:
- Patrick has an ongoing psychosis that only partially responds to medication.
- Polysubstance misuse negatively influences Patrick's psychosis.
- Patrick has some history of physical violence: to stepfather, Bill, and ex-wife's new partner, Jason.

How they may vary:
- In response to life stressors that include the following: access to children which is related to conflicts with Jason; arguments with Bill; difficulties in the relationship with his partner, Sabrina.

How we may affect them:
- Reduce Patrick's psychosis through medication and CBT.
- Assist Patrick with a harm minimisation approach to substance misuse.
- Motivational interviewing to increase his wish for abstinence from substances.
- Help maintain positive access for Patrick to his children.
- Advise and coach Patrick in alternative conflict resolution strategies.
- Liaise with Sabrina's care team.

Assessment-protective

Background protective factors:
- Patrick takes antipsychotic medication.
- Patrick is aware of the links between psychosis and substance misuse.
- Patrick wants to be a good father to his children.
- Patrick has a number of potential social supports: partner, mother, brother, half-sister.

How they may vary:
- Substance misuse may neutralise the therapeutic effects of the antipsychotic medication that Patrick takes.
- Patrick's ability to access the positive fathering part of himself is changeable.
- Patrick's social supports are affected by Sabrina's mental health and Bill's restrictions on his mother, Madge, affecting her ability to help and support.

Assessment of current situation

Where is the balance now? Potential crisis

Warning sign indicators that risk has increased:
- Substance use has increased according to care co-ordinator observations.
- Patrick has told Sabrina that he is hearing more voices.
- Patrick has told Madge and Katie that he is thinking of hitting Jason.
- Phone calls from Sabrina, his mother and Katie expressing their concerns.

Empathetic reasoning

From Patrick's perspective:
I am feeling more desperate as the stresses in my life have increased. Jason tried to provoke me when I visited little Patrick and Rachel. I used

my conflict resolution strategies, but I was still left feeling angry. After the visit I drank more than usual and smoked cannabis. I began to hear more voices that were critical of me but also said that I needed 'to save the children'. Sabrina heard me muttering back to them. I became more confused and distressed. I felt that I had to tell someone and not just act, so I told my mother that I was thinking of hitting Jason. Part of me knows that this will make things worse for me but at least I am asking for help.

Action

Implement short-term interventions:
- Encourage Patrick to increase medication temporarily.
- Encourage Patrick to reduce substance use.
- Encourage him to use strategies from his Wellness Recovery Action Plan (WRAP; Copeland, 1997).
- Help Patrick with conflict resolution strategies in relation to Jason and access to children. Give him praise for using them.
- Liaise with Sabrina, mother and Katie to contain their anxieties.
- Arrange for Patrick to continue to have access to his children without the presence of Jason, e.g. supervised by Madge.

Evaluation

Evaluation of crisis intervention: Crisis averted.

Early indicators: Indicators appear to be good. Patrick, his partner, care co-ordinator and family together gave a good picture of how the situation was changing.

Effectiveness of intervention: No violent incident, no admission and no reduction in social capital.

By conducting the Risk Team Case Formulation the team gained greater confidence in working with Patrick. The team was confident that if and when a crisis should occur they would have some idea about how to manage it in an individualised way. When a crisis did happen, the team had a plan to reduce its length and severity. After the crisis the team were not complacent but reflected on what they could have done differently. Patrick was encouraged to participate in this process as actively as possible to support him to minimise future risk. In doing this the care co-ordinator was aware that they needed to ensure that Patrick did not feel shamed or blamed. As Underhill (2007) points out, linking mental illness and risk can be stigmatising, and in addition the process of conducting a risk assessment can escalate anxiety in clinicians. In contrast, the process of conducting a Risk Team Case Formulation helped to manage the team's anxiety, particularly with its dual focus on protective factors as well as risk factors. The empathetic reasoning exercise helped Patrick to be better understood by the team and went some way to prevent more prejudicial attitudes about him becoming established in the team.

Moving-on Team Case Formulation

Assertive Outreach Teams vary in the length of time they expect to be involved in a client's life. Some teams work to a 'no close' model where the client's time with the team is open-ended. Other teams will take on a client for a set period of time, or for a specific piece of work, after which they are discharged back to another mental health team, or to their GP. Whatever the model followed, for many clients there will come a time when they will move on from the Assertive Outreach Team. The importance of this task has been recognised by the Sainsbury Centre for Mental Health:

> It is extremely important to start preparing clients for discharge several months in advance. Clients should be encouraged to express any fears and feelings of sadness they have about the move. Their successes while engaged with assertive outreach should also be reviewed.
>
> (The Sainsbury Centre for Mental Health, 2001: 14)

In order to bring about a constructive ending to their work with a client, the team can carry out a Moving-on Team Case Formulation.

The Moving-on Team Case Formulation is derived from the ideas of Brief Solution Focused Therapy (de Shazer, 1988; Jackson and McKergow, 2002), and particularly borrows the types of question used in this approach. Here the ideas are applied in a novel way, by using them at the end of a lengthy piece of work, rather than at the start of a brief episode of therapy. However, the solution here can be conceptualised as a response to the problem of how to enable the client to move on and maintain the changes that they have made whilst with the team.

This formulation is organised by eight questions for the team to consider. First the team looks backwards to how they engaged with the client; this will provide useful information for any future clinicians working with the client. Next the team considers what has enabled positive change for the client: a constructive message for the team, anyone working with the client in the future, and potentially the client themselves. As there could always be something more to do, the team then considers what further work they might do with the client had they remained with the team; again this forms guidance for both future clinicians and the client. Next the team considers two linked questions constructing both a hypothetical negative and positive future for the client. Finally, the team considers two more linked questions: five positive messages for the clinicians of the client's new team, and five positive messages for the client. The Moving-on Team Case Formulation can be used as the basis of letters sent to a future team and in an ending letter to the client. The eight questions for this are as follows:

1   What was important for engaging with this person?
2   What do you think has effected positive change for this person?

3   What makes us feel able to see this person move to a new team/return to primary case/be discharged?
4   What would we still be working on if the person stayed with the team?
5   If things went badly for this person, how might they be in ten years' time? (Avoid nightmare scenarios unless very likely.)
6   If things work out well for this person, how might they be in ten years' time?
7   What are the five key messages that we want to pass on to the new team/ GP practice?
8   What are the key messages that we want to pass on to the client?

The Moving-on Team Case Formulation for Patrick is as follows:

What was important for engaging with this person?
- Being aware of how Patrick responds to different genders, and authority, trying not to repeat patterns of the past.
- Flexible engagement patterns in the early work that adapted with time as Patrick wanted more structure and predictability.
- Emphasising his strengths and where he had potential for success.
- Helping him with his goals that include positive access to his children.

What do you think has effected positive change for this person?
- Team providing a source of containment, advice and support.
- Adopting a collaborative medication strategy.
- CBT for psychosis.
- Patrick and his care co-ordinator produced a WRAP that was used in times of crisis.
- Patrick has a social network that can be mobilised to offer support.
- Patrick has retained a sense of hope.
- Generally Patrick has a positive couple relationship with Sabrina.
- Patrick gaining a place on a catering course where the head chef acted as a positive father figure.

What makes us feel able to see this person move to a new team/return to primary care/be discharged?
- The last two years with the team have been ones of great stability for Patrick.
- Patrick has achieved more stability in the relationships within his social network; there is a truce, if an uneasy one, between Patrick and stepdad Bill and between Patrick and his ex-wife's new partner, Jason.
- Patrick has significantly reduced his substance use and now uses only alcohol and cannabis.

What would we still be working on if the person stayed with the team?
- Refinements of the WRAP through experience.
- Ongoing support with vocational issues.

- Substance misuse cessation work (if that is his goal).
- Couple work with Sabrina (if they agree).

If things went badly for this person, how might they be in ten years' time?
(Avoid nightmare scenarios unless very likely.)
Stress from work and his relationship with Sabrina has caused Patrick to
increase his substance misuse, particularly amphetamines. The stress and
substance misuse lead to an increase in his psychosis, the loss of his job
and Sabrina leaving him.

If things work out well for this person how might they be in ten years' time?
Patrick is working as a chef. He has a new family with Sabrina, with
Sabrina's care team giving good support to enable her to parent the child.
He sees little Patrick and Rachel regularly; as they are now teenagers they
choose to spend time with their dad. There have been times when he was
starting to relapse, particularly after the birth of his child with Sabrina,
but he used his WRAP and was not admitted to hospital.

What are the five key messages that we want to pass on to the new
team/GP practice?
- Keep the ball rolling.
- Maintain working relationships with Patrick's social network; even
  if anxious, they are your allies.
- Be aware of how Patrick responds to different staff and when they
  fall into parental roles for him.
- Reinforce Patrick's conflict resolution strategies.
- Let him cook for you, he is very good!

What are the key messages that we want to pass on to the client?
- You are a good dad.
- You are a good cook.
- Use your WRAP.
- Use substances sensibly.
- Use effective conflict resolution strategies – do not hit Jason!

Conducting the Moving-on Team Case Formulation was a positive experience for the team because it allowed them to reflect on the progress that they
had made with Patrick. During the time that they had worked with Patrick
not all of the clients had done so well, and to focus for a while on a positive
outcome helped maintain a sense of hope in their work and job satisfaction.
They were keen not to take too much of the credit, but to acknowledge the
hard work of Patrick himself. The Moving-on Team Case Formulation was
put into an 'ending letter' that was sent to Patrick. At the next home visit that
his care co-ordinator made, Patrick opened the door with a beaming smile on
his face and the letter in his hand.

Issues and discussion

The practice of Team Case Formulation raises a series of issues for further consideration, including those of client involvement and evidence-based practice. One area to consider is how far clients may be involved in Team Case Formulation. Formulation away from the client raises ethical issues and it can feel as if the team are talking behind the client's back. Conversely, to have a client present at a Team Case Formulation may be an exposing and unpleasant experience for them. An allied issue is how to share all, or part, of a Team Case Formulation with a client. While a formulation may help some clients to feel they have been listened to, thought about and understood, for others it may make them feel observed, studied, categorised or even experimented on.

The practice of Team Case Formulation also needs to be considered in the context of the development of evidence-based practice and efficient use of resources. Is it a good use of time and money to have an entire team meet together each week to conduct a Team Case Formulation? This leads to questions about how best to research the direct and indirect benefits of practising Team Case Formulation. Does Team Case Formulation directly lead to changes in client care that are beneficial for them? In teams that practise it, does Team Case Formulation indirectly lead to a movement away from biomedical explanations towards biopsychosocial ones? These are interesting research questions for the future. At present Team Case Formulation represents both a pragmatic and theory-linked way to conduct clinical work in an Assertive Outreach Team, which, on the basis of the responses of both team members and clients, has good face validity.

Conclusion

This chapter has followed the progress of a fictional client, Patrick, through an Assertive Outreach Team to illustrate the use of four types of Team Case Formulation: Engagement, Resources, Risk and Moving-on. Though Patrick is fictional, these four types of formulation can be, and have been, effectively used in a real Assertive Outreach Team.

References

Bartholomew, K. and Horowitz, L.M. (1991) 'Attachment styles among young adults: a test of a four-category model', *Journal of Personality and Social Psychology*, 61: 226–244.

Copeland, M.E. (1997) *Wellness Recovery Action Plan (WRAP)*, West Dummerton, VT: Peach Press.

Cupitt, C. (2005) 'A formulation based approach to engagement', workshop presented at the National Assertive Outreach Forum Conference, Keele University, April.

de Shazer, S. (1988) *Clues: investigating solutions in brief therapy*, New York: Norton.

Drayton, M., Birchwood, M, and Trower, P. (1998) 'Early attachment experience and recovery from psychosis', *British Journal of Clinical Psychology*, 37: 269–284.

Hagan, T. and Smail, D. (1997) 'Power-mapping 1: background and basic methodology', *Journal of Community and Applied Social Psychology*, 7: 257–267.

Hazan, C. and Shaver, P.R. (1994) 'Attachment as an organizational framework for research on close relationships', *Psychological Inquiry*, 5: 1–22.

Jackson, P.Z. and McKergow, M. (2002) *The Solutions Focus: the simple way to positive change*, London: Nicholas Brealey Publishing.

Johnstone, L. and Dallos, R. (eds) (2006) *Formulation in Psychology and Psychotherapy: making sense of people's problems*, London: Routledge.

Kingdon, D. and Turkington, D. (eds) (2002) *The Case Study Guide to Cognitive Behaviour Therapy of Psychosis*, Chichester: Wiley.

Kuyken, W. (2006) 'Evidence-based case formulation: is the emperor clothed?', in N. Tarrier (ed.) *Case Formulation in Cognitive Behavioural Therapy*, Hove: Routledge.

Miller, W.R. and Rollnick, S. (2002) *Motivational Interviewing: preparing people for change*, 2nd edn, New York and London: Guilford.

Morgan, J.F. (2007) *Giving up the Culture of Blame: risk assessment and risk management in psychiatric practice*, Royal College of Psychiatry briefing paper, London: RCP.

Morrison, A.P., Renton, J.C., Dunn, H., Williams, S. and Bentall, R.P. (2004) *Cognitive Therapy for Psychosis: a formulation-based approach*, Hove: Routledge.

Munro, A. (2008) 'Aspects of persecutory delusions in the setting of delusional disorder', in D. Freeman, R. Bentall and P. Garety (eds) *Persecutory Delusions: assessment, theory and treatment*, Oxford: OUP.

Sainsbury Centre for Mental Health (2001) *Mental Health Topics: assertive outreach*, London: SCMH.

Tait, L., Birchwood, M., and Trower, P. (2003) 'Predicting engagement with services for psychosis: insight, symptoms and recovery style', *British Journal of Psychiatry*, 182: 123–128.

Underhill, G. (2007) 'The risks of risk assessment', *Advances in Psychiatric Treatment*, 13: 291–297.

5   Staff stress and burnout

Abi Gray and Alison Mulligan

The previous chapters have explained the context within which Assertive Outreach Teams developed and the client group they cater for. Most teams have access criteria which include repeated hospital admissions, psychotic experiences and the type of interpersonal difficulties that may get diagnosed as personality disorder. There is usually a relatively high level of risk associated with many of the clients: risk to themselves through self-harm, self-neglect or alcohol and substance misuse, sometimes risk to others. In addition, the difficulties experienced by clients can lead to involvement with the police, environmental health and the public, often taking the form of complaints, and with expectations that the health professionals involved will somehow resolve the difficulties. Worried families and friends can want to be involved with the care of the client, sometimes to a far greater degree than the client themselves desire or give permission for.

Consequently, team members can find themselves trying to manage high levels of demand from many different sides, sometimes accompanied by distress and anger. Alternatively, the clients may be so very isolated that it is difficult to maintain contact with them, and staff can spend large periods of time looking for clients about whom they have concern, without much success. However, clients may not wish to be involved with services and may make this very clear, sometimes resenting what can be experienced as an intrusive degree of interest in their lives.

So working as part of an Assertive Outreach Team can be a stressful experience, but does this matter? In this chapter we will suggest that stress is a less important variable than 'burnout', a concept which we examine in more detail below. The long-term nature of the relationship between client and team suggests that a high degree of staff retention is desirable to minimise disruptions to engagement. It is also widely agreed that the health and wellbeing of staff in the NHS is a priority (DoH, 1999; Secretary of State for Health, 1992). In this chapter we will discuss what burnout is and look at some of its causes in relation to Assertive Outreach Teams. In some ways the research findings on Assertive Outreach Teams and burnout are surprising and we will look at why this is, examining implications for both the organisation of teams and the management of individuals within them.

What are burnout and stress and how do they relate to job satisfaction?

The term 'stress' is used by most of us, sometimes on a daily basis, to describe a state of high arousal which may vary greatly in terms of the level of distress it engenders. However, the term does have more specific definitions; for example, Selye (1976) described the physiological and emotional responses to demands from the environment as General Adaptation Syndrome (GAS). These include the slowing of digestion, increased rate of breathing, a rise in blood pressure, and the release of the hormones adrenalin, noradrenalin and cortisol. These physiological changes assist the person in responding to environmental demands and, once the challenge has been overcome, the body returns to its normal state. If, however, the demands do not reduce or disappear and the body remains in a state of arousal for long periods, the implications for both physical and emotional wellbeing can be serious, leading to a state of exhaustion which is often described as 'burnout' (Payne, 1999).

There is no single accepted definition of burnout (Cooper, Dewe and O'Driscoll, 2001) and the concept remains somewhat controversial (Provencal, 1987). There is not sufficient space to consider these issues in depth here (the reader is referred to Cooper *et al.*, 2001 and Onyett, 1998); therefore we will use the definition of burnout proposed by Maslach, Jackson and Leiter in the Maslach Burnout Inventory (MBI) (1996), which is one of the most frequently used measures of burnout. Maslach conceptualises burnout as '. . . a syndrome of emotional exhaustion, depersonalisation and reduced personal accomplishment that can occur among individuals who do "people work" of some kind. It is a response to the chronic emotional strain of dealing extensively with other human beings' (Maslach, 1982: 3).

'Emotional exhaustion' is defined as the depletion of emotional resources. 'Depersonalisation' means the development of a negative and dehumanised view of recipients of services. 'Lack of personal accomplishment' is the feeling that your work objectives are not being achieved. Pines and Aronson (1981) emphasise that in order to burnout, the person must have once been 'on fire'; in other words only those who once had high levels of hope and enthusiasm will subsequently burnout.

Whilst emotional exhaustion overlaps both depression and job stress, Schaufeli (1999) argues that it can be distinguished from them both conceptually and empirically. Whilst depression pervades all areas of life, job stress is work related and includes attitudes and behaviours not typically found in depression. Burnout and job satisfaction are, perhaps obviously, linked (Cooper *et al.*, 2001). However, research remains equivocal about whether burnout causes reduced job satisfaction or vice versa. Lee and Ashforth (1996) found it was only the construct of depersonalisation that correlated with job satisfaction. Schaufeli (1999) succinctly explains the difference between job stress and burnout. He suggests that, whilst stress is a process which is temporarily adaptive in helping people to deal with demands made upon them, burnout is 'a final stage in a breakdown in adaptation' (Schaufeli, 1999: 20).

Burnout and health-care providers

Originally the Maslach Burnout Inventory was designed purely to assess burnout in public sector workers, that is people who do 'people work'. Later, Maslach, Jackson and Leiter (1996) modified the MBI to include a version for use with non-service occupations in which the concepts of depersonalisation and emotional exhaustion were altered somewhat. However, there are particular aspects of working within the caring professions that have implications for burnout.

One aspect of health-care provision is the lack of reciprocity inherent in the relationship between health-care provider and recipient. It is suggested that this is key to understanding the genesis of burnout.

> . . . the former is supposed to give care . . . whilst the latter is supposed to receive . . . Nevertheless, professionals look for some rewards in return for their efforts; for example, they expect their patients to show gratitude, to improve, or at least to make a real effort to get well.
>
> (Schaufeli, 1999: 29)

In addition, the attitude and behaviour of the wider organisation can contribute towards burnout if the organisation is perceived as displaying a lack of reciprocity.

There is some evidence to suggest that staff burnout is associated with the outcomes for the clients of Assertive Outreach Teams. As part of the Pan London Assertive Outreach Study, Priebe *et al.* (2004) looked at the characteristics of staff which were associated with favourable outcomes for clients. Amongst a range of variables, the authors looked at the relationship between staff scores on the three subscales of the MBI: emotional exhaustion, depersonalisation and personal accomplishment (Maslach *et al.*, 1996), and hospital admission rates amongst clients of the service. Results indicated that, whilst job satisfaction did not predict the hospitalisation rates of clients, staff burnout did. Priebe *et al.* (2004) found that low levels of depersonalisation and high personal accomplishment (scores reflecting low burnout) were associated with reduced hospitalisation and fewer compulsory admissions at nine months. In other words, those workers who held less negative views of their clients, and who viewed themselves more positively in relation to their work, were less likely to find their clients admitted to hospital.

For the purposes of this chapter we are considering burnout as comprising the three elements of depersonalisation, a lack of personal accomplishment and emotional exhaustion. We acknowledge the existence of alternative conceptualisations of the construct, but for the sake of brevity, and in order that we can consider research implications for the particular area of

Assertive Outreach Teams, we will retain Maslach's definition. We are not taking a position on which of these factors arises first or which is the most important.

What causes burnout?

Once again, the answer to this question is not simple. Intuitively it may seem that high levels of stress would ultimately result in burnout. However, it has been repeatedly found that the higher social classes, who are often working in highly stressful professions, have low levels of burnout (Caplan *et al.*, 1975). A complex relationship exists between the demands of the job, the resources available to meet those demands and the perceived self-efficacy of the worker (Cooper *et al.*, 2001). Working within a team can be beneficial for mental health but again this has contingencies. If the team is functioning well it can contribute greatly to reduced burnout as well as increased creativity and innovation. However, poorly functioning teams can contribute to burnout and can hinder the effectiveness of workers, sometimes to a catastrophic degree. The relationship between the worker and the wider organisation also has implications for the experience of burnout.

Therefore, we will turn to a consideration of these issues in more detail. In terms of the demands of the job, we will consider the unique nature of the clients who are referred to Assertive Outreach Teams and the way that they impact on both the workers and the society around them. The resources available to meet those demands will be considered as coming from the workers themselves as well as from the teams within which those workers are situated.

The clients

Assertive Outreach Team clients embody several characteristics that may impact on staff experience of job satisfaction and which could theoretically contribute to a state of burnout in the worker. Research suggests that reduced job satisfaction is associated with high level of contact with clients who experience severe and ongoing mental health difficulties (Oberlander, 1990). Maslach (1978) suggested that the seriousness of the client's illness and a degree of either passive dependency or aggressive hostility has a large impact on staff burnout. Threats of suicide and/or violence are experienced as particularly stressful by staff and this is more pronounced amongst staff working in the community (Prosser, Johnson, Kuipers, Szmukler, Bebbington and Thornicroft, 1996). Some suggest that working with psychotic clients is a particularly difficult experience (see chapter six), for example:

> ... that distress is not formed or articulated in words; meaning itself gives way to an experience of meaninglessness. And this is contagious ... psychotic patients rid themselves of the experience by making the staff

feel it instead ... We must accept certain things about working with psychotic people: that they do affect their helpers.

(Hinshelwood, 1998: 19)

In addition, people who are referred to Assertive Outreach Teams tend to be those who have experienced difficulties relating to traditional services and have often been perceived as being difficult to relate to. Many of our clients have diagnoses of personality disorders alongside their primary diagnosis of a psychotic disorder; others may not have been given such a diagnosis but experience ongoing interpersonal difficulties. When we first encounter them they are often detained in hospital and feeling angry with services for this imposition, as well as anxious, suspicious and often frightened. They may have histories that include high levels of abuse since childhood, making it very difficult to trust anyone. Their experience of enforced detainment, often with police involvement, has felt like a further abuse. Little wonder then that these individuals are disinclined to 'engage' in an enthusiastic manner with people who are employed by those same agencies.

These clients, like the rest of us, will have learnt patterns of relating to others throughout their lives, ways of making relationships, but also ways to keep themselves safe within those relationships. For some, the repeated experiences of harm mean that they have given up attempting to relate to anyone. Clients seen by Assertive Outreach Teams are often those with the most complex mental health problems and frequently report difficulties both in early attachment relationships (Dozier *et al.*, 1999) and insecure attachment styles in adult relationships (Berry, Barrowclough and Wearden, 2007; see also chapter two).

It is important to remember that mental health work is about a relationship between at least two people. Whilst the clients are reluctantly positioned as needing help in some way and are expected to benefit from the relationship, we would argue that the worker also brings with them a range of motivations and expectations that interact with those of the client in both helpful and unhelpful ways. The past history of the workers and their own patterns of relating and personal characteristics will contribute to their experience of the work and the likelihood of their burning out.

Worker characteristics

Existentialist perspectives suggest that the origins of burnout can be found in the human imperative to seek meaning in life, and the wish to believe that the things we do as individuals are useful and of value (Becker, 1973; Frankl, 1976). People who enter their professions with such hopes are more likely to expect to derive significance from their work and may make considerable investment in their work (Cherniss, 1995). If experiences at work lead to a sense of failure, then people may feel that their work is meaningless and that they are not making a difference in the way they hoped. Pines (2004) suggests it is at this point there is a risk that people could begin to feel hopeless and helpless and potentially burnout.

If one accepts that people seek to derive a sense of significance from their work, then it is useful to consider the factors which motivate individuals to work in mental health. Hinshelwood (1998) suggests that an awareness of such factors could make a valuable contribution to approaches designed to enhance the mental health of professionals. Psychoanalytic theory has made a significant contribution in explicating the role of the unconscious in the career choices of individuals (Kets de Vries, 1991; Obholzer and Roberts, 1997). Malan (1979) refers to the 'helping profession syndrome', which is viewed as a derivative of Bowlby's (1973) 'compulsive care-giving'. This refers to a situation where the individual 'compulsively gives to others what he would like to have for himself, which . . . leads to a severe deficit in the emotional balance of payments' (Malan, 1979: 161). He suggests that the needs of other people are experienced as demands which they attempt to meet. If they are unsuccessful in their attempts, individuals may be prone to feelings of resentment and subsequently depression. Wilkinson (2003) suggests that, whilst individuals employing such an approach make enormous efforts for their clients, they may be more vulnerable to burnout.

Unconscious determinants of career choice are thought to reflect an individual's personal history. Pines and Yanai (2000) suggest that people choose occupations which allow them to meet needs that were not met during childhood, to realise the dreams and expectations passed on to them as part of family narratives and to recreate significant childhood experiences. Pines (2004) suggests that when the choice of a career involves such significant issues, people enter it with high expectations. The highest expectations or greatest involvement typically relate to areas where there are unresolved childhood issues.

Tillett (2003) suggests that choosing a career in the helping professions may be an attempt to resolve early difficult experiences by taking the opportunity to offer the care and attention to others that was not received during one's own childhood. Fussell and Bonney (1990) argue that, whilst such early experiences may motivate therapists to work in the area, they also have the potential to limit the development of a good therapeutic relationship, either by encouraging avoidance of the client's psychic pain or by excessive care taking and over-identification with the client. The hope may be for resolution of an issue, and success in helping to heal childhood wounds. However, if the work experience repeats, rather than repairs, the childhood trauma, then the individual may be confronted with feelings of failure and the result may lead to burnout (Pines, 2004). Hinshelwood (1998: 2) suggests that such motivations can be particularly problematic when working with people with severe and enduring problems as there will 'always be some degree of failure: there are always clients we cannot help enough'. This may be particularly relevant to assertive outreach work.

Given the emphasis on engagement and relationship building in assertive outreach, we need to consider the factors which might mediate this process and potentially act either as risk or protective factors for the worker. The literature relating to how attachments are formed and maintained seems particularly pertinent to this. Bowlby's (1969, 1973, 1980) developmental theory of attachment proposes that individuals develop internal working models of self–other relationships on the basis of early experiences with primary caregivers. Internal working models are thought to play an important role in the way individuals experience and make sense of their relational world and are presumed to have a continued effect on interpersonal relationships throughout the life span (Svanberg, 1998). Whilst internal working models begin to develop during early childhood, Bowlby acknowledged that they are not static but continue to develop throughout life.

Mackie (1981) suggests that, to provide a secure base for the client, the therapist must be perceived to be genuine, concerned and in touch with the patient's feelings, qualities generally noted to be conditions for good outcomes in therapy. The influence of the worker's attachment style will be relevant if Assertive Outreach Teams are expected both to provide effective therapeutic relationships and offer opportunities to potentially modify and resolve their clients' long-term distress and insecurity. Part of the task is to help clients modify their strategies for approaching interpersonal relationships and regulating emotions, thus promoting more adaptive functioning (Tyrell, Dozier, Teague and Fallot, 1999).

A growing body of research has examined the influence of client and workers' attachment styles on both the process and outcome of treatment. This literature seems highly relevant to assertive outreach given that the primary task of teams is to engage with individuals who frequently have longstanding interpersonal difficulties.

Tyrell *et al.* (1999) examined the fit between the attachment style of worker and client and the impact that this had on therapeutic outcome. These authors found that service users who tended to minimise emotional distress and distance themselves from relationships reported better alliances and functioned better when working with case managers who tended to focus on emotional distress and were highly involved in their relationships. The converse was also true for clients who were more preoccupied with relationships; this group formed better alliances with case managers who tended to minimise their own emotional distress. Overall results indicated that clients and therapists who were dissimilar in their attachment strategies reported stronger therapeutic alliances and generally higher levels of functioning than those who were complementary. The authors suggest this can be attributed to a non-complementary process which allows clinicians to more effectively challenge the habitual interpersonal strategies of their clients.

It is noteworthy, however, that this pattern did not hold for clinicians whose attachment styles fell within the insecure category. The authors suggest that secure clinicians are more likely to be able to manage the potential discomforts associated with responding in a non-complementary manner. This allowed them to respond in a flexible way to the needs of the client, something that clinicians whose attachment strategies fall within an insecure category were not able to do. Acknowledgement of the differences between workers in their ability to engage with clients in Assertive Outreach Teams might usefully consider where each individual's strengths and limitations lie in relation to these factors. Clearly it is neither feasible nor ethical to screen people for their attachment style prior to working in Assertive Outreach Teams. However, in view of the literature described above, it seems important to recognise the areas that people struggle with in terms of engaging and maintaining relationships with clients. Offering regular support via team discussions, supervision and external consultation is important, both as a space for reflection, but also to minimise the potential risk of workers experiencing reduced personal accomplishment in relation to their work, and possibly burnout.

In addition to the influence on relationships, attachment styles are believed to affect psychological wellbeing by acting as mediator between stressful events and mental health (Pielage, Gerlsma and Schaap, 2000). A number of studies indicate that attachment styles influence the way in which people respond to and manage stress and burnout (Mikulincer and Florian, 1995, 1998; Pines, 2004). Individuals with a secure attachment style in childhood are more likely to positively appraise stressful situations and cope adaptively with these in adulthood. Conversely, insecure attachment during childhood has been related to poor coping and increased risk of burnout (Pines, 2004). Mikulincer and Florian (1998) found that people's attachment styles influenced the effectiveness with which they used social support in times of stress. These findings are of interest when considering the potential impact of working long term in assertive outreach.

Alongside the risk factors for stress and burnout, it is important to consider the factors which influence help-seeking behaviour and the forms of support which are valued. In a review of the literature relating to stress and stress management amongst UK clinical psychologists, Hannigan, Edwards and Burnard (2004) reported that many find work demanding and stressful. Up to 40 per cent of clinical psychologists were found to be experiencing 'caseness' levels of psychological distress. Cushway and Tyler (1994) reported that the most commonly cited coping strategies involved cognitive and behavioural strategies, for example talking to colleagues and exercising. Clinical psychologists cited the opportunity to participate in a professional network as a valued source of support and a means of enhancing self-awareness and workload management (Cormack, Nichols and Walsh, 1991). Maintaining links with others working in assertive outreach, for example by means of the Network of Psychologists in Assertive Outreach and the National Forum for Assertive Outreach, might usefully provide opportunities for support and to sound out ideas.

Hannigan *et al.* (2004) acknowledge the additive effects of organisational and client-specific stressors. However, they also highlight the role of therapist beliefs in determining help-seeking behaviour. They suggest that some beliefs held by clinical psychologists may not be conducive to help-seeking and presumably contribute to an increased risk of stress and burnout. Walsh and Cormack (1994) note that perceptions of the idea of support as 'psychologically threatening' appeared to militate against people seeking support. This sense of threat seemed to relate to anxieties about how they, as individuals, might be perceived either by their profession or within the organisation, alongside concerns about being viewed as a client. Psychologists in the study minimised this anxiety by employing 'gate keeping' strategies, assessing the personal qualities of potential support givers and evaluating their perceived skill level.

In summary, a range of individual factors seem relevant to the experience of working within Assertive Outreach Teams. The motivations and hopes that lead people to work in specific settings are likely to have a significant impact on their experience of that work. An ongoing consideration of the influence of these factors, and the use of the full range of opportunities for managing the inevitable stressors associated with the work, might reasonably be expected to reduce the likelihood of burnout. Regular supervision plays an essential role in allowing people to reflect upon, process and manage those issues which might increase the risk of burnout.

Defences and alliance

When clinicians find themselves overwhelmed by the emotions provoked by their clients, the natural response is to invoke emotional defences which allow the clinician to distance themselves from the client and the uncomfortable feelings they provoke. Main (1957) spoke about the way that both clients and staff can collude by ensuring that all the health was projected onto the workers while all the ill health was projected into the client. Menzies (1959) studied hospital staff and found that they used numerous psychological defences to distance themselves from the patients. Main (1957) also drew attention to the risk met with by those clients who do not get better and fail to provide the worker with the satisfaction provided by 'curing' a patient.

Hinshelwood comments that this emotional distancing, which leads staff to treat people 'as if they are not properly alive' (Hinshelwood, 1998: 20), is likely to result in a worsening of symptoms amongst clients, in order for them to register their distress. This corresponds to the burnout literature which suggests that high levels of depersonalisation result in higher levels of re-admissions to hospital (Priebe *et al.*, 2004). In addition, studies suggest that a positive therapeutic alliance has an effect on outcome regardless of the type of therapy administered, including drug therapy (Krupnick, Stotsky, Simmens and Moyer, 1992). The *National Service Framework for Mental Health* (1999) cites Roth and Fonagy (1996), Horvath and Symonds (1991) and Safran and Muran (1996) as providing evidence that, 'The quality of the relationship between patient and professional in psychological therapies can make as much as 25 per cent difference in outcome' (DoH, 1999: 43).

One of the key components for developing this relationship is a positive, empathic understanding of the client, joined with client-centred flexibility, realism and taking a long-term perspective (Perkins and Repper, 1996). However, development of a strong alliance is hindered in people who experience difficulties in social relationships generally or who have a history of poor family relationships (Horvath, 1991). In addition, Maslach describes empathy as a weakness, leaving workers' feelings open and vulnerable (Maslach, 1982).

In the same vein, Pines and Aronson (1981) recommend 'detached concern'. Golembiewski, Munzenrider and Stevenson (1986) emphasise that a level of professional detachment is both functional and ethical, but that this is different from depersonalisation. However, our experience is that this type of 'detachment' is one of the aspects of traditional psychiatric care that Assertive Outreach Team clients have often rejected. In addition, much of the assertive outreach literature actively encourages staff to personalise the relationship and give more of themselves to encounters with their clients (Sainsbury Centre for Mental Health, 1998).

In the previous sections we have considered those characteristics of the worker and the client which may affect the level of depersonalisation, emotional exhaustion and personal accomplishment experienced by the worker. We have suggested that these, in turn, influence the degree to which defences are established to protect the worker from unpleasant feelings and how this can negatively impact on the therapeutic alliance which might, in turn, result in poorer outcomes for the client.

We turn now to those characteristics of the working environment which can influence the psychological health of workers and mediate between a healthy level of stress and the prolonged levels likely to result in burnout. First, we will consider the immediate setting within which the worker is located, most commonly the multi-disciplinary team. This is followed by consideration of the larger organisation, the wider community and the influence of the government on all of these.

Effective team working

Working within teams is a common part of health-care provision. When the team functions well this has the capacity to impact positively on the wellbeing of both staff and patients (Carter and West, 1999). Assertive Outreach Teams are most commonly composed of multi-disciplinary groups of workers, although some areas are using 'bolt on' workers who work from within Community Mental Health Teams (CMHTs). Billings *et al.* (2003) found that, when compared with CMHT staff, assertive outreach workers tended to be more satisfied with their work and reported lower levels of certain aspects of burnout. Whilst these differences were not large, they run contrary to the literature suggesting that work involving clients with more severe clinical and social difficulties is associated with higher burnout (Farber and Heifetz, 1982;

Hare and Pratt, 1988). It is noteworthy that within the Billings *et al.* study the organisation of the team was strongly associated with the degree of emotional burnout experienced by staff. The mean emotional exhaustion score for the majority of teams fell in the average range, but those working in teams with larger caseloads, no available dedicated psychiatrist, and no dedicated inpatient beds, had mean scores falling in the high range.

What are teams?

Onyett (2007) reports that the Healthcare Commission's (2006) *NHS National Staff Survey* showed that 89 per cent of staff responded positively when asked: 'Do you work in a team?' However, only 41 per cent fulfilled the criteria for a clearly defined team. The definition of a team is a group of workers who have shared objectives; who work closely together, but with clearly differentiated roles, to achieve their aims; who have fewer than eight members where there is complex decision making involved; who have a team identity and are recognised by others as a team; and who have opportunities to review performance (West, 2004).

Team working and mental health

The importance of team working in assertive outreach has already been discussed (see chapter two). It seems that the Whole Team Approach has been demonstrated to be helpful to clients in facilitating an effective working relationship with the team, but how helpful is it to staff?

Working within a team has been shown to contribute to improved mental health for team members (Sonnentag, 1996), enhanced performance (Kallerberg and Moody, 1994) and more efficient use of staff (Ovretveit, 1988). However, there are also potential pitfalls; Yan *et al.* (2006) examined the differential effects of well-structured inter-professional team working, versus pseudo-team working and working alone. They found that those working in effective teams were less stressed and more satisfied. Worryingly, they found that:

> those working in inter-professional situations which they define as team working, but which are not well structured via regular meetings, clear objectives and well-defined roles, are likely to report higher levels of errors, stress and lower levels of innovation and satisfaction than those who do not report working in inter-professional teams. In effect, the illusion of inter-professional team working may be placing patients and staff at risk.
>
> (Onyett, 2007: 8)

One of the most interesting elements of effective team working in relation to Assertive Outreach Teams is that of role clarity. Handy (1993) described how role ambiguity contributes to role stress. The importance of role clarity was stressed by Morgan *et al.* (1999) as a means of reducing staff burnout in Assertive Outreach Teams. Consequently, one of the challenges to Assertive Outreach Teams is to find ways to implement the Whole Team Approach, whilst also retaining role clarity. Gray and Lavender (2001) suggested that one way assertive outreach workers maximise their role clarity was in the matching of clients to workers. In this case, although the practical tasks undertaken by different workers may remain similar, the personal roles of each team member may have contributed to a sense of role clarity. It also seemed that some professional role clarity remained, with different professions supporting the daily living of clients in different ways, as informed by their professional training.

A related issue is that of professional identification versus team identification. According to social identity theory (Tajfel and Turner, 1979) too great an identification with one group endangers relations with the other group. The best outcome is achieved when individual practitioners are able to identify with both their own profession and the team. One way this can be enhanced is by clearly identifying the individual goals of each worker, as distinct from the goals of other team members. Another way is through the creation of mutually agreed superordinate goals, but only when every individual's role in achieving these is clear and differentiated from those of other team members (Onyett, 2007).

The issue of autonomy in work also seems important (for a thorough review see Cooper *et al.*, 2001) although the research is somewhat contradictory, with some studies finding a negative correlation between autonomy and burnout (Landsbergis, 1988) while others failed to replicate this (Lee and Ashforth, 1993). Karasek (1979) formulated the Job Demands–Control Model, in which he suggested that posts that contained high job demands, but allowed the individual to exercise high levels of control over important aspects of their work, could be described as 'active' jobs; and these can be beneficial for the worker. Schaubroeck and Merritt (1997) found that high levels of perceived control were only beneficial if workers had high levels of self-efficacy; if not, the combination had negative health consequences.

Does the theory reviewed above provide us with insights into why Community Mental Health Teams tend to score worse than Assertive Outreach Teams in terms of burnout (Billings *et al.*, 2003)? Considering West's (2004) criteria we would hope that all CMHTs have shared objectives and a team identity. However, our experience of CMHT working is that people work less closely together and, perhaps surprisingly, may have less clearly differentiated roles. This seems to have been the case where there has been pressure within the team for everyone to do equal amounts of 'generic' tasks, such as care co-ordinating and covering 'duty'. Also, CMHTs commonly have far more than eight members. Opportunities to review performance will also differ between teams.

Another issue differentiating Assertive Outreach Teams from Community

Mental Health Teams is the relationship between the demands of the job and the resources available to meet those demands. When Gray and Lavender (2001) interviewed assertive outreach workers, they found that staff perceived adequate resources as being essential to the good functioning of the team. Five main categories were identified, namely: time, adequate staffing, skill mix, a sense of position within the wider organisation and the degree of similarity and difference amongst team members. Whilst clinicians in both settings would enjoy similar levels of autonomy, assertive outreach practitioners have protected caseloads of between about 10 and 12 clients. Although these clients often have high levels of need, the team approach means that there are always other team members available to help meet the needs of clients, even if the worker who knows them best is absent. Staff can take leave safe in the knowledge that their absence is covered by their colleagues. So whilst the demands can be high in assertive outreach, the resources tend to be adequate to meet those demands, in contrast to CMHTs, where the demands can also be very high, but where clinicians often feel they are alone in attempting to manage this need. Consequently the demand outweighs the resources available to meet it.

To summarise, Assertive Outreach Teams can help to enhance the mental health of workers by maximising the effectiveness of their team working. To do this they should ensure mutually agreed-upon objectives, with members working closely to achieve these, whilst retaining their individual professional identities and clearly defined roles. Workers should have autonomy to make decisions regarding the organisation of their daily work, combined with a high degree of mastery. They should work in groups of no more than eight members. Where the work group is much larger it may be necessary to break into smaller teams to address those aspects of the work that involve complex decision making. The team should be easily recognisable to others as a team and should be provided with the time and opportunity to reflect on their work and concentrate on ways to improve.

The wider organisation

The structure of the wider organisation is also likely to have an influence on the experience of those working within assertive outreach. Cherniss (1980) extends the notion of burnout to include organisational, personal and cultural factors. He suggests these factors affect the experience of those working in an organisation alongside the experience of client contact. In particular he draws attention to organisational design, suggesting that the way a service is structured in terms of roles and duties, patterns of decision making and authority, as well as the service goals and treatment philosophy, all influence the way individual team members experience a team. He suggests that such factors influence the likelihood that individuals will experience role ambiguity, conflict and potential burnout. In particular lack of social support and feedback was found to be associated with burnout.

Staff perceptions of the organisation they work in have also been linked to burnout. Ellis and Miller (1993) found that perceptions of personal control and a sense of participation in decision making influenced burnout amongst nurses. Manlove (1993) found that burnout was inversely related to a positive perception of the work setting. Leiter (1991, 1992) suggests that client demands are secondary in determining burnout, and proposes that burnout results from the gap between individuals' expectations of their professional roles and the structure of the organisation. This is consistent with the results from a report examining the health of the NHS workforce, which concluded that the main burden of ill health in the NHS is due to psychological illness (Williams, Michie and Pattani, 1998). The main cause of this appeared to be related to poor workplace organisation and employment practices. It seems that, although organisations may agree in principle with the professional goals of their staff, policies may not be supportive of these. Consistent with Cherniss (1980), Leiter (1992) suggests that organisational policies which enhance competence and facilitate the utilisation of employees' skills, while developing their competence, have an important role to play in reducing the likelihood of burnout.

A further influence which seems relevant to the risk of burnout is the perception of the team within the wider system. In the authors' experience, the stigma which is experienced by clients of Assertive Outreach Teams is sometimes felt in a modified form by the team, who are held responsible for the behaviour of the clients. This process appears to take place particularly in relation to hospital admissions. Alongside clients reporting aversive experiences with ward staff, assertive outreach workers may be perceived negatively for bringing 'troublesome and difficult' clients onto the ward. There is potentially a parallel process in operation whereby teams become stigmatised within their organisations in much the same way as clients are stigmatised within society.

Consideration of the wider political and economic context is important when thinking about the factors which affect the experience of those working in assertive outreach. Given the almost continuous reorganisation of services within the NHS, significant changes frequently take place in the form of restructuring and downsizing, in order to maintain the viability of services. Organisational support for professional goals may be viewed as less important under such circumstances. Leiter, Harvie and Frizzell (1998) suggest that, whilst this process may seem to make economic sense for the organisation, the cost in terms of increased disillusionment, exhaustion and cynicism, combined with a corresponding decrease in productivity, may have long-term adverse consequences. In a constantly changing environment there is a risk that Assertive Outreach Teams may feel overwhelmed by the shifting demands placed upon teams, with potentially serious consequences for staff morale.

The wider community

We have seen how a number of aspects relating to the client, the worker, the team and the organisation can contribute to, or protect against, burnout. However, all these factors also exist within the context of the community in which we all live and into which our clients are expected to fit.

Prior to Care in the Community, psychiatric patients were removed promptly from the community as soon as they started to display unusual or disruptive behaviour. Ideally, Assertive Outreach Teams, alongside crisis and home treatment teams, form part of an integrated service designed to support people to remain in the community and out of hospital, thereby trying to avoid the risk of institutionalisation. Consequently, the community is now having to witness and experience close-up the effects of mental disturbance. The community is often not happy with this and our experience is that neighbourhoods, along with the police and Accident and Emergency departments, are struggling, in varying degrees, to find ways to respond.

> We might take the view that the community (society) had a vested interest in 'warehousing' those people who were identified as being mad, bad or useless, if only in order that the rest of us who remained at large could safely project all our mad, bad and useless bits into them, disowning them in ourselves.
>
> (Foster and Zagier Roberts, 1998: 6)

Foster and Zagier Roberts (1998) describe some of the arguments about care in the community and the different beliefs that people have about its purpose: that it is simply a way of saving money, a way of addressing the problems of institutionalisation, of providing more humane treatment, of recognising that it is care and not treatment that is needed, 'or is it a belief that through becoming reintegrated into their communities, those who suffer from mental illness will become more integrated within themselves and so become less disturbed?' (ibid.). However, they also recognise the impossibility of any of this happening should the community be unwelcoming or openly hostile to the client.

Assertive outreach workers have to operate in a situation where the community is often expecting a certain type of response from services when someone appears to be becoming less well; namely for that person to be taken away to hospital. Workers can be on the receiving end of a great deal of expressed concern, and sometimes anger, should that person remain in their home, whilst possibly behaving in a disturbed and disturbing manner. Teams have to balance concerns about risk, either to the client or to others, with therapeutic risk taking. Rules of confidentiality further complicate this situation, as teams are generally unable to explain anything about the individual involved without their express consent.

We have clients who, at times, behave in a way that can be anti-social, including minor infringements of the law. If the police become involved they often seem to be at a loss as to how to manage the situation, given that the person has a diagnosed psychiatric condition. Once again, Assertive Outreach Teams can be expected to remove someone to hospital or to otherwise 'control' the behaviour of the client. The reality is that there are times when we have to make the decision to encourage the police to respond to the situation as they would with anyone else, supporting both police and clients through the process. This can be stressful, with assertive outreach workers receiving angry responses from the client, the police, the client's family and the wider neighbourhood.

It can be very difficult, when put under such pressure, to continue to respond thoughtfully, whilst remaining mindful of all those involved and how best to manage the situation (see Table 5.1).

Avoiding burnout

To conclude, we have shown that, whilst assertive outreach work can be stressful at times, with pressures and demands coming from all sides, research suggests that at present assertive outreach staff are not suffering from high levels of burnout (e.g. Meddings, Perkins, Wharne, Ley, Collins and Wilson, 2007). This would imply that the resources available to most Assertive Outreach Teams are sufficient to allow staff to meet the challenges presented by their work and to feel that they can achieve their goals, thus ensuring a high level of personal accomplishment. However, these conclusions should be viewed with some caution, in view of the relatively small number of studies examining burnout and assertive outreach. Another note of caution relates to the length of time that teams have been established and whether this has any bearing on the levels of burnout observed. It is possible that teams are still burning brightly in terms of enthusiasm for the work as a function of their relative youth. It will be interesting to revisit this area in several years' time to see whether the findings still hold true.

The emphasis on the team approach means that Assertive Outreach Teams are likely to achieve many of those factors described by Onyett (2007) as vital for successful team working, such as close communication, a shared objective and a clear team identity. Care should be taken that the level of generic working should not become so high that role blurring becomes problematic. Our experience of working in Assertive Outreach Teams suggests that they can become very busy at times, and managers should remain mindful of the importance of facilitating opportunities to review performance and to consider the caseload weighting of team members.

If the team is working well together, relationships amongst team members can be vital in containing the emotional impact of the work. Gray and Lavender (2001) found three aspects that staff suggested were vital to a sense of containment. These were:

Table 5.1 Overview of potential factors contributing to burnout

Client characteristics	Worker characteristics	Team	Organisational	Community
History of poor attachments	Attachment style (secure vs. insecure)	Lack of role clarity, pull towards generic working	Lack of clarity regarding decision making, authority, service goals and treatment philosophy	Stigmatising response to mental health difficulties
Severe and ongoing mental health problems	Unfulfilled work expectations and perceived failure to make a difference	Inability to tolerate difference amongst team members	Staff experience of the organisation	Fear and anxiety of AO clients
Longstanding interpersonal difficulties	Disappointed care giving needs	Poorly defined objectives	Team stigmatised within the organisation	
Reluctance to engage in relationship with services	Help-seeking behaviour and beliefs	Unstructured and/or irregular meetings		
	Defensive response to offers of support	Lack of compatibility between worker and team goals		
	Ability to tolerate and engage with psychic pain of clients	Reluctance to allow autonomous functioning of workers		

1   Structural arrangements – having the same base, good management and supervision.
2   Practical team processes – documentation, team meetings, the team approach and debriefing.
3   Informal processes – argument, advice and discussion; support from colleagues; a non-judgemental environment; equality and external support.

Many teams use externally facilitated staff support groups to provide a setting in which staff can safely examine their thoughts and feelings in relation to the work (Carson, Fagin and Ritter, 1995; see also chapter six). Some would suggest that the potential of these groups can be realised only if all team members are involved. Where members are absent, there is a risk that the group serves to increase the possibility of division, scapegoating and projection within the team. Team members within the authors' services have highlighted the value of someone from outside supporting the team to notice and think about things which can be difficult to see when you are in the thick of it. This process can be extremely helpful for the team, providing a means to reflect upon and find a way through the complexities of the work.

Another vital aspect of staff support is that of supervision, both managerial and clinical. Supervision structures vary considerably across teams and will inevitably influence the experience of those working within assertive outreach. A number of studies have found that support from supervisors protects nurses from burnout (Bakker *et al.*, 2000; Leiter and Lashinger, 2006). In relation to nursing staff, the literature suggests that low levels of burnout are found in work environments where staff experience good support and feedback (Melchior *et al.*, 1997). The authors further found that staff reported lower levels of burnout where managers had a leadership style which acknowledged the experiential aspects of the work, such as job satisfaction and wellbeing. Research about stress amongst clinical psychology trainees found that supervision ranked amongst both the top five stressors and the top five coping strategies (Cushway, 1992). This finding was endorsed by the assertive outreach staff respondents to Gray and Lavender (2001), who found managerial supervision either helpful or not, depending on their relationship with the manager. Research suggests that there is a positive relationship between perceived lack of support from supervisors and burnout. Lee and Ashforth (1996) found that support from supervisors explained 14 per cent of the variance of emotional exhaustion, 6 per cent of depersonalisation and 2 per cent of accomplishment (Schaufeli, 1999).

In conclusion, the clients of Assertive Outreach Teams seem to fit the profile of those clients most likely to leave the worker in a state of emotional exhaustion and with a feeling of low accomplishment, owing to the severe and long-term nature of their difficulties. However, in practice, they are often bright, courageous, entertaining and thought-provoking people, whose company we enjoy sharing. The level of challenge they present can often force us to examine our own beliefs and feelings in a way that can prove both positive and rewarding.

References

Bakker, A.B., Killmer, C.H., Siegrist, J. and Schautelli, W.B. (2000) 'Effort–reward imbalance and burnout among nurses', *Journal of Advanced Nursing*, 31: 884–891.

Becker, E. (1973) *The Denial of Death*, New York: Free Press.

Berry, K., Barrowclough, C. and Wearden, A. (2007) 'A review of adult attachment style in psychosis: unexplored issues and questions for further research', *Clinical Psychology Review*, 27: 458–475.

Billings, J., Johnson, S., Bebbington, P., Greaves, A., Priebe, S., Muijen, M., Ryrie, I., Watts, J., White, I. and Wright, C. (2003) 'Assertive outreach teams in London: staff experiences and perceptions', *British Journal of Psychiatry*, 183: 139–147.

Bowlby, J. (1969) *Attachment and Loss, Vol. 1 Attachment*, New York: Basic Books.

Bowlby, J. (1973) *Attachment and Loss, Vol. 2 Separation, Anxiety and Anger*, New York: Basic Books.

Bowlby, J. (1980) *Attachment and Loss, Vol. 3 Loss, Sadness and Depression*, New York: Basic Books.

Caplan, R.D., Cobb, S., French, J.R., Harrison, R.V. and Pinneau, S.R. (1975) *Job Demands and Worker Health*, Washington: National Institute for Occupational Safety and Health.

Carson, J., Fagin, L. and Ritter, S. (eds) (1995) *Stress and Coping in Mental Health Nursing*, London: Chapman and Hall.

Carter, A.J. and West, M.A. (1999) 'Sharing the burden – teamwork in health care settings', in R. Payne and J. Firth-Cozens (eds) *Stress in Health Professionals: psychological and organizational causes and interventions*, Chichester: Wiley.

Cherniss, C. (1980) *Staff Burnout*, Beverley Hills, CA: Sage Publications.

Cherniss, C. (1995) *Beyond Burnout*, New York: Routledge.

Cooper, C.L., Dewe, P. and O'Driscoll, M. (2001) *Organizational Stress: a review and critique of theory, research, and applications*, London: Sage Publications.

Cormack, M., Nichols, K. and Walsh, S. (1991) 'Creating a system for professional development and personal support', *Clinical Psychology Forum*: 37, 8–10.

Cushway, D. (1992) 'Stress in trainee clinical psychologists', *British Journal of Clinical Psychology*, 31: 169–179.

Cushway, D. and Tyler, P.A. (1994) 'Stress and coping in clinical psychologists', *Stress Medicine*, 10: 35–42.

Department of Health (1999) *National Service Framework for Mental Health*, London: Department of Health.

Dozier, M., Tyrell, C., Teague, G. and Fallot, R. (1999) 'Effective treatment relationships for persons with serious psychiatric disorders: the importance of attachment states of mind', *Journal of Consulting and Clinical Psychology*, 67: 725–733.

Ellis, B.H. and Miller, K.I. (1993) 'The role of assertiveness, personal control and participation in the prediction of nurse burnout', *Journal of Applied Communication Research*, 21: 327–342.

Farber, B. and Heifetz, L. (1982) 'The process and dimensions of burnout in psychotherapists', *Professional Psychology*, 13: 293–301.

Foster, A. and Zagier Roberts, V. (eds) (1998) *Managing Mental Health in the Community: chaos and containment*, London: Routledge.

Frankl, V.E. (1976) *Man's Search for Meaning*, New York: Pocket Book.

Fussell, F.W. and Bonney, W.C. (1990) 'A comparative study of childhood experiences of psychotherapists and physicists: implications for clinical practice', *Psychotherapy*, 27: 505–512.

Golembiewski, R., Munzenrider, R. and Stevenson, J. (1986) *Stress in Organizations: toward a phase model of burnout*, New York: Praeger.

Gray, A.S. and Lavender, A. (2001) 'Relationships with clients who find it difficult to engage', unpublished paper.

Handy, C. (1993) *Understanding Organizations*, London: Penguin.

Hannigan, B., Edwards, D. and Burnard, P. (2004) 'Stress and stress management in clinical psychology: findings from a systematic review', *Journal of Mental Health*, 13: 235–245.

Hare, J. and Pratt, C. (1988) 'Predictors of burnout in professional and paraprofessional nurses working in hospitals and nursing homes', *International Journal of Nursing Studies*, 25: 105–115.

Healthcare Commission (2006) *National Survey of NHS Staff*, available online at: www.healthcarecommission.org.uk

Hinshelwood, R.D. (1998) 'Creatures of each other', in A. Foster and V. Zagier Roberts (eds) *Managing Mental Health in the Community: chaos and containment*, London: Routledge.

Horvath, A.O. (1991) 'What do we know about the alliance and what do we still have to find out?', paper presented at the annual meeting of the Society for Psychotherapy Research, Lyon, France, cited in A. Horvath and L.Greenburg (eds) (1994) *The Working Alliance: theory, research and Practice*, New York: Wiley.

Horvath, A.O. and Symonds, B.D. (1991) 'Relation between working alliance and outcome in psychotherapy: a meta-analysis', *Journal of Consulting and Clinical Psychology*, 38: 139–149.

Kallerberg, A.L. and Moody, J.W. (1994) 'Human resource management and organisational performance', *American Behavioral Science*, 37: 948–962.

Karasek, R. (1979) 'Job demands, job decision latitude and mental strain: implications for job redesign', *Administrative Science Quarterly*, 24: 285–306.

Kets de Vries, M.F.R. (1991) *Organizations on the Couch*, San Francisco, CA: Jossey Bass.

Krupnick, J., Stotsky, S., Simmens, S. and Moyer, J. (1992) 'The role of therapeutic alliance in psychotherapy and pharmacotherapy outcome', paper presented at the annual meeting of the Society for Psychotherapy Research, Berkeley, CA, cited in A. Horvath and L.Greenburg (eds) (1994) *The Working Alliance: theory, research and Practice*, New York: Wiley.

Landsbergis, P. (1988) 'Occupational stress among health care workers: a test of the job demands–control model', *Journal of Organizational Behavior*, 9: 217–239.

Lee, R.T. and Ashforth, B.E (1993) 'A longitudinal study of burnout among supervisors and managers: comparisons between the Leiter and Maslach (1988) and Golembiewski *et al.* (1986) models', *Organizational Behavior and Human Decision Processes*, 54: 369–398.

Lee, R.T. and Ashforth, B.E. (1996) 'A meta-analytic examination of the correlates of the three dimensions of job burnout', *Journal of Applied Psychology*, 81: 123–133.

Leiter, M. (1991) 'The dream denied: professional burnout and the constraints of the human service organizations', *Canadian Psychology*, 32: 547–558.

Leiter, M.P. (1992) 'Burnout as a crisis in professional role structures: measurement and conceptual issues', *Anxiety, Stress and Coping*, 5: 79–93.

Leiter, M.P., Harvie, P. and Frizzell, C. (1998) 'The correspondence of patient satisfaction and nurse burnout', *Social Science and Medicine*, 47: 1611–1617.

Leiter, M.P and Lashinger, H.K. (2006) 'Relationships of work and practice environment to professional burnout: testing a causal model', *Nursing Research*, 55: 137–146.

Mackie, A.J. (1981) 'Attachment theory: its relevance to the therapeutic alliance', *British Journal of Psychology*, 54: 203–212.

Main, T.F. (1957) 'The ailment', *British Journal of Medical Psychology*, 30: 129–145.

Malan, D.H. (1979) *Individual Psychotherapy and the Science of Psychodynamics*, Oxford: Butterworth-Heinemann.

Manlove, E.E. (1993) 'Multiple correlates of burnout in child care workers', *Early Childhood Research Quarterly*, 8: 499–518.

Maslach, C. (1978) 'The client role in staff burnout', *Journal of Social Issues*, 34: 111–124.

Maslach, C. (1982) *Burnout: the cost of caring*, New Jersey: Prentice Hall.

Maslach, C., Jackson, S. and Leiter, M. (eds) (1996) *The Maslach Burnout Inventory Manual*, 3rd edn, Palo Alto, CA: Consulting Psychologists Press.

Meddings, S., Perkins, A., Wharne, S., Ley, P., Collins, T. and Wilson, Y. (2007) 'Being assertive effectively', *Mental Health Today*, May: 34–37.

Melchior M.E., den Berg A.A., Halfens R., Huyer Abu-Saad, H., Philipsen H. and Gassman P. (1997) 'Burnout and the work environment of nurses in psychiatric long-stay care settings', *Social Psychiatry and Psychiatric Epidemiology*, 32: 158–164.

Menzies, I.E.P. (1959) 'The functioning of social systems as a defence against anxiety', *Human Relations*, 13: 95–221.

Mikulincer, M. and Florian, V. (1995) 'Appraisal and coping with real life stressful situations: the contribution of attachment styles', *Personality and Social Psychology Bulletin*, 21: 408–416.

Mikulincer, M. and Florian, V. (1998) 'Attachment styles, coping strategies and post traumatic psychological distress: the impact of the Gulf War in Israel', *Journal of Personality and Social Psychology*, 64: 817–826.

Morgan, S., Hemming, M. and Davidson, Y. (1999) *Implementing Assertive Outreach: a joint statement*, London: Sainsbury Centre for Mental Health.

Oberlander, L.B. (1990) 'Work satisfaction among community-based mental health service providers: the association between work environment and work satisfaction', *Community Mental Health Journal*, 26: 517–532.

Obholzer, A. and Roberts, V.Z. (1997) *The Unconscious at Work*, London: Routledge.

Onyett, S.R. (1998) 'An exploratory study of English community mental health teams', unpublished thesis, University of Liverpool.

Onyett, S.R. (2007) *New Ways of Working for Applied Psychologists in Health and Social Care: working psychologically in teams*, Leicester: British Psychological Society.

Ovretveit, J. (1988) *Essentials of Multidisciplinary Team Organisation*, Uxbridge: Brunel University.

Payne, R. (1999) 'Stress at work: a conceptual framework', in J. Firth-Cozens and R.

Payne (eds) *Stress in Health Professionals: psychological and organisational causes and interventions*, London: Wiley.

Perkins, R. and Repper, J.M. (1996) *Working Alongside People with Long Term Mental Health Problems*, Gloucester: Stanley Thornes.

Pielage, S., Gerlsma, C. and Schaap, C. (2000) 'Insecure attachment as a risk factor for psychopathology: the role of stressful events', *Clinical Psychology and Psychotherapy*, 7: 296–302.

Pines, A.M. (2004) 'Adult attachment styles and their relationship to burnout: a preliminary, cross cultural investigation', *Work and Stress*, 18: 66–80.

Pines, A.M. and Aronson, E. (1981) *Burnout: from tedium to personal growth*, New York: The Free Press.

Pines, A.M. and Yanai, O. (2000) 'Unconscious influences on the choice of a career. Implications for organizational consultations', *Journal of Health and Human Services Administration*, 21: 502–511.

Priebe, S., Fakhoury, W., White, I., Watts, J., Bebbington, P., Billings, J., Burns, T., Johnson, S., Muijen, M., Ryrie, I. and White, C. (2004) 'Characteristics of teams, staff and patients: associations with outcomes of patients in assertive outreach', *British Journal of Psychiatry*, 185: 306–311.

Prosser. D., Johnson, S., Kuipers, E., Szmukler, G., Bebbington, P. and Thornicroft, G. (1996) 'Mental health, "burnout" and job satisfaction among hospital and community-based mental health staff', *British Journal of Psychiatry*, 169: 334–337.

Provencal, G. (1987) 'Culturing commitment', in S. Taylor, D. Bilen and J. Knoll (eds) *Community Integration for People with Severe Disabilities*, New York: Teachers College Press.

Roth, A. and Fonagy, P. (1996) *What Works for Whom?*, New York: Guilford Press.

Safran, J.D. and Muran, J.C. (1996) 'The resolution of ruptures in the therapeutic alliance', *Journal of Consulting and Clinical Psychology*, 64: 447–458.

Sainsbury Centre for Mental Health (1998) *Keys to Engagement*, London: SCMH.

Schaubroeck, J. and Merritt, D. (1997) 'Divergent effects of job control on coping with work stressors: the key role of self-efficacy', *Academy of Management Journal*, 40: 738–754.

Schaufeli, W. (1999) 'Burnout', in J. Firth-Cozens and R. Payne (eds) *Stress in Health Professionals: psychological and organisational causes and interventions*, London: Wiley.

Secretary of State for Health (1992) *The Health of the Nation: a strategy for health in England*, London: HMSO.

Selye, H. (1976) *The Stress of Life*, New York: McGraw Hill.

Sonnentag, S. (1996) 'Work group factors and individual well-being', in M.A. West (ed.) *Handbook of Work Group Psychology*, Chichester: Wiley.

Svanberg, P.O.G. (1998) 'Attachment, resilience and prevention', *Journal of Mental Health*, 7: 543–578.

Tajfel, H. and Turner, J.C. (1979) 'An integrative theory of social conflict', in W. Austin and S. Worchel (eds) *The Social Psychology of Intergroup Relations*, Monterey: Brooks/Cole.

Tillett, R. (2003) 'The patient within – psychopathology in the helping professions', *Advances in Psychiatric Treatment*, 9: 272–279.

Tyrell, C.L., Dozier, M., Teague, G.B. and Fallot, R.D. (1999) 'Effective treatment relationships for persons with serious psychiatric disorders: the importance of attachment states of mind', *Journal of Consulting and Clinical Psychology*, 5: 725–733.

Walsh, S., and Cormack, M. (1994) ' "Do as we say but not as we do": organizational, professional and personal barriers to the receipt of support at work', *Clinical Psychology and Psychotherapy*, 1: 101–110.

West, M. (2004) *Effective Teamwork: practical lessons from organizational research*, 2nd edn, Oxford: Blackwell Publishing.

Wilkinson, S. (2003) *Coping and Complaining: attachment and the language of disease.* Hove: Brunner-Routledge.

Williams, S., Michie, S. and Pattani, S. (1998) *Improving the Health of the NHS Workforce: report of the partnership on the health of the NHS workforce*, London: Nuffield Trust.

Yan, X., West, M. and Dawson, J.F. (2006) 'Good and bad teams: how do they affect individual well-being?' Aston Business School working paper.

Part II

Applying models of psychological therapy

6 A psychodynamic perspective

Alf Gillham, Andrew Law and Lucy Hickey

> Society devotes much concern and effort to finding 'care' for the disabled schizophrenic, but avoids contact with him insofar as possible; looks at him in bits and pieces, sees him as the victim of mysterious external forces; denies the inherent validity of his mind and encourages him to do likewise; and at times denies his very psychological existence as a human being.
>
> (Robbins, 1993: 190)

Assertive outreach is not a therapy in itself, but rather a platform to help clients with severe mental illness engage with mental health services. In the UK assertive outreach is designed to aid engagement with people who have previously failed to engage with services, many of whom experience psychosis. The psychodynamic model can provide a helpful framework for understanding the processes involved in making emotional connections with this most challenging client group.

It has been found that Assertive Outreach Teams are remarkably successful in achieving engagement with clients, as reported in the seminar on Assertive Outreach in Mental Health in England (Department of Health, 2005). Defining features of assertive outreach which contribute to this success are the team approach and small, capped caseloads. Both of these features encourage the provision of space and time to reflect. There will always be external forces impinging on this reflective space, such as pressures of workload. However, there is also a personal reluctance to think about the experience of psychosis because of the emotional pain involved for both client and worker. We use a psychodynamic model to facilitate understanding of this emotional pain, expressed in a complex interplay of transference and countertransference, which can enable both worker and client to remain in contact and go on to build a working relationship.

The Whole Team Approach provides group support for the individual worker (see chapter two). The use of daily meetings, regular board planning sessions and weekly reviews provides space for thinking and reflection. Through this process clients are held in mind by all team members, something that does not generally happen in other teams. The fundamental structures inherent in whole team working provide an opportunity for the team to collectively process and understand their interactions with clients within a psychodynamic framework (Navarro, 1998).

Engagement and psychosis

Historically, people experiencing psychosis have been a client group that is difficult to 'think' about and sometimes even our attempts to be helpful can deny their inner worlds. Early in his career Sigmund Freud himself admitted:

> I did not like those patients . . . They make me angry and I find myself irritated to experience them so distant from myself and from all that is human. This is an astonishing intolerance which brands me a poor psychiatrist.
> (Freud in a letter to Istvan Hollos in 1928, cited in Dupont, 1988: 251)

A helpful paper by McCabe *et al.* (2002) highlights the difficulties that junior psychiatrists can have in trying to engage with people experiencing psychosis. This is a 'conversation analytic study' which looks at how doctors engage with clients with psychotic illness during routine consultations. It found that whenever people attempted to talk about the content of their psychotic symptoms, the doctors either hesitated or responded with a question, rather than an answer. And when informal carers were present, the doctors frequently smiled or laughed, indicating a reluctance to engage with the person's concerns about their psychotic symptoms. These junior doctors were clearly unsettled and, like Freud, found it difficult to respond.

Karon (2003) reminds us that therapists can often feel uncomfortable, depressed and angry when talking to someone with psychosis, simply because the client does not react in the way that the therapist wants. In addition, he suggests that the therapist can sometimes feel scared without being sure why. According to Karon, one of the reasons we experience such uncomfortable feelings is that the client is experiencing those very same feelings. In fact this is a form of communication in which the client's feelings are being expressed through our own responses to their feelings. Psychosis can be understood as both an escape from unbearable pain, and a means of communicating the essence of that unbearable pain to another.

The way in which both clients and therapists cope with their emotions is considered to be the key to understanding psychosis from a psychodynamic point of view.

The therapeutic alliance

Early in the development of assertive outreach in the UK, the Sainsbury Centre for Mental Health (SCMH) produced a report on Assertive Outreach (2001). In the section on client engagement it states that:

Effective client engagement is fundamental to the Assertive Outreach model. This involves the development of a trusting relationship with the service user, sometimes referred to by health professionals as the 'therapeutic alliance'. Working with users on their own territory is essential to the development of such a relationship. This is a significant shift from the traditional mental health services that have often been institutionally based.

(SCMH, 2001: 11)

It should be noted that this type of engagement requires the formation of a therapeutic relationship with people who previously had rejected such an alliance and were often psychotic.

In their book *Psychosis: psychological approaches and their effectiveness*, Martindale *et al.* (2000) emphasise the centrality of a good relationship with the patient (and his or her family).

The need for this and the skills required to achieve it are too often neglected. Our evidence points to the need for care of the relationship between the person with psychosis and the key professional(s) to be put back at the heart of the therapeutic endeavour. It is only once this has been achieved that there is a possibility of a range of interventions actually being used therapeutically by the patient.

(Martindale *et al.*, 2000: 26)

In a recent paper, Fakhoury *et al.* (2008) showed that the quality of the therapeutic relationship can be an important predictive factor in the treatment of this client group (see chapter one). Research suggests that the significance of the therapeutic relationship is important not only from the therapist's point of view but also from the patient's perspective (Horvath and Greenberg, 1993). This can create problems for psychotic clients, who may fear any attempts to engage with them. Jackson (2001) suggests that the discovery of meaning in psychosis can actually be dreaded by the psychotic person, whose main priority is to try and get relief from their mental pain.

Psychodynamic theory suggests that, as we attempt to relate to our clients, we often encounter defensive positions and a powerful reluctance or aversion to engage in mental and emotional work. It is not that reality is disavowed, but rather the client mounts a chronic attack on his sensory, perceptual and cognitive capacity to perceive reality. This has been described as an attack on thinking itself (Bion, 1959). Psychosis can therefore be seen not so much as a retreat from reality, but as an attempt at survival, purchased at enormous cost. Grotstein, in his introduction to Jackson's (2001) book *Weathering the Storms*, says:

The Schizophrenic, cut off from his normal world because of its intolerability, seeks to create another one, a parallel world, but one that obeys different rules. It is essentially a psychic retreat. The cost of the retreat is madness; the reward is a new meaning for a virtual life.

(Grotstein in Jackson, 2001: xvi)

Jackson shows how a hatred of reality can be directed at staff, who are seen as the purveyors of 'unwelcome meaning'. This is an extremely helpful insight, one which all workers in Assertive Outreach Teams should know about and understand because of its potential role in bringing about disengagement.

Hingley (1997a) points out that the client's fear of closeness stems from a vulnerability of the ego or sense of self, and problems involving boundaries between self and other. She describes how the perspectives on psychosis emerging within Cognitive Behaviour Therapy (CBT) are closely related to psychodynamic theory, showing, for example, how persecutory delusions can function as a defence against underlying feelings of low self-esteem, although this is still debated by some CBT theorists.

Hingley (1997b) also highlights the importance of defences, without which the ego or self may be unable to adaptively protect itself from the adverse impact of intense affect and internal conflict. She emphasises that we must respect and understand the need for such defences. This has implications for working with a client group, both individually and within an Assertive Outreach Team, where engagement is seen as one of the primary goals.

Three levels of application

Hingley (1997b) suggests that psychodynamic theory can have value in three types of applications. We would like to consider how in particular the third might be used within assertive outreach to complement other aspects of overall care.

1   Intensive long-term psychotherapy:
    Although intensive individual psychoanalytic therapy is not directly applicable to assertive outreach practice, much of this work crucially informs the more supportive, team-based and individual attempts at understanding psychosis.
2   Less intensive and briefer psychotherapy:
    This would be aimed at improving a client's ability to cope with their problems and to relate to other people. This approach makes use of the models and theories described in long-term individual work, such as containment, counter-transference, projection and projective identification.
3   Using a psychodynamic framework:
    This would aim to help staff gain a better understanding of the behaviour and capacities of the client, leading to more constructive and enabling responses from the team, something recommended in the

National Institute for Clinical Excellence clinical guideline for schizophrenia (NICE, 2002).

Psychoanalysis and psychodynamic therapy have much to teach us about helping clients with severe mental illness, despite their relative unpopularity at the coal face of everyday psychiatric practice. Indeed, some recommendations, such as the schizophrenia Patient Outcome Research Team (PORT) treatment recommendations (Lehman and Steinwachs, 2003), actively discourage psychodynamic approaches. In the North American context, PORT Reports carry similar weight to the NICE guidelines. *PORT Recommendation 22* tells us: 'Individual and group psychotherapies adhering to a psychodynamic model (defined as therapies that use interpretation of unconscious material and focus on transference and regression) should not be used in treatment of persons with schizophrenia' (Lehman and Steinwachs, 2003: 143).

However, there is a robust rejoinder to this by Ver Eecke (2003) which also gives a good overview of current psychodynamic approaches to psychosis, and defends their relevance.

Our own NICE (2002) guidelines suggest that there is insufficient evidence to recommend the use of psychoanalytic or psychodynamic psychotherapy in the routine treatment of people with a diagnosis of schizophrenia. This is supported by Roth and Fonagy (2006). However, the guidelines do go on to suggest that psychoanalytic and psychodynamic principles may be useful in helping professionals understand the experience of the individual service users and their interpersonal relationships.

A different way of thinking

The authors hope to show some of the ways in which a psychodynamic understanding can be used in assertive outreach, in much the same way as it has been used to think about working in other settings, such as rehabilitation (Davenport, 2002), acute care (Holmes, 2002) and Community Mental Health Teams (Foster and Roberts, 1998).

Psychoanalysis has always been a way of thinking, not only about the client's difficulties, but also about ourselves and our own feelings and reactions when working with the client. It places a high value on subjective experience, giving much importance to the client's internal worlds, fantasies, dreams, fears, hopes, impulses, wishes, and psychological reactions to symptoms (Gabbard, 2000). At the same time psychoanalysis also emphasises how the client's subjective experience impinges on ourselves and our own internal worlds, fantasies, dreams, fears, hopes, impulses, wishes, and psychological reactions to symptoms.

Example:
Peter had just been admitted to an acute ward and was acutely psychotic, responding to auditory and visual hallucinations. He was visited by an

outreach worker. Peter's conversation was rather rambling and idiosyncratic, full of utterances that didn't appear to make much sense or
bear any relation to reality. The subject of Coca-Cola featured promin-
ently, usually as something being withheld or taken from him. By the
time of the next visit Peter was no longer acutely psychotic. The outreach
worker had been puzzled by his earlier preoccupation with Coca-Cola
and brought two bottles as a gift from the team. Peter was really grateful.
It turned out that this was his favourite drink and he hadn't been able to
get any since his admission!

Making commonsense interpretations like this can be a surprisingly difficult
thing to do when working with clients who are struggling with psychosis.

Multiple models

Psychoanalysis has a complex developmental history and it is impossible
to suggest a single model of psychodynamic therapy for psychosis. Freud
himself changed his theories on three major occasions and there have been
many developments and elaborations since. However, one can say that, essentially, psychoanalysis sees psychosis as a defence against unbearable affect
(Garfield, 1995).

Within psychoanalysis there has been a steady move away from drive theory
towards a relational approach, sometimes called relational psychoanalysis.
Greenberg and Mitchell (1983) describe the way in which the object relationships viewpoint has become incorporated into drive theories of psychoanalysis. The history of psychoanalysis also charts a deeper understanding of
transference and counter-transference and the development of object relations theory, especially through the work of Fairbairn (1952), Klein (1948),
Winnicott (1989) and Bion (1962), which has opened up ways of exploring
this inter-relational space.

In the case of psychosis it is generally agreed that there has been some
damage done to the core of the 'self'. Sutherland (1989) suggests that the
nature and development of the 'self' is the paramount issue for general
psychology as well as psychoanalysis. This is a view that is shared with some
approaches in CBT. For example, Chadwick, Birchwood and Trower (1996)
in their book *Cognitive Therapy for Delusions, Voices and Paranoia* say:

> Thus we believe the building block, the foundation stone, for a personal
> model from which to approach psychotic phenomena is the central
> human endeavour of trying to construct a sense of self that is both
> valued and authentic . . .
>
> (op. cit.: 182)

Naturally one would not expect psychodynamic psychotherapy to be
routinely provided within the context of assertive outreach. Nevertheless, the

psychological work offered in assertive outreach can be usefully informed by the theories and understanding obtained from individual psychodynamic psychotherapy. The literature describing individual work is extensive and gives examples of many practitioners who have worked this way, such as Jackson (2001), Lucus (1993), Robbins (1993), Garfield (1995) and Searles (1986).

Much of what differentiates psychoanalysis from other forms of treatment may be traced to two of Freud's discoveries: the unconscious mind and the transference worked out in the therapeutic relationship. However, these concepts take on extra levels of complexity when applied to working with psychosis.

Freud believed that psychotic clients were not able to form a transference to the therapist because they were 'too narcissistic'. He called this a 'narcissistic neurosis', suggesting that these clients were simply unanalysable (Freud, 1914). It took many years to refute this notion and to reach the position that psychoanalysis now takes with regard to psychosis. As has been pointed out, Karon suggests that psychosis can be understood as a form of communication. Rosenfield (1987) and many other psychoanalytic therapists (in particular Searles, 1986) agree with this.

> It is my conviction that the psychotic patients' speech and behaviour (particularly in sessions) invariably make a statement about his relationship to the therapist . . . it is important to pay minute attention to the patient's communication, and to seek conceptualization and understand what these communications mean in the transference relationship.
>
> (Rosenfeld, 1987: 3)

Jackson (2001) points out that therapists and those trying to help psychotic clients have to be able to tolerate confusing counter-transference states of mind, which requires the capacity to follow multiple, and often paradoxical, threads of communication simultaneously.

Psychoanalytic conceptualisation has attempted to understand and recognise primitive mental mechanisms, as described by Klein (1948) and Bion (1962), particularly splitting and projection, and attempts to understand the intense and yet fragile transferences psychotic clients develop. Klein (1948) described psychosis as the excessive use of normal defence mechanisms as a response to excessive anxiety. These defences exist in extreme forms in psychosis, leading to a distortion of perception, loss of the capacity to think clearly and fragmentation of the self. According to this theory, the aim of the psychotic part of the mind is to relieve itself of emotional pain through projection. One way of understanding this is that whenever a painful feeling arises the mind will evacuate it to produce a hallucination. If the sensation is projected into an object, it becomes a delusion (Bion, 1962).

Bion expanded on this concept, describing an interpersonal process whereby the other person comes to identify with the projections, which then profoundly affect their own emotional state and behaviour. This is called projective identification, a mechanism revealed in fantasies in which the subject inserts his self, in whole or in part, into another person in order to harm, possess or control them.

We need to be aware of these processes in our work. However, Rosenfield (1987) warns that unskilled psychotherapy of the psychoses is a danger to the therapist's personality. We can find ourselves swinging between feelings of helplessness towards our clients and feelings of omnipotence, in which we may believe that we have all the answers and fully comprehend what is going on in their minds. In assertive outreach, where a team approach is used, staff can help each other reach this important insight.

A search for meaning

For grounded and sensitive Assertive Outreach Team members, the challenge is to receive and acknowledge the painful communication; to think and reflect on it, and then to attempt to understand its meaning. From this position it is then possible to construct a working hypothesis about the meaning of the unspoken pain that is somehow being expressed, and to reflect this back to the sufferer. They are then receiving back the pain after it has been considered and clarified by the team, a 'detoxifying process'. In this way the pain and meaning are presented to the person in a more acceptable and less painful format, allowing an understanding to take place.

When this process is carried out, it provides the person experiencing the pain with some important principles:

- It confounds their deeply held and unconscious belief that they are worthless, dangerous and toxic to others. And that professionals, family members and friends always let them down, always desert them, always hate them and wish them harm precisely because they see themselves as dangerous and toxic. The very act of taking in their painful feelings and not running away, but instead coming back with something thoughtful and potentially helpful, gives the person hope that they are worthwhile, that they are lovable.
- It provides a model of thinking and containment. One might say that it models the healthy, depressive position.
- It enhances the belief that their intense pain and anxiety can be contained and are not necessarily destructive.
- It gives the person a sense that their madness/psychosis has meaning, has value and has worth.

Those engaged in the treatment of the person experiencing psychosis also benefit from this process:

- It provides staff with an understanding that pain has value. They can now appreciate that pain is a primary method of communication and not just something to be eradicated.

- It enables staff to spend time in a state of not knowing, with acceptable uncertainty and anxiety. This allows space and time for the emergence of the unconscious awareness of humanity to rise up and propose creative, thoughtful solutions to seemingly intractable problems and dilemmas.
- It allows and encourages deep and meaningful transactions to take place. These transactions enhance the understanding of these experiences rather than simply fuelling the search for an immediate solution.

Practical applications

We can now give some examples of how this approach can be used in the typical experiences of working in an Assertive Outreach Team.

> **Example:**
> Following the particularly traumatic death of one of the service users who had drowned himself, staff in the Assertive Outreach Team met to reflect on their feelings and reactions, assisted by a psychoanalytic consultant. During this discussion one staff member said that he could actually taste the river water in his mouth. This was projection at its extreme, no doubt, but a powerful example of identification and connection with a traumatic and painful death that made everyone want to gag or choke. It was as though everyone wanted to 'spit this experience out' as if it was choking and suffocating them.

This example demonstrates that 'projection as communication' can be a key tool in assertive outreach, but only if the staff group is sufficiently in touch with their own feelings to recognise them as projected feelings coming from the work. Staff need to be sufficiently skilled to recognise a projection and have sufficient space to reflect on it.

> **Example:**
> A young woman, Joanna, told me a story of a traumatic childhood event. On one occasion, the atmosphere was one of horror, dismay and disgust. I felt she was with a small, frightened little girl who did not know what was going on. On another occasion, the story was told again and the emotional tone was quite different: there was an air of triumph, contempt for the alleged abuser. This time, I felt I was sitting in the presence not of a little girl, but of a judge. On a third occasion, the details of the story were quite exciting, and I felt privileged to be the one entrusted with this information . . .

The words are the same, the story is the same; what is different is the experience. The different ways in which the story is told offer glimpses of the different levels of meaning that this particular episode has for Joanna. These are conveyed not by the words she uses, which may be identical each time, but by creating an experience. So, on the first occasion, I felt horrified and desperately sorry for her suffering. The second time, I felt little sympathy, and even somehow guilty, as if I were the one who had committed the offence. I felt dirty and uncomfortable and wanted to get away. By contrast, on the third occasion, I felt rather special and wanted to hear more. These are three very different experiences for the listener, which reflect accurately three different aspects of the experience for Joanna, each requiring understanding.

(Obholzer and Roberts, 1994: 51–52)

The key is to try to become sensitive towards, and in touch with, the 'music behind the words'; to be aware of the likely inner and unconscious experience of the psychotic person and what they might be fearing most; to sense what you need to do or say to reach out to them, so that they can distinguish between what's inside and what's outside, what's real and what's imaginary.

An important aspect of a psychodynamic approach is the necessity of being in touch with our own feelings. We need to be able to recognise when a feeling we are experiencing is related to a client's projection, rather than being simply 'our' feeling. This is astoundingly difficult for many people to see, and understandably so. We are conditioned from a very young age to 'own' our feelings. If I have a feeling inside me, right inside me, how could it come from anywhere else other than from within myself? Over time we can begin to learn to spot a projected feeling by noticing that it is unaccustomedly strong; that its strength or nature doesn't appear to bear any relation to a confirmed and evidenced reality; or that it is puzzling and doesn't feel right and so on. However, even experienced practitioners can fail to recognise the signs of a projection, which is where the importance of the team comes in, by creating a situation where someone else can, as it were, 'see' my unconscious.

Example:

Sarah had been admitted to hospital on a section. She was a remarkable person, with fairly extreme and chaotic bipolar disorder. Sarah was highly intelligent and high achieving. When well, she was capable of great academic achievement and artistic and intellectual prowess. When unwell, she could be depressed to the point of being suicidal or extremely hyper-manic. She would frequently be taken to hospital by the police after running through the streets naked, or showing other extreme disinhibited behaviours. Sarah was visited on a locked ward by an assertive outreach worker shortly after she had been brought in after a typical extreme episode. She appeared settled, but with totally flat affect, was monosyllabic, apparently resigned to her situation, accepting what had happened, and able to speak about it without any distress. The worker spent half an hour or so with her and then left, promising that someone else would visit in a day or two.

The worker got on his bicycle and started to cycle back to the office. Within five minutes, tears were streaming down his face. He felt desperately unhappy and upset. He was totally thrown by what he was feeling, and made absolutely no connection with the visit he had just made. He puzzled over what could have led to this reaction, examining his day and what had been happening in his personal life recently, but remained confused and unable to explain his feelings. On returning to the office for the handover meeting he became acutely upset once again as soon as he started to talk about Sarah. One of the staff said simply, 'It's just like having Sarah in the room'.

Sarah was so totally overwhelmed by such absolutely unbearable feelings that all she could do with them was to unconsciously, and quite violently, 'shove' them into the worker, in the desperate hope that he could hold and contain them for her, until such time as she was able to deal with them. Once the team were able to unpack these unbearable feelings, they were able to go back to Sarah and say how very sorry they were about her recent admission under section, and to acknowledge how desperately sad this made her feel. The team was able somehow to detoxify these feelings and yet retain their essence, and then hand this essence back to her in a form which was no longer overwhelming and potentially destructive. This enabled Sarah to reflect on her experience in a way that helped her to hold onto these feelings as an essential part of herself and her life.

Bion distinguished between psychotic and non-psychotic parts of the personality and explained how they function quite differently. This is also clearly described by Lucus (1993). Both suggest that, because the psychotic part of the personality can't learn through experience, and is intolerant of psychic pain and frustration, the mind evacuates such feelings and those parts of the mind that register them. Thus clients may split off aspects of themselves and project them into the staff members they are working with. We may then experience a fragmenting of our own thought processes, with feelings of deadness, omnipotence, or incredible sadness sometimes being the result. Bion says that this is a form of communication, and that we need to attempt to contain and understand these projections. The staff involved need to try to recognise these experiences as a form of communication, but not act on them. Instead, they need to digest and understand the experiences before reflecting them back to the client in a contained way.

Example:
John had a very severe alcohol problem with a diagnosis of paranoid schizophrenia. He had disturbing thoughts and feelings concerning his

Irish family background and religion, as well as being ambivalent and disturbed by his sexuality. John had a long history of violence and aggressive behaviour and had assaulted a long line of workers, although he had never assaulted any of the Assertive Outreach Team staff. He was, however, often verbally aggressive and threatening towards them.

After the third occasion on which he had been thrown out of a bed and breakfast for violence, it became clear to the team that his violent outbursts were invariably connected to intense drinking sessions complicated by serious abuse of prescribed Diazepam. John would routinely visit the hospital and demand Diazepam with menaces, which the psychiatrist invariably prescribed, as he clearly felt scared by John's propensity for violence. The team contacted the consultant psychiatrist to discuss their concerns and persuaded him not to prescribe any further Diazepam. The following week, John visited the hospital, again demanding Diazepam. On this occasion the psychiatrist refused to oblige, informing John that the Assertive Outreach Team had instructed him not to prescribe this drug any further.

John telephoned the office and left a very threatening message on the answerphone, threatening to kill one of the team. Two team members decided to visit him at work. John was working as a casual labourer on a building site and therefore had easy access to spades, pickaxes and other potential weapons. The two team members felt quite scared, and were also able to connect with and articulate John's fear of himself and others. This enabled John to reflect on how frightened he was much of the time and to see how his aggression and violence were defences against not only terrible feelings, but also the potential of others to damage him. The psychiatrist had been in touch with the fear, but had interpreted it as his own fear rather than John's. His reaction, much like John's ordinary reaction, was to project that feeling somewhere else, placing the outreach team workers in danger.

Here the idea of containment is not seen as something passive. The client has first to feel understood in order to believe that someone can enter into his experience and share some of it without collapsing. The experience of containment can itself lead to the internalising of the containing person, or aspects of that person, and with it the gradual development of the capacity to contain.

Gabbard (2000) has suggested that there are several common threads running through many psychodynamic theories that can helpfully inform our clinical work:

- Psychotic symptoms have meaning (Karon, 1992).
- Grandiose delusions or hallucinations often immediately follow an insult to someone's self-esteem (Garfield, 1985).

- The grandiose content of the thought or perception is the patient's effort to offset the narcissistic injury.

Another common thread is that human relations are fraught with terror for this client group, and any contact with other people can cause intense anxiety, as described by Karon (1992).

One of the most important things we can ever say to a psychotic individual – and indeed something we should almost always say – is 'Don't be afraid, I'm not going to harm you, I'm not going to kill you'. We need to be constantly aware that people experiencing psychosis are almost always highly anxious, highly afraid and often paranoid.

An example of a psychodynamically informed supportive approach is described in 'When the going gets tougher: the importance of long-term supportive psychotherapy for psychosis' (Meaden and Van Marle, 2008). This paper argues that not all clients are helped by psychosocial approaches. It suggests that long-term psychodynamically informed supportive therapy offers a valuable approach in cases where the current psychosocial interventions are ineffective or where unhelpful team reactions are obstacles to care. This implies that assertive outreach combined with psychodynamically informed supervision can be effective.

A framework for team working

Hinshelwood (2004) skilfully takes quite complex psychoanalytic theories of psychosis and applies them to workers trying to care for psychotic people, showing how both clients and staff are affected by this. He reminds us of the deadening effect of past institutionalism and how its effect on staff mirrored the internal world of their clients. He also stresses the importance of not repeating this same pattern in a community setting and warns that we can all too easily fall into ritualistic patterns of working which keep us away from any real contact with our clients (Menzies, 1988).

Hinshelwood further outlines why we need to become aware of the different ways in which we can be made to feel and act when working as a team. If these feelings and reactions are not brought into awareness then we may simply enact them within the team. There are times, however, when they have to be enacted within a team before they can be understood. This is why external consultants are sometimes needed.

The difficulties team members experience in trying to think about this mirrors the inability of the patient to reflect. We need to create a space for 'not knowing' within the team, to avoid a premature attempt to fill what is apparently meaningless with too ready-made an understanding.

In our experience, the most important lesson a psychodynamic perspective can give is to show how the staff team, managed by a skilled manager and with the skilled support of an external facilitator, can act as a key container for the unbearable pain of the people we work with. If we can take in that unbearable pain, if we can reflect on that pain without leaping into or avoiding action; if we can share our fantasies and our reactions to that pain without judgement and without filtering, we can allow our unconscious awareness of human interactions and human experience to emerge.

This allows space for tentative hypotheses to emerge, and the team can offer up these initial thoughts and reflections to the client to enable a common search for meaning. We often have to be in a state of some anxiety and not knowing in order to do this, but this is the only place from which true and really effective thinking can take place. One might argue that the ability to say 'I don't know, I really don't know' is the greatest and most important ability that anyone who works in health and social care can develop. This is an especially important, and difficult, position for a manager to take up, particularly in assertive outreach where the service users are often high risk, presenting with complex and apparently urgent needs, often in crisis and where the pressure to 'do something' is almost unbearable. The team constantly looks to their manager to rescue them from anxiety, to say 'It's easy, all we need is to do this and that and it'll be fine!' The greatest gift a manager can give to their staff team when they are clamouring for an answer is to say 'I don't know. I really don't know' and then to remain silent and stay with the anxiety that follows. Out of this anxiety comes possibility and, above all, thinking.

A manager of one Assertive Outreach Team has two quotes posted on his office wall: 'At those times when you feel most pressure to act, to do something which seems logical, urgent and necessary – stop. Take space and think. It may be that you are about to be swept into an unconscious enactment of someone else's problem.' The second is: 'I cannot contain the staff. The system contains the staff. I manage the system.'

The most important thing staff members can do is to get in touch with those vague, lingering hunches and thoughts, which are the stirrings of the unconscious when it reacts to projections and unconscious communications from the client. When these tentative stirrings manifest themselves, staff should nurture and share them with others, as they invariably represent an important insight into the experience of the service user.

Example:
We had been working with a male service user, of mixed parentage, for some time. One of our white female workers tentatively put forward her experience that when visiting Simon she often felt anxious and threatened. She wasn't sure whether it was a sexual thing or not. Her views were initially dismissed as they were not shared by any other members of the team and did not resonate with anyone else. However, being persistent, she continued to raise her experiences.

Eventually, it struck us that she was the only white woman on the team and that this might be a factor in her experience. Instead of raising the issue with Simon directly, we decided to 'act out' our hypothesis that Simon had issues with white women. We did this by visiting Simon in a variety of pairs, a not unusual practice. After each paired visit, the white female member of staff reflected on how she had felt during the visit and the team thought about this. The experience of the other member of the pairing was also reflected on. After a series of such visits, the most powerful experience, in terms of splitting and projection, was one where the white female staff member had paired with a black male worker. The white female worker had felt a strong sense of anxiety and the black male worker had felt 'blanked'. During this visit there was a strong sense of both disengagement and hostility from Simon.

When we considered this visit back in the team, we were convinced that this powerful and sexual combination of black man and white woman had generated considerable anxiety within Simon. On the next visit the black male worker was able to initiate a conversation about relationships during which Simon was able to tentatively reflect on his own mixed parentage and the confusions and tensions this created in him. This was a real breakthrough in our relationship with Simon and in our ability to create a safe space within which he could begin to explore his fear of mixed parentage relationships as it related to his hidden and defended positions.

Many of the feelings and experiences that people in extreme pain hold are felt to be so dangerous as to risk destroying themselves and others. The result of holding in these thoughts and fantasies is to split people off from reality, as these thoughts and experiences cannot be shared, explored and tested out. Hinshelwood (2004) suggests that 'we are all in the same boat' and that to understand our clients we inevitably have to suffer something of our patients' suffering, so that they come to see that we may know something of their world. He argues for a truly reflective psychology of care which requires some inner emotional labour, and stresses that this is not easy.

Hinshelwood goes on to suggest that reflection can operate in the minds of carers in three ways:

- a reality of small successes
- not knowing
- moral judgement.

We need to be aware that we will judge our patients emotionally and try to reflect on this. At times we will like or even hate our clients (Winnicott, 1959) but what is important is to try to be honest about this, using it in a way that allows us to reflect on what they may be trying to communicate. By doing this we can enable our clients to find their own space and eventually allow them to reflect on themselves.

Conclusion

We hope that we have shown how a psychodynamic perspective and ways of thinking can assist Assertive Outreach Teams in trying to work with people who experience psychosis. We have described a way of thinking about working with psychosis that can enable us to see psychosis as an attempt at communicating something which is hard for the individual, the team and society to receive. The ability of a staff team or individual to detoxify such dangerous thoughts on behalf of the person in pain, and then to present them back in a potentially manageable form, is one of the most important functions we can perform on behalf of others.

The assertive outreach model, with its Whole Team Approach and small, capped caseloads, provides the space to think about and process difficult feelings. It allows space for staff to reflect on both their clients and themselves. At a time when many Assertive Outreach Teams are under pressure to increase workloads or to merge with other teams, the need to defend this space and time for reflection is paramount.

References

Bion, W.R. (1959) 'Attacks on linking', *International Journal of Psychoanalysis*, 40: 308–315.
Bion, W.R. (1962) *Learning from Experience*, London: Heinemann.
Chadwick, P., Birchwood, M. and Trower, P. (1996) *Cognitive Therapy for Delusions, Voices and Paranoia*, Chichester: John Wiley & Sons.
Davenport, S. (2002) 'Acute wards: problems and solutions. A rehabilitation approach to in-patient care', *Psychiatric Bulletin*, 26: 385–388.
Department of Health (2005) 'Assertive Outreach in Mental Health in England: report from a day seminar on research, policy and practice', 7th October.
Dupont, J. (1988) 'Ferenczi's "madness"', *Contemporary Psychoanalysis*, 24: 250–261.
Fairbairn, W.R.D. (1952) *Psychoanalytic Studies of the Personality*, London: Tavistock.
Fakhoury, K.H., White, I. and Priebe, S. (2008) 'Be good to your patient. How the therapeutic relationship in the treatment of patients admitted to assertive outreach affects rehospitalization', *Journal of Nervous and Mental Disease*, 195: 789–791.
Foster, A. and Roberts, V. (1998) *Managing Mental Health in the Community: chaos and containment in community care*, London: Routledge.
Freud, S. (1914) 'On narcissism', *The Standard Edition of the Complete Psychological Works of Sigmund Freud*, 14: 73–102, London: Hogarth Press.
Gabbard, G.O. (2000) *Psychodynamic Psychiatry in Clinical Practice*, Washington, DC: American Psychiatric Press.
Garfield, D. (1985) 'Self-criticism in psychosis: enabling statements in psychotherapy', *Dynamic Psychotherapy*, 3: 129–137.
Garfield, D.A.S. (1995) *Unbearable Affect: a guide to the psychotherapy of psychosis*, New York: John Wiley & Sons.
Greenberg, J. and Mitchell, S.A. (1983) *Object Relations in Psychoanalytic Theory*, Cambridge, MA: Harvard University Press.

Hingley, S.M. (1997a) 'Psychodynamic perspectives on psychosis and psychotherapy I: Theory', *British Journal of Medical Psychology*, 70: 301–312.

Hingley, S.M. (1997b) 'Psychodynamic perspectives on psychosis and psychotherapy II: Practice', *British Journal of Medical Psychology*, 70: 313–324.

Hinshelwood, R.D. (2004) *Suffering Insanity: psychoanalytic essays on psychosis*, London: Brunner-Routledge.

Holmes, J. (2002) 'Acute wards: Problems and solutions. Creating a psychotherapeutic culture in acute psychiatric wards', *Psychiatric Bulletin*, 26: 383–385.

Horvath, A.O. and Greenberg, L.S. (1993) *The Working Alliance: theory, research and practice*, New York: John Wiley & Sons.

Jackson, M. (2001) *Weathering the Storms*, London: Karnac Books.

Karon, B.P. (1992) 'The fear of understanding schizophrenia', *Psychoanalytic Psychology*, 9: 191–211.

Karon, B.P. (2003) 'The tragedy of schizophrenia without psychotherapy', *Journal of the American Academy of Psychoanalysis and Dynamic Psychiatry*, 31: 89–118.

Klein, M. (1948) *Contributions to Psychoanalysis, 1921–1945*, London: Hogarth Press.

Lehman, A.F. and Steinwachs, D.M. (2003) 'Evidence based psychosocial treatment practices in schizophrenia: lessons from the Patient Outcomes Research Team (PORT) project', *The Journal of the American Academy of Psychoanalysis and Dynamic Psychiatry*, 31: 141–154.

Lucus, R. (1993) 'The psychotic wavelength', *Psychoanalytic Psychotherapy*, 7: 15–24.

McCabe, R., Heath, C., Burns, T. and Priebe, S. (2002) 'Engagement of patients with psychosis in the consultation: conversation analytic study', *British Medical Journal*, 325: 1148–1151.

Martindale, B., Bateman, A., Crowe, M., *et al.* (eds) (2000) *Psychosis: psychological approaches and their effectiveness*, London: Gaskell for ISPS.

Meaden, A. and Van Marle, S. (2008) 'When the going gets tougher: the importance of long-term supportive psychotherapy in psychosis', *Advances in Psychiatric Treatment*, 14: 42–49.

Menzies, I. (1988) *Containing Anxiety in Institutions*, London: Free Association Books.

National Institute for Clinical Excellence (2002) *Schizophrenia: core interventions in the treatment and management of schizophrenia in primary and secondary care*, London: NICE.

Navarro, T. (1998) 'Beyond keyworking', in A. Foster and V. Zagier Roberts (eds) *Managing Mental Health in the Community: chaos and containment*, London: Routledge.

Obholzer, A. and Roberts, V.Z. (1994) *The Unconscious at Work: individual and organizational stress in the human services*, London: Routledge.

Robbins, M. (1993) *Experiences of Schizophrenia: an integration of the personal, scientific, and therapeutic*, New York: The Guilford Press.

Rosenfield, H.A. (1987) *Impasse and Interpretation*, London: Tavistock Publications.

Roth, A. and Fonagy, P. (2006) *What Works for Whom: a critical review of psychotherapy research*, New York: Guilford Press.

Sainsbury Centre for Mental Health (2001) *Mental Heath Topics: assertive outreach*, London: Sainsbury Centre for Mental Health.

Searles, H.F. (1986) *Collected Papers on Schizophrenia and Related Subjects*, London: Maresfield Library.

Sutherland, J. D. (1989) *Fairbairn's Journey into the Interior*, London: Free Association Books.

Ver Eecke, W. (2003) 'The role of psychoanalytic theory and practice in understanding and treating schizophrenia: a rejoinder to the PORT Report's condemnation of psychoanalysis', *Journal of the American Academy of Psychoanalysis and Dynamic Psychiatry*, 31: 11–29.

Winnicott, D. (1959) 'Hate in the countertransference', *International Journal of Psychoanalysis*, 30: 69–74.

Winnicott, D. (1989) *Psycho-Analytic Explorations*, London: Karnac Books.

7 Family and systemic work

Sara Meddings, Inger Gordon and Debbie Owen

Approximately 50 per cent of those with severe mental health problems live with family or friends (Dept of Health, 1999a). It is estimated that up to 1.5 million people in the UK care for a relative or friend with a mental illness (Rethink, 2003). The physical and psychological wellbeing of relatives is inevitably affected by living with someone with a serious mental health problem (Fadden, 1998), yet relatives can also play an important role in their recovery. Many assertive outreach clients and their family and friends may benefit from support to improve relationships, understanding and mental wellbeing.

This chapter focuses on people experiencing psychoses, the predominant mental health difficulties facing people who use assertive outreach services. Nevertheless, we recognise that people who use assertive outreach may experience a range of other difficulties, often concurrently. Family therapy draws on different traditions – including structural, social constructionist, narrative, behavioural – each with its different strengths. We are aware that different approaches and trainings have been in conflict in the past, yet in practice we have found that they can work well together and complement each other. There is also a growing consensus about the benefits of integrating psychosocial interventions and systemic family therapy (Burbach, 1996; Burbach and Stanbridge, 1998; Carr, 2000; Fadden, 1998; Meddings *et al.*, 2007). So rather than considering them separately, we will present integrated practice, all delivered with an outreach perspective.

Families, for us, include not only parents, partners, children, siblings and extended family, but also other groups of people living in family-like settings, such as shared houses, and wider social networks such as friends and colleagues. The latter may especially be important for people receiving assertive outreach services, who may have become isolated from their families of origin and have only tenuous contact with their friends. Working with such groups may facilitate continuing friendships and wider social participation.

The policy and research context

Government policy initiatives have made families and 'carers' a high priority. *The Carers (Recognition and Services) Act 1995* (Dept of Health, 1996) established carers' rights to an assessment and required local authorities to provide services for carers. The contribution that families make in caring for their relatives was formally recognised in *Caring About Carers: a national strategy for carers* (Department of Health, 1999b). It acknowledged that 'helping carers is one of the best ways of helping the people they are caring for' (Department of Health, 1999b: 12) and outlined plans to provide better information, support, and care for carers.

The National Service Framework for Mental Health (Dept of Health, 1999a: 69), standard six: 'caring about carers', recognises the impact that caring for someone with a mental health problem can have on carers' own physical and mental health and that they have a right to access services in their own right. The related *Policy Implementation Guide* (Dept of Health, 2001) suggests that, within assertive outreach, there should be provision of psycho-education to families and others, family therapy, practical support and care plans for carers.

The NICE guidelines for schizophrenia (NICE, 2002) recommend:

> Family interventions to be offered to 100 per cent of families of individuals with schizophrenia who have experienced a recent relapse, are considered to be 'at risk' of relapsing, or who have persisting symptoms, and are living with or in close contact with their family.
>
> (NICE, 2002: 54)

The Healthcare Commission audit in 2006 found that approximately half of people with schizophrenia had received NICE-guided family interventions. In Assertive Outreach Teams the level is generally much lower (Department of Health, 2005), but in our team we have achieved 60 per cent (Beeton, Meddings and Gibbins, 2007), demonstrating that it is possible to deliver family interventions routinely in this context.

The evidence for family work

Family therapy is one of the most effective interventions for psychosis. Literature reviews suggest that both behavioural family management and systemic therapy are effective and reduce relapse in long-term cases by about 30 per cent – a similar efficacy to Cognitive Behaviour Therapy or Clozapine (Burbach, 1996; Alanen, 1997; Fadden, 1998; Jones, 1987; Seikkula and Arnkil, 2006). In assertive outreach, McFarlane *et al.* (1996) have demonstrated that family involvement reduces re-hospitalisation, and enhances rehabilitation and family-related outcomes.

The concept of expressed emotion (EE) has been influential in the development of family work since the early 1970s (Vaughn and Leff, 1976). EE comprises emotional over-involvement, criticism and hostility. In a comprehensive review of 26 studies, with an overall sample of 1,323, Kavanagh (1992) found the median relapse rate in a low EE environment to be 21 per cent compared with 42 per cent in a high EE environment, suggesting it to be as important as medication. It is not only relatives who are vulnerable to showing high EE. Approximately 40 per cent of staff are 'over-helpful' or critical of clients, e.g. for being unmotivated, non-compliant or not following advice, and could be designated high EE (Repper and Perkins, 2003). Clearly in Assertive Outreach Teams where staff have frequent and sometimes prolonged contact with their clients this could be an important variable.

However, EE is not a stable trait. For nearly half of relatives, EE fluctuates over time without intervention (McCreadie *et al.*, 1993). In their critique, Smith and Birchwood (1990) advocate seeing families as facing problems rather than as problem families with high expressed emotion and suggest that 'EE is an operational "thermometer" of stress in a *particular* relative–sibling (or spouse) relationship at a *particular time*' (Smith and Birchwood, 1990: 657). Likewise in teams staff may at times become high EE as a result of stress which is poorly managed (see chapter five). Support, helping people's understanding and reattributing challenging behaviours to the psychosis rather than personal character traits, may help reduce critical comments and emotional involvement, reducing everyone's stress.

A sizeable literature describes the negative impact or 'burden' of caring for someone with serious mental health difficulties (Fadden, 1998). When feeling burdened, relatives of assertive outreach users say they value education and information; support and expressions of concern, especially at times of crises; workers taking time to learn about and understand the family; willingness to meet in their environment; flexibility of approach, and sharing responsibility for monitoring their relative's mental state (Hughes, 2007). Burden is also affected by how people perceive their roles and responsibility, how they create meaning and their sense of reciprocity (Schwartz and Gidron, 2002). Families who see positives in their situation use more social support, make sense of their experiences and are more able to cope (Stern *et al.*, 1999). Families report that their relatives with serious mental health problems make positive contributions: they provide companionship, news about family and friends, listen to problems and give advice (Greenberg, Greenley and Benedict, 1994); they contribute to the personal growth of family members: to a familial sense of increased appreciation and closeness; patience and perspective; self-value and purpose; life satisfaction and practical support (Lukens *et al.*, 2004; Schwartz and Gidron, 2002; Coldwell, 2008).

People who use assertive outreach services are especially vulnerable to social exclusion. At times of crisis, families are generally pulled closer together by centripetal forces (Rolland, 1990). This pull is normal and adaptive in families at certain points in the lifecycle e.g. family births and deaths, short-term illnesses. However, when faced with long-term illness or disability it becomes problematic, especially when it coincides with centrifugal periods such as adolescence, as psychosis often does. People can then lose touch with their wider social network and supports, which impedes recovery (Ohaeri, 1998). Many assertive outreach clients describe experiences of surviving alone, disconnected from family as well as services (Lukeman, 2003). It is therefore particularly important that teams actively work to preserve and promote family and social networks.

It is crucial that we work with service users and relatives to further their own recovery goals and not just those of professionals. Clinicians prioritise symptom reduction more than service users and their relatives (Repper and Perkins, 2003). People who use rehabilitation and assertive outreach services see recovery in terms of improved wellbeing, improved mental state and relationships with family and others, as well as empowerment, work, independence and coping, and material wellbeing (Meddings and Perkins, 2002). They emphasise choice and control (Read, 1996), practical support, counselling and help with social networks (Shepherd *et al.*, 1995).

Frameworks for family work

We have found it helpful to think about our work with families in terms of intervening at different levels. We use higher levels where there are more complex needs, distress, concurrent problems or life transitions for other members, relationship difficulties, or where someone from the family has requested it.

Levels of working

1. Information and assessment
Everyone can benefit from being offered general information about the Assertive Outreach Team, crisis or out-of-hours support and other services, or about mental health difficulties. This may include practical support such as care breaks. Relatives are entitled to carers' assessments to identify their needs.

Where the person using the service consents, we can share more individualised information, and collaborate more with relatives in reviews and less formal settings. Likewise Team Case Formulations benefit from information offered by relatives (see chapter four).

A specialist family work practitioner leads on this in our service, but the whole team is involved. Workers provide information leaflets and collate contact details early on so relatives may be involved in meetings appropriately. Relatives work in partnership with the assertive outreach service. In this way consideration of relatives' perspectives and needs forms part of routine practice.

2. Basic family work
2a. Most relatives of assertive outreach users benefit from psycho-education, basic family interventions and support. This involves communication training, ways of coping with the impact of having a relative with serious mental health difficulties and helping people to understand what is going on for their relative. It might follow a manualised treatment plan (e.g. Kuipers, Leff and Lam, 2002).

Family work might be provided by psychologists or team members with psycho-social interventions training. Alternatively, some relatives find independent carers' workers or support from independent sector providers, such as Rethink, more helpful.

2b. Many families access relatives' and carers' groups where they gain peer support. These can be arranged within services, or families can access support groups and carer education and training programmes run by Rethink.

2c. Ongoing family work can follow any intervention to help families maintain progress. Carried out by any Assertive Outreach Team member with supervision, it may occur only every few months or when needed.

3. Family therapy

Some families benefit from family therapy which draws on multiple traditions within systemic family therapy and psycho-social interventions.

This work is carried out by two therapists, one of whom must have a two-year family therapy training or equivalent. In our service, one of the therapists is always a member of the Assertive Outreach Team to facilitate integration with team work. Another option is to develop a semi-separate family therapy service (e.g. Burbach *et al.*, 2007).

Supervision

It helps to promote a coherent and clinically robust approach if all staff attend general team supervision and formulation groups, reflective practice and seminars. These should routinely include consideration of family work. In our service, staff involved in levels two and three attend a monthly family work supervision group with the team psychologist and a family therapist.

How can we engage families?

Assertive outreach is invoked when traditional services have not been able to engage with people. Consequently it is crucial that we pay attention to how we engage and form therapeutic relationships with both individuals and their families.

Barriers to engagement

There are many reasons why families find it difficult to engage. First, relatives feel guilt and worry that it is their fault that they have a relative with a serious mental health problem. Being offered family work itself might be perceived as signifying blame. Clear messages that it is not their fault and that we are seeing them because they can support recovery may be helpful, alongside allowing them to talk about their feelings.

There may also be family stories about being let down in the past. Many of the people we work with have insecure attachment patterns as a result of feeling let down when they were much younger. This has been repeated in multiple social contexts, e.g. school, family, and ultimately mental health services. Such experiences inhibit people from forming new relationships where they risk being let down once more (see chapter two). Families may choose not to engage due to negative experiences with services, including hospital admissions, family therapy, social services or other authorities, and not necessarily in relation to the person with mental health difficulties. Family therapy itself has sometimes been perceived to blame families (Smith, Gregory and Higgs, 1997). We find it helpful to acknowledge these experiences, and the possibility that we too may let them down, but offer to experiment and see how we get on. We reflect with them on how we can learn and try to do things differently. After living with, or caring about, someone with a psychiatric disability for so long, some people may also have become resigned to how things are and to have lost hope in the possibility of recovery. This can be exacerbated by misinformation about recovery rates. We find it helpful to give information about recovery and about the evidence base for family work in a user-friendly, hopeful, realistic manner.

Another source of difficulty is that families do not always want to share information openly with each other. There can be real dilemmas about consent, confidentiality and the competing needs of users and their relatives.

Finally, there may be practical reasons why people are not able to engage with family work. Appointment times, transport and other access issues can be difficult for any family or wider group to negotiate and manage.

Forming a relationship is a two-way process. Mental health services can create barriers to engagement. A key barrier is a perceived lack of 'suitable' families, perhaps due to therapists' attitudes or engagement skills, which must be addressed through training (Burbach and Stanbridge, 1998; Fadden, 1997). Families in assertive outreach may be especially vulnerable to being perceived as unsuitable. It is crucial that we seek supervision and opportunities for reflective practice to overcome this. Management must also allow space for this kind of reflection, and for family work itself, in staff workloads.

Reaching out to families

Within assertive outreach, it is important to have a philosophy within the team that all workers engage with families and the wider social network in an opportunistic and informal manner, especially in terms of information sharing and support.

Example:

A support worker was accompanying Gino in relation to a short-term work placement. Gino was unsure about whether he wanted to continue with the placement as his mother had told him there was 'no point as it wasn't going to lead to a proper job'. It seemed that his mother was becoming anxious and being dismissive and critical of him. One day the worker arrived when Gino's mother happened to be there and mother and son were arguing about the work placement. The worker later reported at the team meeting that he 'just listened to what both of them were saying, helped them to calm down, and listen to each other'. He helped Gino and his mother to manage their stress by supporting them to listen to each other, articulate their worries and problem solve. He also gave them verbal information about recovery and about the vocational service. Gino was able to tell his mum how important the opportunity was to him, which was something he had not been able to say before. He went on to successfully complete the work placement.

Sometimes, this form of impromptu support is all that the family want or need. At other times, it can lead to more formalised work in terms of carers' assessments or basic family work. Sometimes it can help the team or the family to consider engaging in family therapy.

Example:
Mrs Smith phoned the Assertive Outreach Team most days for emotional support, to check that the team was aware of how her son was and to discuss his recovery or setbacks. She did not want formal family work. Then it happened that the same person took her call for several consecutive days and they were able to suggest and arrange a regular time twice a week for telephone contact. It allowed the team to offer more consistent and containing support.

For many families it is a question of finding the right time to offer family work. Families are more likely to accept help and engage in family work at times of crisis, for example when their relative is in hospital (Barrowclough and Tarrier, 1997). Other opportunities for engagement include times when family members phone frequently for ad hoc support or liaison; when there is conflict or stress within the family; when there has been a transition or change such as someone leaving home; or when a member of the family or social network request work. In the latter instance, it might be important to respond relatively quickly whilst the person or family is highly motivated.

It is important to have a genuinely positive attitude to families and to acknowledge the skills and expertise of the family, including the service user, within a recovery-orientated approach. Relatives of people with psychosis report the most important aspects of family interventions to be emotional support, backup, reassurance/encouragement, and information (Budd and Hughes, 1997). Systemic therapy recognises people's positive intentions and that current problems may often be due to attempts to solve past problems (Fisch, Weakland and Segal, 1982). For example, a well-meaning attempt to encourage someone to tidy their room may be perceived as criticism and lead to stress in the family.

There are different schools of thought about the benefits of seeing family members together or separately. A general principle in family therapy is to invite everyone living in the household (Burnham, 1986). Seeing people together from the outset promotes a sense of openness and working together. It enables all stories and hopes and worries about the sessions to be shared by the system as a whole. Everyone can see how the others relate to each person and their accounts. It begins a process where all members see how each one of them is valued by the therapists.

A behavioural family therapy approach advocates meeting people individually in the first instance, and then bringing them together (Falloon *et al.*, 2004). This enables individuals to feel heard and to express their own needs and hopes for the sessions without worrying about the response of other family members. Sometimes people want to talk about issues which they do not want other members to hear. Whilst there may be advantages to providing such a space for individuals, and some family members we work with value this, it can create secrets between the therapist and individuals, encourage paranoia in others and counter the sense of the family working therapeutically together. Usually we meet with the family as defined by them, often a group who live together. We take a flexible approach and consider, as a whole team, the pros and cons of initially seeing people together or individually. In these discussions it can be helpful to analyse network roles: referrer, customer who asked for the referral, identified client, primary supportive figures such as parents and partners, other professionals and also people's attitudes to change (Carr, 2000).

Family therapy is more effective if the person with psychosis joins the sessions (Barrowclough and Tarrier, 1997). However, should that person choose not to attend, we can still find ways to work with their relatives, or indeed a single relative, without disclosing personal information about them (Slade *et al.*, 2007).

Example:
Pete asked that someone work with his mother as he was struggling with her criticisms. He did not consent to our sharing any personal information about him with her, including his diagnosis. Nor did he want to attend sessions. We worked with his mother by finding out what she had noticed about her son. She worried about him hearing voices, believing he was a famous footballer and leaving his flat dirty. We helped her to explore what might be going on, including sharing understandings about voices and delusions, which were neither her nor his fault. By considering the wider system, we realised that she was an especially tidy person. We normalised messiness in young men, whilst also checking with the rest of the team that he wasn't self-neglecting. She talked with friends about their young adult sons who were also untidy despite not being assertive outreach users. She found the sessions supportive. Several months later Pete told one of us that his mother had been less critical since family work and he recommended it to a friend.

With one family, the parents had divorced and the client lived with his father, seeing his mother daily. The parents disagreed about aspects of his care, so we worked individually with family members as preparation for meeting together. We also found it helpful to engage members of the wider family network, who played mediating and supportive roles.

We need to remain aware of power imbalances within families as well as between workers and families. Family histories can include one member abusing another. Many assertive outreach clients have previously been abused and/or stigmatised in society. We discuss feeling safe within sessions and help people to find their voice. We pay particular attention to whether or how to include children in the family – considering potential parentification and child protection issues – in consultation with Child and Adolescent Mental Health Service colleagues.

Basing family therapy clearly within the team, as a routine part of the team's function, generally facilitates engagement. It normalises need for family support, allows personal introductions and enables everyone to have an idea of who we are and what to expect before we start work. We negotiate the best time for appointments and stick with that, finding this to be containing and pragmatic. We write to each member of the family separately. This demonstrates the importance to us of everyone attending and means that we need not rely on one person to pass a message on to another. We offer open invitations to anyone else the family may choose to invite. During the actual sessions we work with whoever is present.

At an early stage we need to consider when and where best to meet. To help people to regain their independent lives we may need to provide some after-hours appointments for working people or those with other care commitments. We need also to consider other access needs e.g. physical disabilities, transport, providing interpreters. Most people are seen either in a clinic setting or in the assertive outreach client's home. If the assertive outreach user is in hospital we usually see the family in a room on the hospital site. When booking other clinic rooms, we try to book them conveniently near to people's homes, making it more likely that they can make their way to the session independently. Seeing people at home can feel less threatening for people and alter the power balance. We advocate seeing families in the assertive outreach client's home rather than in a relative's home for this reason, and because it promotes their adult status. Seeing people at home may also be necessary for reasons of access or to allow flexibility over how much they join in. It may help to engage someone who is reluctant to join family therapy.

Example:
Paul was ambivalent about family therapy. He sat in another part of the room, apparently making a model. We noticed that he was also listening to what we were saying and occasionally joined in the conversation. We saw Paul's decision to sit separately like this as a way for him to manage his stress in a crowded room, enabling him to decide how much he

wanted to participate. He was worried about his mother and wanted her to benefit from our support. On one occasion, he was waiting for us but his mother had forgotten and he went to find her.

Home visits offer us a wealth of information, such as observing where people usually sit, or about overcrowding when an adult has returned to live with parents. On the other hand, clinic settings provide safe space where we are in more control of interruptions and boundaries; more neutral ground if there is potential conflict; and the possibility of people leaving a session or not arriving. At times seeing people in a clinic can allow us to think more clearly, but whether this is also true for the family would need to be explored.

One of the advantages of working in assertive outreach is that we are able to draw on the knowledge and expertise of the whole team when reflecting on who best to invite and how best to go about inviting people and engaging them in family interventions.

Formulating

What we do in family therapy sessions is determined by the individual family, the therapists, and our shared hypotheses and curiosities about what is going on, in terms of strengths, problems and exceptions. In assertive outreach the process of formulating, for both clients and therapists, begins prior to the first meeting, through conversations with other team members.

Formulation in family therapy draws on ideas from a number of models and is illustrated by Carr (2000), Johnstone and Dallos (2006) and Burbach *et al.* (2007). Models we find particularly helpful include:

- Stress vulnerability, including biological determinates of an 'illness' – the idea that mental health problems develop when there is a current life stressor or trauma, in the context of vulnerabilities associated with upbringing, socio-economic context or biology (Zubin and Spring, 1977).
- Recovery and the importance of hope, social inclusion and quality of life – including ideas that people can recover and find meaning in life even when their symptoms persist and that everyone's recovery journey is unique (Repper and Perkins, 2003).
- Strengths approach – valuing and building on the strengths and resources of each individual family member and of the family and system as a whole, rather than focusing only on deficits and problems (Ryan and Morgan, 2004).
- Circular causality and hypotheses about patterns of relating which are systemic, and concern the total relational system – questions can make constructs visible, challenging family belief systems and interactional patterns to promote flexibility and change (Selvini-Palazzoli *et al.*, 1980).
- The idea that many problems facing families arise from well-intended

failed solutions as people try to deal with prior difficulties – for example, a parent might try their best for their son with psychosis by looking after him and doing everything for him, perhaps even leaving work to do so, but this in itself might create new difficulties (Fisch, Weakland and Segal, 1982).

- The roles of language and culture: problems may occur when dominant narratives and stories people have available about themselves do not accord with their lived experience – for example, when the only stories told about people with psychosis are of inadequacy, a re-authoring of individual stories of achievement is needed to create visibility and wider scope for competence (White and Epston, 1990).
- Context, including the family life cycle and the impacts of social inequalities and poverty, gender, race and culture (Carter and McGoldrick, 1989; Jones, 1994).
- Attachment, loss and transition, including the importance of relationships, endings and containment (Byng-Hall, 1996).
- Reflexivity – recognising our own context, values and assumptions and the multiple realities about which we can be curious (Cecchin, 1994; Burnham, 2005).

Formulating with families is an ongoing process carried out by therapists and families together. Hypotheses guide what interventions to use and interventions inform formulation. We often draw a formulation diagram, such as Figure 7.1.

Example:
Kate's psychosis developed in the context of vulnerabilities and stresses, including losses experienced by the whole family. Similarly we understood the struggles of Kate's father, Bob, in the context of these life-events, leading him to feel that he was coping alone.

When Bob noticed Kate becoming more paranoid and easily agitated, he became more anxious himself. He expressed his concerns frequently to the health team and to Kate. When they seemed not to act, he sought solutions to help her. Kate perceived Bob's reactions as him pursuing and criticising her. She felt more stressed, causing the psychosis to worsen and leading her to find a solution through withdrawing.

Exceptions were co-created by Bob and the Assertive Outreach Team. Bob used his social networks and was able to support Kate at a level of intensity she could manage. Bob's anxiety felt contained and Kate felt less stressed. The blip ended.

Within a specific session, we set an agenda collaboratively and balance issues arising from ongoing hypotheses with the family's pressing concerns. We have found that we need to be especially flexible, adapting any plans and

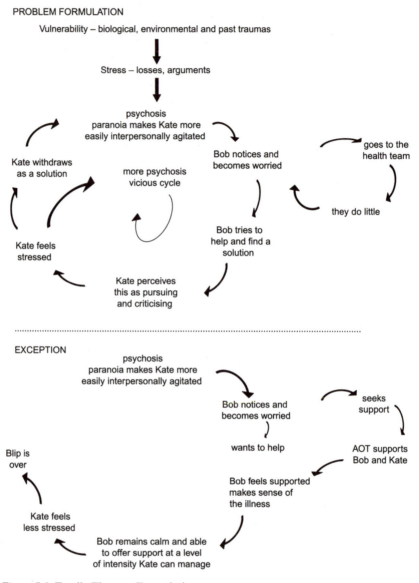

PROBLEM FORMULATION

Vulnerability – biological, environmental and past traumas

Stress – losses, arguments

psychosis
paranoia makes Kate more
easily interpersonally agitated

Kate withdraws
as a solution

more psychosis
vicious cycle

Bob notices and
becomes worried

goes to the
health team

they do little

Kate feels
stressed

Bob tries to
help and find a
solution

Kate perceives
this as pursuing
and criticising

EXCEPTION

psychosis
paranoia makes Kate more
easily interpersonally agitated

Bob notices and
becomes worried

seeks
support

wants to help

AOT supports
Bob and Kate

Blip is
over

Bob feels supported
makes sense of
the illness

Kate feels
less stressed

Bob remains calm and able
to offer support at a level
of intensity Kate can manage

Figure 7.1 Family Therapy Formulation

interventions to reflect the family situation on the day. The examples we give
here are some of the interventions we find ourselves using most frequently in
an assertive outreach setting. They are not intended to be an exhaustive list of
what might be done in family work; nor are they a list of things that must
always be done.

Interventions

We often hypothesise about the importance of loss and grief. People and their families need time for sharing narratives and processing emotions associated with a family member developing mental health problems, including loss of hope, meaning and identity (Repper and Perkins, 2003). The relapsing nature of psychosis and associated stigma make it harder to move through normal grief processes. The development of severe mental illness has been described as a 'catastrophic event' for families (Burbach and Stanbridge, 1998). This may be exacerbated when families are already coping with other losses. Denial, high emotional involvement and criticism may have adaptive functions in helping people cope with a relative developing psychosis. Working through loss, grief and acceptance helps people move through denial phases and reduces criticism (Patterson *et al.*, 2005). Listening to families, creating a space for everyone to take stock and orientate, can facilitate receptivity to further work.

Service users and relatives have consistently asked for more information (Read, 1996; Shepherd *et al.*, 1995). Relatives perceive the increase in knowledge and understanding as one of the most valued aspects of family work (Budd and Hughes, 1997). Families of assertive outreach clients may have lacked access to information more than most, as a result of their relative's disconnection from services. Information sharing is appropriate at all levels of family intervention (Birchwood, Smith and Cochrane, 1992; Barrowclough and Tarrier, 1997).

Rather than just 'provide' information or education, we generally find it more helpful to have conversations with families where we each share information. We value the expertise that assertive outreach clients and their relatives bring, whilst acknowledging our own, different, expertise. Some families find leaflets and factual information to be containing, whereas others value telling their story, sharing what has and has not worked, and exploring different perspectives. Some want to focus on what might cause psychosis; others on potential treatments, including medication and what they can do themselves; others on the details of local services, such as how to get help in a crisis, what vocational services are available or the implications of being detained under a section.

Example:

We gave Mary information about the nature of her son's difficulties, including the view that relatives do not cause schizophrenia, but can greatly enhance recovery. We discussed problems with diagnostic labels, and ways of re-framing Delroy's problems. Delroy described how it felt for him and how he was troubled by his experiences. When he expressed worries about taking medication, we gave him information about the possible benefits and side effects and the importance of taking it as prescribed. Mary was able to find new ways of caring for her son by becoming less involved, encouraging him to do things for himself and to go out with members of the Assertive Outreach Team.

Living with psychosis is stressful and ways of coping with it, such as withdrawing or shouting at voices, often cause stress in relatives, who may become over-caring or critical, causing yet further stress for clients. This cycle can be reduced by tackling the problem itself, developing problem-solving skills and drawing on the multi-disciplinary skills of the Assertive Outreach Team in medication, individual psychological therapy, socially inclusive work and structured activity. It is helpful to integrate individual psychological approaches into work with the whole family (Burbach and Stanbridge, 1998). Sometimes the referred client is able to teach these strategies to their relatives. Relatives can also act as a resource of potential strategies, helping the client to use them as necessary.

As well as intervening with the problem directly, families may need other stress management approaches, including relaxation, diary keeping, exploring beliefs about symptom-related behaviours, or helping relatives to see that withdrawal and low motivation are symptoms of psychosis.

Example:
Marianne had personalised her partner Jane's strategy of withdrawal as simply avoiding contact with her. She realised in family therapy that this was Jane's way of coping with persecutory voices. This reduced stress for both of them.

Sometimes, as a result of the impact of psychosis, families have drifted apart and stopped communicating effectively. Disengagement from services may have exacerbated this and created no-go areas for discussion. Therapy sessions create a reflective space to practise new ways of communicating and generate exceptions to fixed patterns. Ground-rules help such as:

- one person speaking at a time
- talking to, rather than about each other, e.g. 'That's interesting, would you like to tell your daughter that directly?'
- sharing time equally within the session and listening to each person in turn
- reminding people to listen to each other, e.g. 'Did you hear what your sister said?' (Kuipers, Leff and Lam, 2002).

Positive communication patterns can be modelled and encouraged, such as clear ways of making requests or expressing disappointments; acknowledging difficult feelings *and* noticing positives; reconnecting to what relatives have always appreciated about each other.

Families tend to be pulled together centripetally when faced with illness or crisis (Rolland, 1990), yet where there is high EE, reducing face-to-face contact with that person to below 35 hours a week has been shown to reduce relapse (Vaughn and Leff, 1976). Practical interventions such as teaching independence skills, providing respite or accompanying people on trips out can help. This is easily arranged where family work is embedded within an Assertive Outreach Team. Structural interventions, like changing seats during sessions, can also help shift family structures and boundaries to reduce rigidity, enmeshment and disengagement (Minuchin, 1974; Yang and Pearson, 2002). This is especially powerful when done in people's home environment.

Example:
Family therapy sessions were arranged to include the extended family network once Delroy returned home. Mary, Delroy and Vivienne (Mary's sister) and Michael (Delroy's cousin) attended. A structural task was given to strengthen the relationships between Mary and her sister, and Delroy and his cousin. The two sisters and two cousins were asked to sit next to each other and to plan something that they would like to do that day. The sisters went on a church outing together, the men watched football. This facilitated social support, helping Delroy and his mother to separate from each other, challenging the enmeshed cross-generational relationships. Outside the family therapy sessions, the team taught Delroy new skills such as sandwich making and provided respite. His mother noticed gains. When asked directly, Delroy couldn't see any improvements, but was able to do so through circular questioning: Therapist – 'If I were to ask your mother how you are doing, what do you think she'd say?' Delroy – 'She'd say I'm doing a bit all right.'

Work on attachments and multi-generational patterns can help people to improvise new scripts (Byng-Hall, 1995). Developing coherent narratives, especially about reparation, reduces criticism (Stern *et al.*, 1999). Drawing family trees enables us to learn new information, and to notice patterns within the family. It enables us to normalise issues around transitions and the family life cycle.

Example:
Drawing a family tree with Mary and Delroy allowed support networks to become more visible, helping them to re-access support from their extended family.

Family trees can help demystify the psychosis and place it more within people's understandable experience. For assertive outreach clients, drawing a family tree can be less stressful than talking about themselves and can facilitate participation, as it moves the focus to a piece of paper, away from interaction or the sense that they are a 'problem'.

Byng-Hall (1995: 200) argues there are 'more important shifts in family functioning arising from praising the family's struggle to manage better than from any other intervention'. Anderson and Goolishian (1988) suggest problems can be dissolved through conversations which generate new meanings.

Example:
We re-framed Bob's frequent phone calls to the team as positive moves to help his daughter and manage his own anxiety, so that he could speak with her without feeling stressed. Together we re-framed Kate's reluctance to engage with work as her managing her stress levels and keeping safe. We took a both/and position – that we could both recognise the value of work and hope for the future, and also accept that at present, Kate's life is better than it has been for many years.

White and Epston (1990) argue that people reify problems as if they are stable and enduring. They advocate exploring exceptions when the problems did not occur, and externalising problems to stop cycles of guilt and blame. We talk about 'the psychosis' and 'the voices', recognising that they are a problem facing the whole system, which we can tackle together, rather than the problem being the client themselves. When families have been blown apart by one member's experience of psychosis, this approach can help unite the family once more.

Reflecting teams

We use a team approach to family therapy and the model of live supervision without a one-way screen (Smith and Kingston, 1980). We adopt the reflecting techniques of Andersen (1987, 1992). One person leads a session whilst the other observes and is then able to offer reflections and different ideas. Reflections are offered in the form of a conversation between the therapist and reflector, watched by the family. 'During the reflecting processes . . . the family and the team are together all the time and all that is spoken is spoken openly' (Andersen, 1992: 87). Afterwards the family responds, saying what they liked and disliked about that conversation and what they want to explore further. Comments are made tentatively, with suggestions that are 'different enough but not too different' from previous discussion (Andersen, 1987: 417). This allows new ideas to be considered without any obligation to accept them. Reflections are always appreciative and creative in their intent. They gently invite the family to be curious about their ways of seeing and doing things. They try to connect to narratives and metaphors used by family members and in their comments embrace significant social contexts like culture and gender. The therapy team tries to avoid taking a strong position in which one idea is thought to be better than another. By presenting both sides of a dilemma, using *both/and* rather than *either/or* language, various descriptions can live on simultaneously, and with equal value, until they are ready to be assimilated into a shared story. Families get used to modelling these multiple possibilities and to talking openly and straightforwardly. This process seems to put families more at ease, which can be especially important when working with clients vulnerable to paranoia, and families whose ties with each other are under particular strain.

Example:
At a session with Cezar, his family and keyworker from the residential home, his mother discussed how she felt stressed by Cezar visiting her sometimes several times a day. She found it difficult to say 'no'. Sometimes this pressure led them to shout and exchange insults. We explored ways of managing this, including the suggestion that she would appreciate Cezar phoning first and not visiting if it was inconvenient. Staff offered to support Cezar with this. Cezar raised how he felt his independence and privacy were not being respected by staff when they encouraged him to go to bed at set times. Everyone expressed their needs and emotions around this before a reflecting conversation was observed:

Reflector – 'It was interesting that both Cezar and his sister seemed to feel able and safe to express anger at different times today.'
Therapist – 'Yes and that it seemed to be shared with the others without an argument developing.'
Reflector – 'I wonder if it was also positive for Cezar to hear this from his family?'
Therapist – 'There seems to be a change since the last meeting.'
Reflector – 'I have also been conscious of a strong theme running throughout today's meeting about a shared need for respect.'
Therapist – 'Mmm I think this was particularly evident for Cezar and his mother. I wonder if being able to express themselves and being respected are related.'

We invited comments in response to these reflections:

Sister – 'Respect is very important to us and it is important in our culture.'
Mother – 'Yes, respect is important to our family' (smiling).
Cezar nodded agreement.

Working with the wider system

We work with wider social systems in similar ways to families, e.g. workplace, college or residential home. Bringing the family and professional systems together from the outset of referral facilitates ongoing dialogue about treatment plans. Seikkula and Arnkil (2006) invite the whole system, including client, family, mental health services, employer, neighbours and friends, to regular meetings to find out what each needs and can offer to help. This is where all decisions are made. By working collaboratively with the wider system, the Assertive Outreach Team creates a framework in which responsibility for change is shared. We find that pooling ideas about how the system is operating, and reflecting on how practitioners feel they are invited to adopt particular views, can lead to a consolidated team approach and more robust interventions.

Example:

We worked with Bob and Kate to reach a shared formulation about what was going on for the family and team. We had understood the relationship between Kate's deteriorating mental state, centripetal forces and increased stress. The family enabled us to see the role of services in the formulation. A vicious circle had been exacerbated by services either seeing withdrawal as a relapse signature and pursuing Kate, or also withdrawing. Service responses heightened Bob's anxiety. Kate suggested that she would be all right and that she wanted less, not more contact with her family. We learned that her history of reducing contact with her family and services just prior to relapse might have been a solution to the problem of stress. We respected this solution and worked with it. By working together as equal partners, we were all able to learn from one another's perspectives.

We shared this re-formulation with the rest of the team. We suggested the team act as a container for Bob's very real worries, allowing him to telephone at times of anxiety and to remain separate, rather than getting caught in the vicious circle with his daughter. The team agreed with Kate a level of contact low enough for her to tolerate, yet high enough for the team to monitor her mental state. Bob was able to take a holiday for the first time in years without worrying about her too much.

A systemic approach to team processes and team work

Systemic formulation can inform the work of the whole team and wider system, not only those directly engaged in family work. For example, when communication seemed to be an issue, we changed the structure within the team building so that people spent more time in shared offices and had to talk with each other in new ways. We provided in-house training where we learned from each other and also brought in external trainers. We gain ongoing support and inspiration from local and national assertive outreach networks and from other networks of teams and professional groups who work with similar client groups: our extended 'family' network.

Working systemically enhances team relationships and collaborative working. Individuals accustomed to witnessing each other, both in the interviewing position and whilst reflecting during tricky or uncertain moments, can develop close bonds. The positions that can divide the different professions can be re-examined in the light of increased respect, and sustaining alliances can be built. Peer supervision groups provide a reflective space for the issues to be explored further and good practice to be articulated and shared with the wider team.

Embedding a systemic approach within an Assertive Outreach Team can create a synergy between individual and family-based interventions. For example, a systemic formulation about the importance of boundaries led to our team social worker arranging for a bedroom door to be fitted for one client. Systemic reflections can also facilitate thinking about how teams relate with each other and the systems which might promote this.

Example:
A member of the Early Intervention Team talked about a family where the parents of the young man had been divorced and there was disagreement between them about what was best for their son. In the reflections we noticed how this was potentially mirrored by disagreements between this team and the Assertive Outreach Team who were about to take over his care. We thought about how, as with the family, shared conversations might help. This highlighted the usefulness of inter-team discussion, joined-up care planning and shared formulation.

Assertive Outreach Teams can get caught up in family processes and dynamics just as families can get caught up in team processes and dynamics. Teams may use reflecting teams in clinical meetings when discussing crises or new referrals, to enable them to think and notice patterns. In reflective practice we have considered our own attachment relationships, including tendencies to over-care. The reflective tools of systemic practice facilitate a creative space to free up fixed perceptions and patterns.

Conclusions

People's recovery can be greatly enhanced by the involvement of their families and wider social networks. By supporting such networks, family therapy can lead to improved wellbeing for clients, their relatives, friends and those in wider networks. Careful attention needs to be given to engagement, in reaching out to individuals and families who have previously chosen not to engage with mental health services.

'Family sessions are very important – like a form of therapy for us all.'

'We talk about our circumstances, specific problems and abilities to handle them, which change over time.'

'It helps us and the Assertive Outreach Team to understand each other better and what's going on for Sam and for us as a family.'

'It helps us to recognise the positives in each other and to all work as a team.'

(Reflections from a family about consultations offered by assertive outreach)

Acknowledgements

With thanks to all the families with whom we have worked and from whom we have learned so much. Thanks also to Emily Skye, Ann Glaister and Becky Whitfield for critical reading of earlier drafts.

References

Alanen, Y.O. (1997) *Schizophrenia: its origins and need-adapted treatment*, London: Karnac Books.

Andersen, T. (1987) 'The reflecting team: dialogue and meta-dialogue in clinical work', *Family Process*, 26: 415–428.

Andersen, T. (1992) 'Relationship, language and pre-understanding in the reflecting process', *A.N.Z. Journal of Family Therapy*, 13: 87–91.

Anderson, H. and Goolishian, H. (1988) 'Human systems as linguistic systems: evolving ideas about the implications for theory and practice', *Family Process*, 27: 371–393.

Barrowclough, C. and Tarrier, N. (1997) *Families of Schizophrenic Patients*, London: Chapman and Hall.

Beeton, L., Meddings, S. and Gibbins, J. (2007) 'Audit of NICE guidelines schizophrenia, Sussex Partnership NHS Trust', available from the authors.

Birchwood, M., Smith, J. and Cochrane, R. (1992) 'Specific and non-specific effects of educational intervention for families living with schizophrenia. A comparison of three models', *British Journal of Psychiatry*, 160: 806–814.

Budd, R.J. and Hughes, I.C.T. (1997) 'What do relatives of people with schizophrenia find helpful about family intervention?', *Schizophrenia Bulletin*, 23: 341–347.

Burbach, F. (1996) 'Family based interventions in psychosis – an overview of, and comparison between, family therapy and family management approaches', *Journal of Mental Health*, 5: 111–134.

Burbach, F., Carter, J., Carter, J. and Carter, M. (2007) 'Assertive outreach and family work', in R. Velleman, E. Davis, G. Smith and M. Drage (eds) *Changing Outcomes in Psychosis: collaborative cases from practitioners, users and carers*, Oxford: BPS Blackwell.

Burbach, F.R. and Stanbridge, R.I. (1998) 'A family intervention in psychosis service integrating the systemic and family management approaches', *Journal of Family Therapy*, 20: 311–325.

Burnham, J.B. (1986) *Family Therapy*, London: Routledge.

Burnham, J. (2005) 'Relational reflexivity: a tool for socially constructing relationships', in C. Flaskas, B. Mason and A. Perlesz (eds) *The Space Between*, London: Karnac Books.

Byng-Hall, J. (1995) *Re-writing Family Scripts*, New York: Guilford Publications.

Carr, A. (2000). *Family Therapy: concepts, process and practice*, Chichester: Wiley.

Carter, B. and McGoldrick, M. (1989) *The Changing Family Life Cycle: a framework for family therapy*, Boston: Allyn and Bacon.

Cecchin, G. (1994) *The Cybernetics of Prejudice in the Practice of Psychotherapy*, London: Karnac Books.

Coldwell, J. (2008) 'A grounded theory of how people with a diagnosis of schizophrenia contribute to their family', unpublished thesis, Salomons, Canterbury Christ Church University.

Department of Health (1996) *Carers (Recognition and Services) Act 1995: Policy Guidance*, London: Department of Health.

Department of Health (1999a) *A National Service Framework for Mental Health*, London: Department of Health.

Department of Health (1999b) *Caring About Carers: a national strategy for carers*, London: Department of Health.

Department of Health (2001) *The Mental Health Policy Implementation Guide*, London: Department of Health.

Department of Health (2005) 'Assertive outreach in mental health in England: report from a day seminar on research, policy and practice', 7 October.

Fadden, G. (1997) 'Implementation of family interventions in routine clinical practice following staff training programs: a major cause for concern', *Journal of Mental Health*, 6: 599–612.

Fadden, G. (1998) 'Family intervention in psychosis', *Journal of Mental Health*, 7: 115–122.

Falloon, I.R.H., Fadden, G., Mueser, K., Gingerich, S., Rappaport, S., McGill, C., Graham-Hole, V. and Gair, F. (2004) *Family Work Manual*, Birmingham: Meriden Family Programme.

Fisch, R., Weakland, J.H. and Segal, L. (1982) *The Tactics of Change*, London: Jossey-Bass.

Greenberg, J., Greenley, J. and Benedict, P. (1994) 'Contributions of persons with serious mental illness to their families', *Hospital and Community Psychiatry*, 45: 475–480.

Hughes, H. (2007) 'Relatives' experiences of assertive outreach', unpublished thesis, University of Surrey.

Johnstone, L. and Dallos, R. (2006) *Formulation in Psychology and Psychotherapy*, Routledge: London.

Jones, E. (1987) 'Brief systemic work in psychiatric settings where a family member has been diagnosed as schizophrenic', *Journal of Family Therapy*, 9: 3–25.

Jones, E. (1994) 'Gender and poverty as contexts for depression', *Human Systems*, 5: 169–183.

Kavanagh, D.J. (1992) 'Recent developments in expressed emotion and schizophrenia', *British Journal of Psychiatry*, 160: 601–620.

Kuipers, E., Leff, J. and Lam, D. (2002) *Family Work for Schizophrenia: a practical guide*, 2nd edn, London: Royal College of Psychiatrists.

Lukeman, R. (2003) 'Service users' experience of the process of being engaged by assertive outreach teams', unpublished thesis, Salomons, Canterbury Christ Church University.

Lukens, E.P., Thorning, H. and Lohrer, S. (2004) 'Sibling perspectives on severe mental illness: reflections on self and family', *American Journal of Orthopsychiatry*, 74: 489–501.

McCreadie, R.G., Robertson, L.J., Hall, D.J. and Berry, I. (1993) 'The Nithsdale schizophrenia surveys. XI: relatives' expressed emotion stability over five years and its relation to relapse', *British Journal of Psychiatry*, 162: 393–397.

Meddings, S., Owen, D., Burbach, F. and Thomas, M. (2007) 'Three journeys towards integrating models when working with families and psychosis', *Context*, 93: 13–16.

Meddings, S. and Perkins, R. (2002) 'What "getting better" means to staff and users of a rehabilitation service', *Journal of Mental Health*, 11: 319–325.

Minuchin, S. (1974) *Families and Family Therapy*, London: Tavistock.

National Institute for Clinical Excellence (2002) *Schizophrenia: core interventions in the treatment and management of schizophrenia in primary and secondary care*, London: NICE.

Ohaeri, J.U. (1998) 'Perception of the social support role of the extended family network by some Nigerians with schizophrenia and affective disorders', *Social Science and Medicine*, 10: 1463–1472.

Patterson, P., Birchwood, M. and Cochrane, R. (2005) 'Expressed emotion as an adaptation to loss', *British Journal of Psychiatry*, 187 (supplement 48): s59–s64.

Read, J. (1996) 'What we want from mental health services', in J. Read and J. Reynolds (eds), *Speaking Our Minds: an anthology*, Milton Keynes: Open University Press.

Repper, J. and Perkins, R. (2003) *Social Inclusion and Recovery*, London: Balliere Tindall.

Rethink (2003) *Who Cares? The experiences of mental health carers accessing services and information*, Kingston upon Thames: Rethink.

Rolland, J.S. (1990) 'The impact of illness on the family', in R. Rakel (ed.) *Textbook of Family Practice*, Philadelphia: Saunders.

Ryan, P. and Morgan, S. (2004) *Assertive Outreach: a strengths approach to policy and practice*, Edinburgh: Churchill Livingstone.

Seikkula, J. and Arnkil, T.E. (2006) *Dialogical Meetings in Social Networks*, London: Karnac Books.

Selvini-Palazzoli M., Boscolo, L., Ceccin, G. and Prata, G. (1980) 'Hypothesizing – circularity – neutrality: three guidelines for the conductor of the session', *Family Process*, 19: 3–12.

Schwartz, C. and Gidron, R. (2002) 'Parents of mentally ill adult children living at home: rewards of care-giving', *Health and Social Work*, 27: 145–154.

Shepherd, G., Murray, A. and Muijen, M. (1995) 'Perspectives on schizophrenia: a survey of user, family carer and professional views regarding effective care', *Journal of Mental Health*, 4: 403–422.

Slade, M., Pinfold, V., Rapaport, J., Bellringer, S., Kuipers, E. and Huxley, P. (2007) 'Best practice when service users do not consent to sharing information with carers', *British Journal of Psychiatry*, 190: 148–155.

Smith, D. and Kingston, K. (1980) 'Live supervision without a one-way screen', *Journal of Family Therapy*, 2: 379–387.

Smith, G., Gregory, K. and Higgs, A. (2007) *An Integrated Approach to Family Work for Psychosis*, London: Jessica Kingsley.

Smith, J. and Birchwood, M. (1990) 'Relatives and patients as partners in the management of schizophrenia: the development of a service model', *British Journal of Psychiatry*, 156: 654–660.

Stern, S., Doolan, M., Staples, E. and Szmukler, G.L. (1999) 'Disruption and reconstruction: narrative insights into the experience of family members caring for a relative diagnosed with serious mental illness', *Family Process*, 38: 353–369.

Vaughn, C.E. and Leff, J.P. (1976) 'The influence of family and social factors on the course of psychiatric illness', *British Journal of Psychiatry*, 129: 125–137.

White, M. and Epston, D. (1990) *Narrative Means to Therapeutic Ends*, New York: Norton.

Yang, L.H. and Pearson, V.J. (2002) 'Understanding families in their own context: schizophrenia and structural family therapy in Beijing', *Journal of Family Therapy*, 24: 233–257.

Zubin, J. and Spring, B. (1977) 'Vulnerability: a new view of schizophrenia', *Journal of Abnormal Psychology*, 86: 103–126.

8 Cognitive Behaviour Therapy

Caroline Cupitt

Cognitive Behaviour Therapy (CBT) is now a well-established psychosocial intervention for people with psychosis and complex mental health problems. Many of the NICE Guidelines recommend individual CBT, not just for common mental health difficulties such as anxiety and depression, but also for schizophrenia (NICE, 2002; 2009). Since the majority of people receiving assertive outreach have received a diagnosis of schizophrenia, this guideline is of huge importance for the effectiveness of Assertive Outreach Teams. What is extraordinary is that, despite evidence for the effectiveness of both assertive outreach and CBT, so little is known about how to combine them effectively. Others have commented on this (e.g. Hemsley and Murray, 2000; Lehman *et al.*, 2003) but still the literature remains scarce. Perhaps it should therefore come as no surprise that the National Study of Assertive Outreach found that the number of teams which can actually deliver CBT according to the NICE guideline for schizophrenia remains pitifully small (Wright, 2005).

The Mental Health Policy Implementation Guide outlined in detail a service model for assertive outreach in the UK (Department of Health, 2001). It includes CBT as an assertive outreach intervention, stating that a range of CBT techniques should be available from within the team. The inclusion of CBT is presumably based on evidence of its effectiveness when provided to people with psychosis, either on an outpatient basis (e.g. Sensky *et al.*, 2000) or on acute wards (e.g. Drury *et al.*, 1996). To my knowledge no one has evaluated the effectiveness of CBT for psychosis when provided from within an Assertive Outreach Team. Although CBT can sometimes be practised in a conventional way within Assertive Outreach Teams, very often it needs to be significantly adapted to overcome difficulties with engagement. Two authors have commented on this. Freeman (2000) identifies a need to emphasise the collaborative aspects of CBT and integrate the intervention into care plans. Mills *et al.* (2004) further suggest that CBT should be delivered within a recovery-orientated framework, in order to bring about engagement with people who may be more inclined to resist therapy. However, neither author is explicit about adaptations required, nor how barriers can be overcome.

NICE recommends that everyone with the diagnosis of schizophrenia who experiences ongoing symptoms should receive individual CBT of at least 16 sessions (NICE, 2009). This is based on the existing evidence from trials which deliver CBT to people who are not only willing to receive therapy but also to complete the numerous measures involved in clinical trials. People receiving assertive outreach are likely to be at best ambivalent about therapy, require a much longer period of initial engagement and perhaps a different approach to therapy itself. This chapter aims to describe some of the adaptations which may be required.

A range of Cognitive Behavioural Therapies

As other chapters in this book suggest, a range of psychological skills are required within Assertive Outreach Teams. Even within a CBT framework, a wide range of skills are relevant. In my own work I have found the following to be useful:

- general CBT skills (in particular for psychosis, depression and anxiety)
- strengths-based approaches
- Motivational Interviewing
- schema-based CBT skills (in particular for working with interpersonal difficulties)
- family work, which could include systemic therapy.

The last is the subject of a chapter in its own right, so this chapter will focus on adaptations of the first four. There are of course other approaches which may also be occasionally useful. For example, a small number of people may wish to engage in an intensive therapy such as Cognitive Remediation Therapy (Cupitt *et al.*, 2004; Wykes and Reeder, 2005).

A unique setting

The clinical trials on which the evidence for CBT is based have generally been conducted with a motivated group of participants who agree to or seek referral, in a clinic or hospital setting and using a therapy protocol which follows a structured format. In assertive outreach we see people who are by definition difficult to engage in collaborative relationships, need to be visited on an outreach basis and frequently dislike formal interventions, structured interviews and paper tasks, all of which are commonly considered part of CBT. This might make CBT seem like a formidable task. However, there are also many factors favouring a CBT approach in assertive outreach. For example, there are plenty of opportunities for in-vivo work. Seeing people in their own environments mean that we can often literally see the extent of their difficulties and work directly with the situation. Generalisation is much less of a problem than in clinic-based CBT.

Example:

I visited Derek for a regular weekly session of CBT. However, his benefit money had not arrived as expected and he had nothing to eat. Responding to this took priority and we went together to the local benefit office to request an immediate payment. Derek had previously spoken about difficulties with anger, and this became apparent as he confronted staff with such aggression that they were likely to refuse to serve him. I was able to calm Derek, discuss what had occurred and immediately begin some anger management training in vivo.

In addition, when a CBT therapist is working as part of a whole team, the assessment process is enriched by the contributions of other team members who may have very different professional or personal perspectives. Team colleagues can also be drawn into the therapeutic process, creating opportunities for multi-faceted interventions. To some degree this can take the place of what would be called 'homework' in conventional CBT.

Perhaps the most important role of the team is in maintaining engagement and overcoming obstacles. People using assertive outreach services often have personal histories of rejection and abandonment by significant others, frequently combined with low self-esteem. The powerful emotions provoked by the intensity of a therapeutic relationship can make engagement falter at a very early stage. However, because in Assertive Outreach Teams people generally have relationships with a number of different staff, their engagement with the team can be maintained through periods when CBT sessions are impossible (see chapter two). What is more, other team members can often find out what has triggered the person to disengage from therapy, address the difficulty and support them to re-engage (Cupitt, 1999). In most other settings the person would be lost to follow-up and their assumptions about others confirmed yet again.

To make the most of the advantages team working offers in assertive outreach, and to allow as many people as possible to receive CBT, it needs to be fully integrated into team practice. In an ideal team all members will have some knowledge of the principles of CBT and be able to use a variety of simple techniques. However, there may be only one or two staff qualified as CBT therapists.

Integrating CBT techniques into assertive outreach

The Mental Health Policy Implementation Guide (Department of Health, 2001) lists a wide range of team functions to which all staff contribute. These do not necessarily imply a CBT approach, but all can be enhanced by using CBT principles and techniques. For example:

- assessment
- problem solving

- activities (i.e. the B of CBT)
- co-morbidity: substance misuse, common mental health problems
- social systems: maintaining and expanding social networks
- relapse prevention: individualised, shared plans
- advocacy and assertiveness
- care planning.

For such integration to be effective, training and supervision are important for all staff. This may occur on a number of levels, supporting the interests and abilities of individuals.

- Some staff have had no contact with CBT and need access to training in basic CBT skills.
- Some staff are keen to use CBT skills or techniques learnt on short courses. They need supervision to apply these skills effectively.
- Some staff have had formal CBT training and need ongoing supervision of therapy work. Such staff are normally employed as CBT therapists, counselling or clinical psychologists.

Managers need to be aware that formal training in CBT requires some time working with people whose difficulties are not complex in order to develop basic skills. This can mean that staff in Assertive Outreach Teams have to take training cases from other teams, before they can begin to work therapeutically with the team's own clients.

Everyday CBT skills

Staff who are trained to use specific CBT techniques or trained to deliver therapy will find many everyday opportunities for practice within an Assertive Outreach Team. Almost any sources of distress in a person's life could potentially become treatment targets for CBT. As a person raises issues of distress, it is possible to begin to take a CBT approach, for example by asking for the thoughts, feelings and behaviours associated with the problem. Someone who has developed CBT skills can then introduce specific strategies for coping such as:

- relaxation for anxiety
- coping strategies for voice hearing
- activity scheduling for depression
- sleep hygiene for insomnia.

The use of such CBT skills-based interventions can be extremely helpful in introducing a psychological approach to distress. However, it is important not to underestimate the degree to which such approaches can surprise people who have not encountered them before.

Example:
Tanya had been an inpatient on an acute ward for many months, receiving many pharmacological treatments. She was hearing voices telling her to harm herself and frequently acting on these by cutting her arms. Despite trying a range of medications, her voices and self-harm continued. When I visited and began to talk with her about psychological strategies she could use to cope with her distressing voices, she told me that such strategies would not work as her voices were caused by a chemical imbalance in her brain. When I suggested that we find out by giving them a try anyway, she threatened to report me to the ward doctors. She refused to see me the following week.

Such skills-based CBT can of course be delivered by staff who have attended short training courses on specific techniques. However, there are advantages in delivering them as a therapist. For this reason many assertive outreach psychologists like to spend a proportion of their clinical time participating in the generic work of the team, for example by doing some of the regular weekly visits to people not currently identified as in need of CBT. This kind of visit will very often provide opportunities to introduce psychological perspectives and perhaps begin a skills-based intervention which can later become the basis for an episode of therapy. When working on such a generic basis, a psychologist may be asked to help with a variety of tasks, including delivery of medication. Clearly it is important that association with other modalities of treatment does not limit a psychologist's ability to take a psychological approach. Whether or not delivering medication creates a problem will depend on many factors and it makes sense to decide on an individual basis. In some cases delivering medication may be interpreted as privileging pharmacological solutions to distress; in other cases it can helpfully open up the issue for discussion.

Example:
I visited Ben as part of a team strategy to offer him daily support through a period of distress. I had been asked to deliver some new medication recently prescribed. When I arrived I placed the medication on the table in front of us saying, 'Dr X asked me to give you this'. As the conversation developed, Ben expressed his ambivalence about the medication and we explored many different ways to understand what was happening to him. Rather than limit this exploration, delivering the medication appeared to have opened up the discussion.

Going further

Sometimes a skills-based approach does not work. For example, it may be that activity scheduling cannot raise someone's low mood because paranoid thoughts and feelings prevent them from doing the very activities that would help. A thorough initial assessment would have revealed this, but very often this has not been possible. In my experience the majority of people receiving assertive outreach services reveal the extent of their difficulties only gradually, and are especially sensitive to reactions of staff.

However, an initial attempt to use a simple skills-based approach can build engagement even if it is not successful in addressing the target problem. The attempt acknowledges the person's difficulties at the level to which they have shared them and explicitly seeks ways to address them. This alone can allow the conversation to broaden out to explore other related areas of difficulty. Such a step-wise approach to CBT does not follow the treatment manuals, which generally suggest one should move logically from a full assessment to formulation and intervention. Rather, it allows the client to remain in control of the process, deciding how much to reveal to the therapist at any one time. For this to be successful the therapist needs to be flexible in their approach, and able to adapt interventions in the light of new material at any stage. This process of adaptation can be made collaborative, with the therapist thinking aloud with the person about how to review their approach each time significant new information is aired. It normally means that the formulation remains either very tentative, or single-problem-focused in the early stages of therapy. Indeed, it may be that an overall case formulation cannot be developed until the end of the episode of therapy, or even in some cases at the end of multiple episodes of therapy.

Example:
Robert spoke to the team of a terrifying sound he was hearing on waking each morning. He identified this as the sound of the nuclear siren. He responded by remaining in bed for most of the morning.

The initial approach was to look for ways to enable Robert to feel more in control of the experience. Since the noise occurred every morning and yet nuclear war had not occurred, Robert was open to exploring ways of changing its meaning. He was able to identify the sound as the first note of a favourite piece of music, and so I suggested he use it to trigger this tune in his mind, thereby evoking pleasant feelings. Robert tried this and said it didn't work. However, he then began to talk about how he was feeling depressed and felt his life was over. These feelings were worst in the mornings. It was then possible to formulate a relationship between his interpretation of the sound and his low mood. This led to a much longer piece of therapeutic work which sought to reconnect him to sources of meaning in his life.

Providing Cognitive Behaviour Therapy

If an initial piece of skills-based CBT has been provided by another member of the team, the process of introducing a therapist can take a little longer. It is often helpful to hold joint sessions, or to arrange for the therapist to meet with the person in very informal settings in the early stages. Inevitably the therapist's personal qualities are going to have more influence on the engagement process than would normally be expected. Most psychologists in this situation find themselves revealing more about themselves than they have been trained to do. Many would also argue that when working with people whose lives are socially impoverished it is unethical not to offer a real sense of relationship. Perkins and Dilks (1992: 15) suggest that 'some self-disclosure, real two-way interaction and sharing, is essential in forming an effective relationship with someone who has few, if any, other close relationships'. Finding common interests or experiences can create very valuable opportunities, not only for engagement, but also as a means to begin the process of assessment. When working like this it is vital that ethical issues and professional boundaries are explored regularly in supervision (see chapter ten).

Example:
Alex was a very isolated and lonely young woman, who described intense anxiety and panic attacks in social situations. She found it difficult to meet the team psychologist and was reluctant to talk about herself, always preferring to redirect the topic of conversation to the subject of others. She spent a lot of time watching TV and was very involved in a current series of Big Brother. The psychologist shared this interest and they talked extensively about the different people on the show. By exploring the way Alex felt about these people and their problems, the psychologist was able to build up a detailed picture of Alex's own concerns. Over time, as Alex began to trust the psychologist, it became possible for her to talk more directly about her own difficulties.

When making the transition from a skills-based approach to an episode of therapy, it is also important to consider the location of meetings. Although it is a general principle of assertive outreach that contacts should occur on the client's own territory, most commonly their home, this is not always the best place for therapy. For some people there is no doubt it is ideal, particularly if they find going out difficult and/or mental health centres unpleasant. However, others have little or no privacy at home and certainly not a room in which they can talk uninterrupted for an hour. Home may be associated with violence or intimidation either in the past or present, which makes it a difficult place to explore feelings about those very experiences. I have found that very often someone will identify these issues themselves, saying, 'I would rather come to you'. However, one should not assume that the environment of a mental health centre is ideal either. Other options need to be explored and a mutual agreement negotiated. This is often the first task on which therapist and client need to collaborate and can be important in setting the tone of the therapy.

Another consideration in negotiating a venue for CBT sessions is possible risk to the therapist. All Assertive Outreach Teams have clients whom they only visit in pairs, or who are never visited by women alone for safety reasons. It is possible to conduct CBT on home visits accompanied by another member of the team, but unless the other team member happens to have a background in CBT themselves, this can lead to less focused sessions. It is often preferable to find a venue where a one-to-one meeting is safe. This may be the local mental health centre, but could also be a number of other community venues provided they meet the basic requirements of safety, privacy and accessibility. On this basis I have conducted CBT sessions in cafés, pubs and parks. It is generally best to choose either unpopular places or unpopular times to ensure one is not interrupted. A fast food outlet may be almost completely empty mid-morning, but very busy over lunchtime.

In keeping with the informality of the settings, CBT sessions may be accompanied by cups of tea or even meals. Most Assertive Outreach Teams have a fund which can be used to pay for such courtesies. Sharing food and drink with someone can be an important way to establish engagement and the process of negotiating the making or paying for it can provide an opportunity to reinforce the collaborative nature of the exercise – for example, by agreeing to alternate who pays for coffee each week.

In contrast to the flexibility of setting, it does appear important for people to keep to a regular day and time to meet. Many people receiving assertive outreach have felt let down by services in the past and fears about this can present as a major obstacle to engagement in therapy. Arranging a regular time and planning sessions in blocks of perhaps six or eight at a time can help to convey the therapist's commitment to the process. The therapist needs to be prepared to keep to such arrangements, for example by turning up as agreed even during periods when it seems unlikely that the other person will attend. When combined with the flexibility to share in ordinary human activities such as eating and drinking, the therapist is thus able to form a very genuine but safe therapeutic relationship. When appropriate, this kind of arrangement can be extended beyond an episode of therapy to create occasional opportunities to meet in order to maintain or boost progress.

When it is possible to achieve all the above and negotiate target problems for CBT, an episode of therapy provided by an Assertive Outreach Team may then be able to follow one of the established approaches. In the case of psychosis this might take six to nine months (e.g. Fowler, Garety and Kuipers, 1995; Chadwick, Birchwood and Trower, 1996; Morrison, 2001; Gumley and Schwannauer, 2006). However, some people will require a longer engagement period, extending the period to more like 12 months. It may also prove very difficult to agree therapy goals which take psychotic experiences as the focus. A more flexible approach may be required, which perhaps targets depressed mood or anxiety initially, just touching on psychotic experiences or leaving them out entirely. The degree of adaptation needed will vary and needs to be carefully considered by the therapist in order to maximise the therapeutic gain for the client.

Functional goals in CBT

CBT for psychosis has sometimes been criticised for over-focusing on symptom reduction, and certainly this has been a preoccupation of clinical trials (Birchwood and Trower, 2006). Studies such as Sensky *et al.* (2000), which is generally cited as evidence of the effectiveness of CBT, also demonstrate that supportive counselling is generally very beneficial to people with a diagnosis of schizophrenia. In response to this, Penn *et al.* (2004) have asked whether it is possible to harness some of the most effective aspects of supportive therapy to improve outcomes in CBT. Interestingly, under the heading of supportive therapy he includes Assertive Community Treatment, which he describes as an example of a psychosocial approach to providing people with support in daily living. His analysis implies that CBT delivered within an assertive outreach setting may in fact be more effective than a stand-alone CBT intervention.

Penn *et al.* (2004) go on to describe what they call Functional CBT (FCBT). In this approach symptom-focused CBT techniques are used in the context of working on functional goals. The early sessions focus on identifying functional goals such as working, education or social activities which serve to decrease stress, increase feelings of productivity and promote social connectedness. The ways in which psychotic symptoms interfere with these goals is also explored. These symptoms are then treated using CBT in the usual ways, based on an individualised case formulation. The idea of embedding CBT within a framework of life goals is also described by Mills *et al.* (2004) in the context of a recovery-orientated approach to assertive outreach.

In many ways FCBT is simply good CBT, but its explicit emphasis on people's life aspirations may be especially helpful for people receiving assertive outreach services. Perhaps the person does not wish to focus on their psychotic experience, or does not see past psychotic episodes as relevant to their future. Whenever the initial barrier to engagement rests in identifying a meaningful goal for therapy, this kind of approach is likely to be more successful than purely symptom-focused CBT.

Example:

Ahmed is a British Muslim who did well at school and became the first member of his family to go to university. He describes enjoying the freedom of life away from home and starting to use both alcohol and drugs heavily. In his final year, under the pressure of exams, he became psychotic and was admitted to hospital. He was able to retake his final year and he got his degree. After graduation he got a good job, but soon became unwell again. Following his second breakdown, he returned to live with his parents and became very anxious and fearful. He was initially very reluctant to discuss what had happened to him, but happy to talk of the possibility of returning to work. By focusing on this goal it was possible to discuss how his anxieties had become a barrier to work and begin therapy.

Sometimes a person's most pressing functional goal is disengagement with services. It is also not uncommon for people to identify a specific goal, such as coming off medication or getting discharged from a section of the Mental Health Act. This can present an interesting starting point for CBT, and I have found myself teaching people assertiveness skills to use when negotiating with other team members, in particular psychiatrists. When done in the context of a team approach and using a shared formulation, this can be very helpful and creates the possibility of improved engagement with the team. However, care needs to be taken to ensure that the work of the team does not fragment into different strands, working in opposition to each other. It is also important that such work creates genuine opportunities for people to play a more active role in their treatment and does not become tokenistic.

Occasionally someone identifies a functional goal which is linked to very unusual beliefs, for example the goal of finding a local church where the priest can cure schizophrenia. It would be a mistake to ignore such goals, but attempts to pursue them need to take place alongside other work that seeks to develop an alternative version of the goal which has more hope of success. It is much easier for all of us to let go of unhelpful beliefs if we have a position to move to which offers hope. Research by Phillips *et al.* (2007) indicates that people use a wide range of causal explanations for psychosis, including, in rank order: 'out of the ordinary factors' (psychotic phenomena); nerves; brain problems; life events; practical problems; childhood experience; personal factors; relationship difficulties; physical factors; hormonal factors; genetic factors; deserving of problems. These are generally not mutually exclusive and exploring a range of causal explanations can be the best way to begin CBT for psychosis for some people.

Example:
Clinton said he wanted to find a priest to cure his schizophrenia. He believed that his problems stemmed from a spiritual cause and therefore only priests could perform the healing necessary. Wishing to acknowledge the spiritual dimension of his experience, I helped him to contact the hospital chaplain. At the same time we discussed how his aversive childhood experiences had affected him and made him wish for a world in which magical powers were everyday phenomena.

Motivational approaches

There are occasions when functional goals can be identified, but it may be difficult for someone to find the motivation to work towards them. Many people have experienced repeated knockbacks in life and cannot easily find the energy to try again to achieve an old ambition. In this scenario it is helpful to draw on strategies from motivational interviewing, aimed at enabling people to move from pre-contemplation to contemplation of change (Prochaska and DiClemente, 1982; DiClemente and Velasquez, 2002).

In motivational interviewing ambivalence is viewed as a potential source of motivation and not as an obstacle (Miller and Rollnick, 2002). It is important to elicit and explore both sides of the ambivalence in a non-critical, non-focused and open way. The most common mistake is for staff to simply focus on, and attempt to reinforce, the person's reasons for change. If the person is genuinely ambivalent this can inadvertently encourage them to express the other side of the ambivalence, namely the reasons to remain exactly as they are. This in turn can trigger staff to attempt more vigorously to persuade the person to change. Inadvertently, staff have then actually reinforced the status quo and reduced motivation for change.

Instead, what is required is a light touch which informs rather than seeks to persuade, one that explores all angles. It is important to listen carefully to the client's perspective and draw out the implications of their position. For example, at times it may be helpful to agree that it is easier to let things stay as they are, in order to provoke the person to voice a wish for change that expresses the other side of their ambivalence. This is often referred to as 'de-emphasising the message' and can be more powerful than any attempts to persuade.

Motivational interviewing was first developed for work with people with alcohol problems, but has since been applied to a wide range of other areas of behaviour change such as smoking, HIV, weight control and exercise. It has been used in mental health to encourage adherence to treatment (Kemp *et al.*, 1998), but can be extended to support CBT for psychosis and other conditions. Baker and Hambridge (2002) describe how it may be used to support someone struggling to engage in an exposure-based treatment for anxiety, or to begin the process of challenging delusional material.

Strengths-based approaches

It can be difficult to begin conventional CBT because of the tendency for CBT to take a problems-based approach. Indeed, in many CBT manuals the very first task is to draw up a problem list (e.g. Hawton, 1989). Often people receiving assertive outreach have been viewed by services as little more than lists of problems for a long time and reject this approach. Others may have a sealing-over recovery style to psychosis which means that they do not wish to engage in any form of therapy that requires them to explore psychotic experience (Drayton *et al.*, 1998). In both these scenarios a strengths-based approach can be helpful.

Ryan and Morgan (2004) describe in detail what a strengths-based approach might entail within an assertive outreach setting. They advocate using a strengths model as an 'organizing philosophical framework for mental health practitioners and for their organizations'. They describe a strengths-based care planning process as opposed to a problem-based one, in which there is a focus on identifying the person's wants and the resources available to them. However, whereas Functional CBT would then use this as a platform from which to explore how symptoms interfere with goals, it is possible to proceed with a strengths-based CBT approach without making reference to any symptoms as such. Thus the therapy seeks to build on someone's strengths using resources around them as a means to undermine their difficulties, rather than address the difficulties directly.

Example:
Sajit had a long history of psychosis including insulting voices which never went away. He led an isolated life, actively avoiding the company of others. He never spoke directly about any of his difficulties, but appeared to have very low self-esteem. An obvious starting point would be to help Sajit find strategies to cope with the voices, but he refused to discuss them. Taking a strengths approach to promote engagement, the psychologist spent several weeks discussing Sajit's strengths and abilities. He identified an interest in and ability at football, which led to them jointly attending a weekly football session. This provided low-intensity social contact for Sajit and a much needed experience of success. He was subsequently able to acknowledge that when he played football the frequency and intensity of the voices reduced. Thus the psychologist had in fact taught Sajit two well-recognised coping strategies for voices, but without ever discussing voices directly.

The use of a strengths-based approach is very common in Assertive Outreach Teams, with a general aim of increased engagement and wellbeing. However, as the above example illustrates, it can also be used specifically to address distressing symptoms within an overall CBT formulation. For someone who has a sealing-over recovery style, this may be the only CBT approach with which someone will want to engage (Startup *et al.*, 2006).

Schema-focused approaches

Although most people receiving assertive outreach services have a primary diagnosis of a psychotic disorder, most will also have profound emotional and interpersonal difficulties as well. Their difficulties in maintaining engagement with mental health services often reflect much broader difficulties with relationships and many people are as isolated from family and friends as they are from services (Lukeman, 2003). Such emotional and interpersonal difficulties can be formulated in terms of cognitive schema, and such a formulation can be helpful as a guide to the engagement process. In time it may also lead to an episode of schema-focused cognitive therapy.

Most of the therapy literature referring to cognitive schema relates to personality disorders and in particular borderline personality (e.g. Beck *et al.*,

1990; Layden *et al.*, 1993; Linehan, 1993; Young, 1990). Whilst people using assertive outreach services are unlikely to have a primary diagnosis of personality disorder, many would meet the diagnostic criteria if they were applied. Ranger *et al.* (2004) found that 92 per cent of the users of their inner city Assertive Outreach Team met diagnostic criteria for personality disorder. Nevertheless, it may not be helpful for the team to use the language of personality disorder since it can be experienced as pejorative and alienating. However, the literature is helpful in understanding some of the emotional and interpersonal difficulties that people are experiencing. These can be the most significant barrier to engagement for some people.

Leahy (2001) describes a model of resistance to cognitive therapy which includes a strong emphasis on schema level factors. He points out the deep need we all have to remain consistent with the past, including the way we have come to view ourselves, for example as victims, moral champions or helpless individuals. These factors may make change appear impossible and if the therapist is not careful their attempts to challenge dysfunctional beliefs will actually be experienced as an assault on the person's core values. In the same way staff in assertive outreach need to be aware that their messages of hope and optimism may at times provoke resistance rather than ameliorate it.

For some people there is an obvious self schema which relates to difficulties with engagement. Perhaps the most common would be a sense of personal worthlessness which makes it difficult to accept help, particularly if it is offered with genuine kindness. Anyone who has grown up in an abusive or invalidating environment is likely to have developed a self schema of worthlessness. It may also be accompanied by an interpersonal schema of mistrust, expressed as a view that other people are basically hostile. When schema such as these make engagement difficult, therapy is also a challenge. Leahy (2001) has described this as 'schema resistance' within cognitive therapy.

Example:
Peter grew up in a large family with parents who were often in conflict. He didn't do well at school, was bullied and left without qualifications at 15. At the age of 17 he had his first psychotic breakdown and was admitted to hospital. There is very little information about his psychotic experiences as he rarely confided in anyone. He remains socially isolated. His contact with the team is erratic and he often seems to deliberately avoid staff. He does not even want help to claim social security benefits. One possibility is that he has come to believe he is worthless and does not deserve help. There is a danger that the team's overt efforts to help are actually consolidating his view that he is beyond help.

Often a more complex formulation is required which includes attention to the interactions between staff and service users. Both parties will hold core cognitive schema and at times the interactions between them will provide important information about how the person has become disengaged from services. Attention to interpersonal process in this way has increasingly become a part of cognitive therapy, in particular following the influential book by Safran and Segal (1990). Leahy (2001) similarly does not view cognitive therapy as a process of simply following a manual of procedures, but of a deeply human relationship in which the therapist will inevitably experience their own personal reactions to the client. Like Safran and Segal (1990), he encourages cognitive therapists to make use of this material, rather than dismiss it merely out of a wish to create distance from other therapeutic models such as psychoanalysis.

In assertive outreach not only do we have our own responses to service users as a valuable source of information but the whole team's reactions, which can be digested in team meetings and supervision. Attention to these interpersonal processes can enrich an individual psychological formulation and provide important mechanisms to ensure that the team works as a consistent whole to promote engagement (see chapter two).

There is no doubt that the clients of Assertive Outreach Teams can provoke very strong reactions in staff. There are perhaps three principal traps that staff can fall into, related to interpersonal schema. Firstly, staff can find themselves involved in an over-identification with the person they are seeking to help. Clearly some identification is necessary for empathy and engagement to occur. However, since many health-care workers have themselves experienced some kind of childhood abuse, this may leave staff with their own schemas of worthlessness or mistrust which can easily become activated by hearing of the experiences of the person they are trying to help. The result can be intense emotion which is not necessarily helpful to the engagement process, or either person's mental health.

A second common interpersonal trap occurs when staff find themselves re-enacting the role of the other in the person's past. For example, a staff member might find themselves tremendously irritated by and angry with the helplessness of someone who has a history of physical abuse. They may have linked into the person's interpersonal schema and taken the role of abuser, which in turn reinforces the person's role as abused and helpless. Without reflection and careful attention to the interpersonal processes, the roles reinforce each other and any genuine engagement is quickly lost.

Example:
Charlotte had experienced physical abuse from both parents as a child, and as a young adult began to isolate herself from others. By the time she was referred to the team she was living as a hermit, never leaving her flat and seeing no one. It took many months to establish contact, but when this was achieved several staff spoke about how irritated and angry they felt during visits. It appeared that her extremely avoidant interpersonal style had triggered the same response in others that it had initially developed to avoid. The team were able to agree that only staff who

found her likeable should visit to avoid confirming her interpersonal schema and disrupting the initial engagement.

The third possibility is that the staff member has strong core schema themselves and are not able to prevent these impacting on the people they try to help. This is less common, but when it does occur it is arguably the most damaging interpersonal scenario. Staff with strongly dysfunctional interpersonal schema can be very challenging to manage within assertive outreach and are probably best helped to look for work in less emotionally demanding settings.

Conflictual schema

Many people receiving assertive outreach are not wholly resistant to services, but in fact ambivalent. Lukeman (2003) interviewed nine service users who had become well engaged with Assertive Outreach Teams, about the process of their engagement. She found that the beginning of a new relationship with the team created a dilemma since the service was both imposed but also offered aspects of collaboration. As the relationship developed, and the person began to depend on the service, another dilemma was created since within this dependence there were also aspects of empowerment. Lukeman found that this latter dilemma never resolved, but remained active and ongoing. This dilemma may also be familiar to staff who are concerned about the degree to which the service encourages dependence versus independence. To some extent perhaps this dilemma is always a part of someone's contact with any part of mental health services, but for people receiving assertive outreach services it appears to be particularly acute. The relationship is not an easy one, and at times staff may inadvertently trigger a period of disengagement in their enthusiasm to provide help.

> **Example:**
> Francis had experienced several episodes of psychosis but believed that the most recent would definitely be his last. He felt things had started to go his way for once and he wanted to get on with his life without services. His confidence was not shared by the team, who were anxious to offer as much continued support as possible. However, Francis found the team's efforts intrusive and disappeared. Later the team discovered that he had left the country to stay with relatives abroad. On reflection the team wondered if they might have achieved more by explicitly acknowledging Francis' wish for independence and agreeing a structured reduction in service which allowed some ongoing contact.

Ruptures in engagement are generally experienced in terms of either withdrawal or confrontation. Dramatic withdrawal, as in the above example, is quite rare. What is perhaps more likely is a change in the quality of the relationship, which becomes less confiding. When a team identifies that this has occurred, a consideration in terms of interacting conflictual schemas can be very helpful to address the difficulty and bring about re-engagement. Likewise, if the rupture is characterised by confrontation, there is also likely to be a schema-level conflict that can be identified, although if the confrontation is dramatic, the team may not immediately be able to address the interpersonal issues. Initially the most important task is for the team to reflect and develop an interpersonal formulation. This generally requires some protected time such as a reflective practice group or team supervision session, facilitated by a psychological therapist. Once an understanding has been reached, the use of whole team working, at times drawing on the help of staff from other teams, for example at inpatient facilities, can be helpful in trying to re-establish engagement.

For people whose early relationships have been very abusive, there may be much greater difficulties. The literature on borderline personality (e.g. Layden *et al.*, 1993; Young, 1990) describes a characteristic set of seven schema: dependence, lack of individuation, emotional deprivation, abandonment, mistrust, unlovability and incompetence. These schemas often act in incongruent or antagonistic ways producing severe internal conflict. For example, it is not unusual for someone to have both a schema of dependence and of mistrust. This might result in help-seeking behaviours alongside rejections of services.

> **Example:**
> Karen describes her early life as very difficult. She was very close to her mother, but they both lived in fear of her father, who was physically violent. Sometimes they would try to flee the home, but in the end always returned. As an adult Karen developed psychosis and when in acute distress would make many calls to emergency services desperate for help, whilst at the same time refuse contact with the Assertive Outreach Team. Staff in the team felt very frustrated by their inability to support Karen when she seemed to need it most. One way to understand her behaviour was that she had both dependence and mistrust schema.

There is the possibility of a whole team adopting a CBT approach to interpersonal difficulties by taking up specific training, for example by undertaking whole team training in Dialectical Behaviour Therapy (DBT; Linehan, 1993). There are a few examples of Assertive Outreach Teams which have integrated DBT into their model specifically to meet the needs of people diagnosed with borderline personality, for example the Queensway ACT team (Basevitz and Aubry, 2002). There are also a few teams in the UK who have used schema-focused CBT approaches (e.g. Cupitt, 1999).

Barriers to therapy

Although the majority of people receiving assertive outreach can be offered CBT in some form which is both acceptable and beneficial, there remain barriers for others. It is not uncommon to meet people who appear to value specific CBT skills when introduced in the context of more general support, but do not welcome a shift towards more structured or formal sessions. A dislike of formal interventions may relate to a number of factors, not least prior experiences of CBT.

Davies (2008) interviewed people who had used assertive outreach services and asked about experiences of talking therapies, in particular CBT. She found that about a third of participants wanted access to formal talking therapies, but two-thirds expressed a preference for more informal emotional support, in which present difficulties were listened to and understood in the context of an ongoing relationship with outreach staff. It is therefore important not to try to formalise CBT when more informal support is preferred. However, a decision not to attempt individual CBT does not mean that a Team Case Formulation cannot be helpful in enhancing the quality of emotional support offered by the team (see chapter four).

There are times when someone experiences such extreme personal disorganisation and cognitive problems accompanying psychosis that it is very difficult to use CBT approaches. For example, severe thought disorder may make ordinary conversation almost completely unintelligible. However, emotional themes are still often apparent and reflection on these may be helpful in seeking to resolve communication. A great deal of patience is required in the early stages and often a greater emphasis on using written materials and behavioural approaches.

Example:
Robert had a very long admission with a psychosis triggered by an assault. His thinking was so disordered that it was impossible to follow his conversation, but his fear of the outside world was tangible. I spent many weeks listening to him talk about his fears without understanding anything he said, but still able to reflect back to him an understanding of his terror. Slowly his conversation became more intelligible and we were able to discuss a graded approach to re-engaging with the outside world which allowed him to test out his fears.

When thought disorder or impairments to memory and concentration make it difficult to maintain continuity from one session to another, memory aids can be used such as written summaries, diagrams and notebooks.

Breadth and depth of therapy

Most of the people who receive assertive outreach have complex and long-standing mental health difficulties. It is therefore likely that they will require more than one episode of CBT for psychosis to achieve significant progress. At the end of each episode of therapy, significant problems are likely to remain and could become the focus of subsequent therapy. I have generally found that working over multiple periods of six to 12 months is helpful, rather than meeting with someone continuously for years. This allows CBT to be offered to more people on the team's caseload and also explicitly acknowledges that there are times when psychological change is possible and times when it is not. For example, it may be that the costs of change are so great that someone does not wish to tackle the difficulties in their family relationships whilst they are living at home. However, an admission to hospital may create the opportunity to review this and ask again whether there could be benefits from trying to change long-established patterns of communication. Such careful negotiations become easier over time as greater trust develops and the interrelationships between the issues in someone's life become more apparent.

It can at first be very difficult to judge when to offer CBT and how much psychological change is likely to be possible in the often very difficult circumstances in which people live. Such judgements are necessarily very individual and often real clarity about timing only emerges with hindsight, having developed an overall psychological formulation. For some people an acute crisis is the very best time to intervene, when factors which normally seem insurmountable suddenly shift. For others only the quieter and calmer periods of life offer the opportunity for reflection and insight. In trying to determine the best timing for an intervention, the most important principle is collaboration, with the therapist sharing their questions and dilemmas with the client as much as possible so that a joint decision about how to proceed can be reached.

There are other benefits to repeated episodes of therapy, such as the chance to review and refine strategies developed in previous episodes. Some people specially request regular follow-up sessions to support a change instigated during a previous episode of therapy. At the end of therapy I explicitly talk about the possibility of further sessions in the future, encouraging the person themselves to initiate this when they feel ready. Thus over time the clients themselves increasingly take responsibility for the timing of CBT interventions.

Conclusions

CBT has become not only a valuable but an essential part of assertive outreach in the UK. It can be integrated into a team approach and provided in a step-wise fashion that acknowledges the degree of engagement present at any particular point in time. It is unlikely to be a once only intervention due to the complex and long-standing nature of people's difficulties. For some it will become a recurrent aspect of their care.

It seems reasonable to assume that CBT can be at least as effective when provided within assertive outreach settings as in conventional clinics. What is more, since assertive outreach is in itself a form of psychosocial intervention, one could imagine that there might be a synchrony leading to enhanced effectiveness of both. However, a word of caution is needed here.

The effectiveness of CBT is based on clinical trials, each of which has clear exclusion criteria. Assertive outreach by definition provides a service to many people who have been excluded from other kinds of services, most notably by their difficulty in maintaining consistent contact. This presents the first challenge, and this chapter has sought to outline some of the ways people can be engaged in CBT who might more normally be excluded from receiving such services. However, once engaged, there is a further challenge to effectiveness. In all clinical trials and in routine clinical services, there is a dropout rate, which may be 30–50 per cent of the initial referrals. In assertive outreach, because of active engagement work, the dropout rate is virtually nil. Thus a CBT therapist in assertive outreach cannot be expected to replicate the results of clinical trials, and may not even be able to produce the same treatment effects as routine services. Any outcome data collected by services must bear this in mind. Nevertheless, this does not mean that there isn't a genuine synchrony between the two models, such that CBT enriches the practice of assertive outreach and assertive outreach allows people to receive CBT who would normally be excluded from psychological therapy services.

References

Baker, A. and Hambridge, J. (2002) 'Motivational interviewing: enhancing engagement in treatment for mental health problems', *Behaviour Change*, 19: 138–145.

Basevitz, P. and Aubry, T. (2002) *Providing Services to Individuals with Borderline Personality Disorder in the Context of ACT: research base and recommendations.* Ottawa: Centre for Research on Community Services, Faculty of Social Sciences, University of Ottawa.

Beck, A.T., Freeman, A. and Associates (1990) *Cognitive Therapy of Personality Disorders*, New York: Guilford Press.

Birchwood, M. and Trower, P. (2006) 'The future of cognitive-behavioural therapy for psychosis: not a quasi-neuroleptic', *British Journal of Psychiatry*, 188: 107–108.

Chadwick, P., Birchwood, M. and Trower, P. (1996) *Cognitive Therapy for Delusions, Voices and Paranoia*, Chichester: Wiley and Sons Ltd.

Cupitt, C. (1999) 'Key factors in engaging with people with severe personality disorder', *Mental Health Care*, 2: 386–388.

Cupitt, C., Byrne, L. and Thompson, N. (2004) 'Delivering cognitive remediation therapy in a clinical setting', *Clinical Psychology*, 37: 10–14.

Davies, R. (2008) 'Effective involvement in mental health services: the role of assertive outreach and the voluntary sector', presentation to the Network of Psychologists in Assertive Outreach, Bristol University, May.

Department of Health (2001) *The Mental Health Policy Implementation Guide*, London: Department of Health.

DiClemente C.C. and Velasquez, M.M. (2002) 'Motivational interviewing and the stages of change', in W.R. Miller and S. Rollnick (eds) *Motivational Interviewing*, 2nd edn, New York: Guilford Publications, Inc.

Drayton, M., Birchwood, M. and Trower, P. (1998) 'Early attachment experience and recovery from psychosis', *British Journal of Clinical Psychology*, 37: 269–284

Drury, V., Birchwood, M., Cochrane, R. and Macmillan, F. (1996) 'Cognitive therapy and recovery from acute psychosis: a controlled trial. I. Impact on psychotic symptoms', *British Journal of Psychiatry*, 169: 593–601.

Fowler, D., Garety, P. and Kuipers, E. (1995) *Cognitive Behaviour Therapy for Psychosis: theory and practice*, Chichester: John Wiley and Sons.

Freeman, J. (2000) 'A cognitive behaviour therapy approach in an assertive outreach team', *Mental Health Practice*, 3: 12–15.

Gumley, A. and Schwannauer, M. (2006) *Staying Well After Psychosis: a cognitive interpersonal approach to recovery and relapse prevention*, Chichester: John Wiley and Sons.

Hawton, K. (1989) *Cognitive Behaviour Therapy for Psychiatric Problems: a practical guide*, Oxford: Oxford University Press.

Hemsley, D. and Murray, R. (2000) 'Commentary: psychological and social treatments for schizophrenia: not just old remedies in new bottles', *Schizophrenia Bulletin*, 26: 145–151.

Kemp, R., Kirov, G., Everitt, B., Hayward, P. and David, A. (1998) 'Randomised controlled trial of compliance therapy: 18-month follow up', *British Medical Journal*, 312: 345–349.

Layden, M.A., Newman, C.F., Freeman, A. and Byers Morse, S. (1993) *Cognitive Therapy of Borderline Personality Disorder*, Boston: Allyn and Bacon.

Leahy, R.L. (2001) *Overcoming Resistance in Cognitive Therapy*, New York: Guilford Press.

Lehman, A.F., Buchanan, R.W., Dickerson, F.B., Dixon, L.B., Goldberg, R., Green-Paden, L. and Kreyenbuhl, J. (2003) 'Evidence-based treatment for schizophrenia', *Psychiatric Clinics of North America*, 26: 939–954.

Linehan, M. (1993) *Cognitive-Behavioural Treatment of Borderline Personality Disorder*, New York: The Guilford Press.

Lukeman, R. (2003) 'Service users' experience of the process of being engaged by assertive outreach teams', unpublished thesis, Salomons, Canterbury Christ Church University.

Miller, W.R. and Rollnick, S. (2002) *Motivational Interviewing: preparing people to change addictive behaviours*, 2nd edn, New York: Guilford Press.

Mills, J., Grant, A., Mulhern, R. and Short, N. (2004) 'Working with people in assertive outreach', in A. Grant, J. Mills, R. Mulhern and N. Short, *Cognitive Behavioural Therapy in Mental Health Care*, London: Sage Publications.

National Institute for Clinical Excellence (2009) *Core interventions in the treatment and management of schizophrenia in primary and secondary care update*, London: NICE.

Penn, D.L., Mueser, K.T., Tarrier, N., Gloege, A., Cather, C., Serrano, D. and Otto, M.W. (2004) 'Supportive therapy for schizophrenia: possible mechanisms and implications for adjunctive psychosocial treatments', *Schizophrenia Bulletin*, 30: 101–112.

Perkins, R. and Dilks, S. (1992) 'Worlds apart: working with severely socially disabled people', *Journal of Mental Health*, 1: 3–17.

Phillips, C.M., Cooke, M.A., Cooke A. and Peters, E.R. (2007) 'Identity and cause of problems: the perceptions of patients with a diagnosis of schizophrenia', *Behavioural and Cognitive Psychotherapy*, 35: 237–240.

Prochaska, J.O. and DiClemente, C.C. (1982) 'Transtheoretical therapy: toward a more integrative model of change', *Psychotherapy: Theory Research and Practice*, 19: 276–288.

Ranger, M., Methuen, C., Rutter, D., Rao, B. and Tyrer, P. (2004) 'Prevalence of personality disorder in the case-load of an inner-city assertive outreach team', *Psychiatric Bulletin*, 28: 441–443.

Ryan, P. and Morgan, S. (2004) *Assertive Outreach: a strengths approach to policy and practice*, Edinburgh: Churchill Livingstone.

Safran, J.D. and Segal, Z.V. (1990) *Interpersonal Process in Cognitive Therapy*, New York: Basic Books.

Sensky, T., Turkington, D., Kingdon, D., Scott, J.L., Scott, J., Siddle, R., O'Carroll, M. and Barnes, T. (2000) 'A randomised controlled trial of cognitive-behavioural therapy for persistent symptoms in schizophrenia resistant to medication', *Archives of General Psychiatry*, 57: 165–172.

Startup, M., Wilding, N. and Startup, S. (2006) 'Patient treatment adherence in cognitive behaviour therapy for acute psychosis: the role of recovery style and working alliance', *Behavioural and Cognitive Psychotherapy*, 34: 191–199.

Wright, C. (2005) 'Assertive Outreach – what's really going on in England?', workshop presented at the annual conference of the National Forum for Assertive Outreach, Keele University, April.

Wykes, T. and Reeder, C. (2005) *Cognitive Remediation Therapy*, London: Routledge.

Young, J.E. (1990) *Cognitive Therapy for Personality Disorders: a schema-focused approach*, Sarasota, FL: Professional Resource Exchange.

9   Community psychology

Sara Meddings, Becky Shaw and Bob Diamond

Community psychology has developed as a response to the limitations of traditional approaches. It is not a specific therapy or technique nor a distinct model of working in mental health services. It draws upon theories and practices which recognise the relationship between disadvantage, discrimination and distress, seeking explanations beyond the individual. It recognises that the conditions that contribute towards distress are ecological and multi-faceted. In this chapter we consider community psychology approaches which we find useful in assertive outreach. We outline our understanding of community psychology by describing its values, how it is practised alongside those who use services, and the use of its principles in community and service development.

It is crucial that mental health services reach out to people so that they want to engage, rather than coercing them through compulsory treatment. There has been some confusion about the term 'assertive', which has sometimes been understood to mean aggressive outreach within a medical approach (Meddings and Cupitt, 2000). Community psychology is one way of supporting services to engage with people on their own terms. In Nottinghamshire and Sussex we have tried to establish assertive outreach services built on the values and practices of community psychology alongside recovery and strengths approaches. We believe that this works well because it enables constructive and empowering relationships to be developed with those very people whom mental health services find most difficult to reach. In order to do this we must first consider the contexts of mental distress.

Contexts of disadvantage and discrimination

> Mental health workers need to accept the implications of the research on inequalities and mental health, and refuse to provide care based on causal models which ignore the effects of abuse, discrimination and disadvantage.
> (Williams, 1999: 44)

Traditional mental health services, particularly psychiatry, are founded on concepts of illness, diagnosis and treatment. Psychiatry has primarily focused on mental illness as residing within the individual and treated it pharmaco-logically. Psychotherapy has similarly emphasised the focus of intervention on the individual. Explanations for distress tend to be sought from within the person through such concepts as dysfunctional behaviour, faulty cognitions or ego strengths. It is not unknown for psychiatric mental health services to fail people and, on occasion, attribute the blame for such failings to the people receiving care. Smail (2005: 7) suggests the private and public worlds have turned inside out and an illusion exists that we can simply reinvent ourselves through 'magical voluntarism'. Psychology has played its part in this process. This can lead to people feeling themselves responsible if they do not benefit from psychological interventions. Prilleltensky and Nelson (2002: 85) suggest that, 'In ignoring the larger social and political context, traditional approaches often unintentionally blame the victims of oppression for their oppression.'

The causal link between social factors, stresses and vulnerabilities, and the development of, and recovery from, mental health problems is well estab-lished (Cochrane, 1983; Williams, 1999; Orford, 1992; Zubin and Spring, 1977). Recent studies have shown that increased risk of developing psychosis is associated with increased levels of deprivation at birth and father's social class (Harrison *et al.*, 2001); higher perceived levels of social isolation (van Os *et al.*, 2000); migration (Cantor-Graae and Selton, 2005) and other childhood socio-economic indicators of social exclusion, including rented housing, parental unemployment and single parent households (Wicks *et al.*, 2005). Wicks *et al.* (2005) estimate that about 20 per cent of the risk of develop-ing psychosis could be attributable to adverse social conditions. Again, 69 per cent of women and 59 per cent of men with psychosis have been physically or sexually abused as children and over half as adults (Reed *et al.*, 2005).

Cromby and Harper (2009) argue that paranoia can be understood as co-constituted by social, relational, material and subjective factors. Paranoia makes sense in the context of experiences of living with job insecurity, relative deprivation or increased risks of violence. In order to understand endur-ing mental health difficulties, we need to consider social circumstances and contexts beyond the individual.

> Service users want a service that takes account of the whole range of attitudes to emotional distress or mental illness . . . We need to recognise that racism and sexism can drive you mad.
>
> (Read, 1996: 177)

The added stigma of serious mental health problems adds to disadvantage. People with mental health problems are more likely to be unemployed (Social Exclusion Unit, 2004). This may be due to disabilities, low self-confidence, the side effects of medication and fears about losing benefits, but also prejudice and discrimination, and the low expectations and support from professionals.

Such disadvantage may be especially significant for assertive outreach clients: an audit of two assertive outreach teams found only 5 per cent of clients were currently married, or in a civil partnership; 33 per cent had a close friend; 12 per cent were at college or in paid or voluntary work and no one was working more than half-time; all were on benefits (Meddings *et al.*, 2006). Women, people from black and minority ethnic groups, and lesbians and gay men may be additionally victimised within mental health services, including the sexual assault of inpatients (McFarlane, 1998; Read, 1996; Thomas, Bartlett and Mezey, 1995; Commission for Audit and Healthcare Inspection, 2007; Healthcare Commission, 2007).

Example:
Sayid, an assertive outreach client, experienced a number of traumas when younger and is now struggling to find a positive identity as a gay Muslim. His mental health deteriorated after witnessing a traumatic event in the Middle East. This was exacerbated when, following the London bombings, whilst he was in hospital other patients were paranoid about him, leading to racist abuse. His recovery was further hampered by stresses due to waiting and uncertainty over housing. He used the only power that he did have to rebel in ways which, in turn, abused women. He found a self-help group helpful because he was given the opportunity to use his voice and was listened to. It also allowed him to demonstrate that he was a caring man.

Mental health services tend to underestimate the significance of social and material contexts on wellbeing, preferring to understand distress as an internal state existing within the individual. If the origins of distress are considered to exist within the individual, it becomes easy to inadvertently link cause and responsibility together. If someone does not engage with services, it can be considered the individual's fault for lack of engagement. Similarly, with 'non-compliance'. People who choose not to take prescribed psychiatric medication may be considered non-cooperative, despite the fact that the general population frequently do not complete a full course of prescribed medication. Assertive outreach clients are especially likely to be stigmatised by labels such as 'difficult to engage', 'non-compliant', 'manipulative', 'self-defeating', or 'unmotivated'.

Values of community psychology

Community psychology advocates a broader view of distress:

> Community psychology aims to correct this individualistic bias by aiming always to consider people within the contexts of the social settings and systems of which they are parts or which influence them.
>
> (Orford, 1992: 6)

It turns the focal gaze away from limitations and faults within the individual and towards the potential for strengths and abilities that might assist a person to link up in any number of ways with their environment.

The salient characteristics of community psychology are:

- Working with communities as well as individuals: with groups that share common interests; building alliances with marginalised groups; recognising that peer support can be mutually beneficial and an effective means to change.
- Encouraging collaborative and participative involvement of both individuals and communities. Such involvement may contribute to developing practical activities as well as new knowledge.
- Seeking to develop people's strengths rather than focus on concepts such as diagnosis or categorising symptoms.
- Acknowledging the importance of influences such as housing, income, social circumstances, as well as personal histories, on wellbeing.
- Emphasising prevention as well as reaction or treatment. This may take the form of education, facilitating social support, influencing public policy.
- A commitment to devolve professional power and to work towards sharing control and decision-making.
- Working together to improve our service systems and society.
- Recognition of social injustices. Aiming to effect social change in a broad context by actively influencing social policy that facilitates the empowerment of disadvantaged and disenfranchised people.

Rather than representing a technique or specific intervention, community psychology is built around a framework of principles. The applications in practice may look different and unique to each setting. Community psychology is committed to working towards greater social equality and embraces particular values such as inclusion, justice, freedom and respect. There are many examples of community psychology in practice and, whilst it is not the remit of this chapter to consider them in detail, these include housing environments (Kagan, 2007), debt and poverty (Bostock, 2004), people who use mental health services and their involvement (Diamond *et al.*, 2003), women's health (Holland, 1992), employment and local groups (Fryer, 1990, 1992), and research (Serrano-Garcia, 1990).

In this chapter, our focus is on the value of, and relationship between, community psychology and assertive outreach. Assertive outreach services were created to serve the needs of people who hitherto were not engaging with mental health services. The aim of such services:

> is not only maximising access to helpful professional resources, provided in a coordinated and consistent way, but also acting as a gateway for reaching into the wider network of community services and supports

that, in the longer term, will provide the more permanent relationships and usual life opportunities for personal development and achievements.

(Smith and Morris, 2003: 22)

People receiving support from assertive outreach services may have little involvement and connection with many of the established social structures in society. Community psychology attempts to redress this imbalance. It offers a framework for understanding what we need to consider when searching for the forces contributing to human misery and distress (see Figure 9.1).

Prilleltensky and Nelson (2002) describe values within community psychology that can also be seen to underpin a more just society. These include participation and self-determination, acceptance of human diversity and social justice. Such issues are relevant at the personal and societal levels. People exist through a social-material embodied history that is located within both the relational context of family and friends and ultimately bound within a social context of culture and ideology.

Hagan and Smail (1997) highlight the centrality of power to distress. They show how access to social and material resources is linked to wellbeing. They map the impact of people's social environment on their lives and help people and teams to understand why they perceive and relate to the world in the way they do. This de-mystification may relieve distress in itself. They outline the reality of the current and past situation, and highlight areas where we can support people to redress this.

It is important for services to acknowledge that people are often trapped by their social, historical and material circumstances and may have little power to effect change. We need to be aware of this when considering empowerment and be cautious not to inadvertently direct people into other forms of oppression. Community psychology encourages links between groups of people who are marginalised, creating possibilities for people to have more influence over their lives. By joining in solidarity with others in similar situations, people may increase their confidence, gain social validation and friendship. Practically, they may apply for funding to increase their material power, for example to cover costs of meeting.

Example:
One of the stumbling blocks for a self-help group of assertive outreach clients in a rural area of East Sussex was that members were poor and could not afford to meet. The group and allies obtained funding from the Assertive Outreach Team to pay for a community venue in which to meet, for travelling expenses and refreshments. The group enabled people to meet each other and form friendships and to find ways in which they could promote their own recovery, for example through talking, day trips and walking.

Figure 9.1 Cartoon by Dave Shaw (reprinted by permission from the artist)

Recovery rates from schizophrenia have been found to be higher in so-called 'developing countries' than in the west and this is hypothesised to be because people are less stigmatised, more supported by extended families and more likely to be in employment (Warner, 1994). Recovery is enhanced by social support, decent housing, employment or other meaningful roles (Orford, 1992; Warner, 1994). Practice that supports people to get better housing, or develop interests through leisure or employment and encourages social networking, is at the heart of community psychology and effective assertive outreach.

If we are to understand what it is to have mental health problems and why they occur, we need to recognise social and economic position, power and discrimination. People who use assertive outreach services have experienced alienation and marginalisation from society. They are likely to have little if any access to positions of privilege and power. Community psychology encourages us to share this information and consider opportunities for people to be supported to exert whatever influence is feasible over their living circumstances. As workers we can challenge the oppression and exploitation that perpetrate inequalities and distress.

Our critical eye should include our own professional practice and the professions from which we base ourselves. If we are to reach out creatively and try to engage with those who feel most disempowered and dislocated from society, we must start by constructively challenging how we each use our own positions of power and privilege. To do this we must increasingly listen to and act on the opinions of people who are using mental health services.

Working with experts by experience

What supports recovery?

People are recovering, not only from life traumas or symptoms but also treatments, negative attitudes and prognoses of professionals, devaluing and disempowering services, lack of opportunities to engage in valued activities and discrimination and social exclusion (Repper and Perkins, 2003).

Discourse on recovery has been developed by 'experts by experience'. Both recovery and community psychology are strengths-led, move away from illness models, devolve power and expertise, and privilege the accounts of people who use services and are experts by experience. Yet they differ in that recovery-based approaches have a greater emphasis on hope, personal responsibility and individuals being able to bring about change alone. Recovery has been criticised for being too individualistic; however, in the UK it has also been grounded in the wider anti-discriminatory and disability movements. In this section we explore recovery through a community psychology lens and show how applying the principles of recovery contributes to the field of community psychology and its relation to assertive outreach.

Psychological interventions have an important role to play in supporting people's recovery as highlighted by other chapters in this book. The evidence base shows that about a third to half of people with psychosis are helped by individual therapy. However, this leaves at least half who are not helped by it (Roth and Fonagy, 2005; Read, Mosher and Bentall, 2005). The outcome evidence for individual psychotherapies is more modest than often considered (Epstein, 2006; Moloney, 2006). People who have received psychotherapy say they find the contact satisfying, yet also often report that disturbing experiences continue. People who use services do value and ask for talking treatments. However, talking can be with friends, relatives and peers as well as professionals.

Users also want a more holistic approach which takes account of mental, emotional and spiritual factors (Mental Health Foundation, 1997). Users stress the importance of information, advocacy, choice, accessibility and equal opportunity, self-help, help with practical problems, involving family and friends, developing outside activities including work and leisure, income, and user-involvement including user-employment and service monitoring (Read, 1996; Beeforth *et al.*, 1994).

People value help in making sense of their problems and in coming to terms with their difficulties; practical support with housing and finance; social networks, and physical health, whereas professionals place greater emphasis on professional support, treatment and monitoring. However, there is some general consensus, especially about the importance of information (Shepherd, Murray and Muijen, 1995). Meddings and Perkins (2002) found some similarity between how users and staff of rehabilitation and assertive outreach services construed 'getting better': both emphasised improved mental state, wellbeing, relationships, confidence and self-worth and greater engagement in work and valued activities. Yet significantly more service users also saw getting better as involving improved material wellbeing, especially housing and finances.

Recovery-oriented services may promote self-management and the use of personal recovery plans; value the expertise of people who have personal experience of mental health problems, sometimes by employing them within services; and support people to reach the different kinds of life goals they are aiming for – such as work, social networks and reducing discrimination. Psychologists need to support people's recovery on their own terms, *both* through psychological therapies *and* through community psychology approaches which can support them in working towards other things they want, like community networking or social and material inclusion.

Effective assertive outreach services may be grounded in recovery and community psychology approaches. Sam has written about her experiences:

> 'Before assertive outreach it was awful. I had problems and a very long history. I heard voices from the dead. I was in hospital for 12 years – six different places – from 17 years old. The nurses used to say "You will never get out" and you become institutionalised. They diagnosed me with so many things – personality disorder, paranoia, schizophrenia.

They pumped me full of drugs. Being gay in hospital was difficult – the first person I told was a doctor who told me I wasn't gay, I was ill. It's another extra thing to deal with.

I have been with assertive outreach for six years. I moved in my flat in 2000. Just because I have a mental health problem doesn't mean my life has to stop. I've spent hardly any time in hospital since assertive outreach. I made a full recovery and do not take medication now.

In assertive outreach they visit you in your home. You don't feel threatened and you don't feel there's a barrier. You're known better and you have a much better relationship with people. It's about trust. They make you feel you can achieve what you want to achieve. One of the things that most helped me was seeing a psychologist. What I needed was to sit down and make sense of what was going on in my head. It was hard work – horrible sometimes. Work has helped me too. It's given me confidence to know I could do this.'

(Meddings *et al.*, 2007: 36)

The concept of recovery was developed by the survivor and service user movements and has been adopted by professionals (e.g. Deegan, 1988; Leete, 1989; Anthony, 1993; Repper and Perkins, 2003; Roberts and Wolfson, 2004). The recovery literature highlights the importance of hope; being believed in; taking responsibility for our own lives; grieving and learning about ourselves, and finding new meaning and sense of purpose. It can occur without professional interventions, and even though symptoms may remain (Young and Ensing, 1999; Anthony, 1993). Recovery might mean living with the presence of distressing symptoms yet coping with them and living well. Recovery does not mean that people stop accessing services – many people recover and lead fulfilling lives precisely *because* they receive ongoing support from assertive outreach or elsewhere. It is crucial that we support people to define their own recovery aims and offer the support they want to achieve this. Both community psychology and recovery emphasise the importance of listening to people who use services, and the potential for workers to learn from them.

Recovery, or discovery, is a lifelong process led by the person themselves:

'One of my moments of discovery was discovering that professionals don't know it all, aren't god and that I know better than they do about me as I have lived with myself a lifetime. But that also professionals can be a very useful resource for information and support when I need it.'

(Service user, Nottingham, 2007)

Community psychology approaches may offer people who use services support in their journeys of discovery and recovery, without being confined to individualistic models or therapies. Community psychology has developed independently of the recovery approach yet is congruent with it. Both look at broader issues which survivors say are important, including the recognition that professionals do not necessarily have the answers. This includes a broader conceptualisation of recovery and the role of social, material and political factors.

Supporting self-help and peer support networks

Community psychologists can support disadvantaged and oppressed groups to develop social support networks and friendships. One way of doing this is by supporting people to develop self-help or peer support groups. These groups also provide alternative views of the world and may be particularly attractive to people who do not want to get involved with mainstream service provision. For example, assertive outreach service users might want to be part of recovery groups, women's groups, groups for survivors of sexual abuse or campaigning groups. While they may benefit from help in accessing or developing groups, it should be noted that peer support pre-dates, and is independent of, community psychology. Such groups can and do develop without support from psychology and we must take care that psychology does not become imperialistic and take recognition away from survivors themselves.

The amount and kind of support psychologists provide needs to be tailored, depending on the skills and confidence of survivors, with ownership and control remaining with group members. In keeping with a community-building approach (Kretzmann and McKnight, 1993), it needs to promote people's own capacities, skills, assets and aspirations, adding additional resources, whilst allowing communities to maintain control. Professionals can support people to start, run and maintain groups without taking over. One of us (Becky) started a general mental health group 11 years ago:

> 'I felt alone with my difficulties and frustrated with the service I received. I received more help from other patients than staff. I learnt how to cope with many symptoms, and with the service; to get what help I needed and learn to readjust to a newer life, through the support received from other patients during hospital admissions and the group I had set up in the community. An essential part of the group was that true friendships were formed – something many people lack and services cannot give. Having people in your life that truly care, that aren't just there because they are paid to be there, is essential.'

The Hearing Voices Network links patients, non-patients, professionals and other allies who share the belief that there is no one cause or treatment for voices and that they are not necessarily a sign of psychiatric problems. It is committed to raising awareness and acceptance of voice hearing, creating spaces to talk freely about voices and to understand, learn and grow from the experience (Downs, 2001).

Sussex Hearing Voices groups were developed at the request of three people who were using assertive outreach services and wondered if there were others who shared similar life experiences and heard voices. They asked that psychology support them to start a network. Funding was obtained for a project worker who had experience of hearing voices and of mental health services. Groups were developed in two phases: they were initially set up and facilitated by professionals including the project worker and psychologists; they then progressed to self-help and facilitation by members. The ethos was always of an emerging self-help group following the philosophy of the Hearing Voices Network (Downs, 2001; Romme and Escher, 1993). Members set agendas, supported one another and shared ideas about coping with their experiences. Several assertive outreach service users attended. Others received the newsletters and felt part of a collective, with at least one person reporting how helpful he had found this, saying that the sense of not being alone in having these experiences made him feel less crazy.

Another member said, 'Realising you're not strange, a weirdo, it happens to other people. Members of the group have enabled me to normalise and to know you can have a fulfilling life, even with voices.'

Members increasingly facilitated the groups and staff withdrew, providing arm's-length support, offering consultation and help with arranging training or funding.

Members of Sussex Hearing Voices Network were asked what they thought the role of community psychology was in supporting hearing voices groups:

'Psychologists should be there in the background – not attending groups every week, but be on call so if there's a problem you can contact them for advice. Some people don't want to talk about their problems when there are professionals there. It's helpful to meet for supervision, guidance for the facilitator is extremely useful e.g. if I have a problem getting people to join in, how I go about things, having a general talk about mental health, or what to do if there's a crisis. They should be available to help set up the group, to help with funding for rooms and refreshments.' Julia

'I think it'd be good to have psychologists there. It's nice to have professional people there to say what can be harmful or whatever. To have the group come up with ideas and the psychologist then put the professional point of view as well – something the group hasn't thought of. And safety: making sure that the group is safe and noticing anything dangerous . . . information like pointing out services that are available – like direct payments and alternatives to going into hospital.' Chris

'Community psychology needs to address not so much *what* it does, but *how* it does it . . . I don't think psychologists should be facilitating hearing voices groups, I feel they should support people with the experience to facilitate them themselves. Practical support can be offered, for example securing a room to meet, funding, admin help.' Lou

(Sussex Hearing Voices Groups, 2007)

Different people may look for different types of groups and there are many types of peer support groups. There is no right or wrong way for a psychologist to support a group, as long as it is the group that leads on what support it needs. Sometimes it is not about holding someone's hand all the time but giving them the confidence so that they can walk on their own.

Promoting user-led research

It is extremely helpful for services, psychologists, and service users to understand what is working well and what could be improved. It becomes even more valuable when the research questions and topic areas are designed and asked by the service users themselves. Assertive outreach clients have chosen not to engage with traditional services for a number of reasons. Understanding those reasons can provide a useful tool for identifying how assertive outreach services can do things differently. User-led research may pose new kinds of questions, methodologies and ways of presenting findings, and have a greater degree of meaning and value for both clients and services. It may provide new information which does not emerge in traditional research.

An assertive outreach client may ask very different questions of the service, and be interested in different outcomes, opening the door to new conversations, and raising ideas not normally considered. By researching questions which are important to service users, we may well develop services better tailored to their needs.

> We felt the involvement of service users would improve the quality of the information generated. What we got was a whole lot more: energy and clarity of vision so often lacking in professionals who are bogged down by bureaucracy and the needs of the service; a determination to see the task through and pave the way for the future work of others, and a principled yet realistic and pragmatic approach. By working in partnership with service users, the Chichester AOT has learnt considerably more about itself, its functioning and the likely value of greater involvement of service users in its thinking/activity.
>
> (Hayward *et al.*, 2004: 28)

The benefits may not be restricted to services and the people who use them, but also include those users involved in the research process itself – increasing their confidence, self-esteem and skills, but most importantly, shifting the balance of control and power.

In the past service users have primarily been seen as 'subjects' of research. We argue that actively involving people who have used services at all levels creates better, more valuable research, with more meaningful outcomes and arguably higher ethical standards.

SURGE (2005) outlines three levels of user-involvement in research and evaluation:

- Consultation – service users are consulted about research projects, for example, commenting on questionnaires. Service users have little power or control over the research planned.
- Collaboration – professionals and service user researchers jointly run a project. It may be professionally, service-user or jointly initiated. Power is equal.
- Control or user-led – users have the power over research questions and methodology, undertaking interviews themselves with little professional involvement.

One approach to user-controlled research can be seen in the development of user-focused monitoring by the Sainsbury Centre for Mental Health. This is led by Diana Rose, an experienced researcher and user of mental health services. It is based around the premise that:

> if the evaluation of services was genuinely to reflect the concerns and views of the people who use them, rather than those of providers, then users should lead the process at every stage: from the questions asked, through the collection, analysis and interpretation of data, to the final reporting of the results and development of recommendations for change.
> (Repper and Perkins, foreword to Kotecha et. al., 2007: 4)

There are several key issues, whatever the level of involvement:

- Resources should be in place to cover time and expenses, before the project begins.
- Service users should be involved right from the beginning of the project.
- Sensitivity, flexibility and open-mindedness are needed throughout by all.
- Emotional, practical and research-based support and training should be provided.
- Jargon should be avoided and key terms explained.
- Clarity and transparency about what is wanted from participants, and what is being offered, are essential from the beginning.
- Findings and recommendations should be shared with all participants in ways which are accessible to them.

If the positive attitudes and values generally associated with assertive outreach were to be implemented, services would become much more needs-led, leading to better outcomes for people using those services and a better working environment for staff. This requires a change in attitudes by both staff and management. Service-user involvement in research is a first step to finding out what services are needed and the style of working preferred by the client group.

Service development and community psychology

Opening up new discourses

Wallcraft and Michaelson (2001) argue for the development of a 'survivor discourse' to replace professional discourses and to reclaim language. Survivor-led movements challenge dominant discourses, e.g. Mad Pride and the Hearing Voices Network. The Sussex Voice newsletter includes a regular feature about famous people who have heard voices.

Social disability approaches help people to work within their own frame of reference, to reclaim the kind of life they want to lead, sometimes through the use of prosthetic aids (Repper and Perkins, 2003). One man was helped to cope with the aliens watching him from above by wearing hats and sunglasses. Previously housebound, this enabled him to go to the shops, pub and to use other community resources. Another person used a piece of lead in his breast pocket to stop harmful rays, whereas before he had resorted to using his arms and legs, often distressing other people, who were afraid of being kicked.

We can work towards devolving power by respecting people's own accounts of their lives and recovery. NICE (2002) advocates a diversity of views within medical records, including the accounts of people who use services, and requires professionals to support people to find meaning and to write their own account of their mental health problems for the notes.

> **Example:**
> Dan, an assertive outreach client, has written his own life story, which describes the reasons for the development of mental health difficulties and what he has found helpful for his recovery. We supported him to access resources such as a computer and then helped by typing and proof reading for him. His story has been placed as a report within the psychiatric record, amongst reports by other kinds of experts.

Seikkula and Arnkil's (2006) 'Open Dialogue' approach brings together professionals, families, employers, friends and other members of people's social networks alongside the person with a diagnosis of psychosis, to generate dialogues about the experiences, explanations and ways of supporting the person with the diagnosis, as well as each other. Their privileging social inclusion and psychological approaches over medication resulted in only 29 per cent of people being prescribed neuroleptics. Both symptomatic and social recovery was high.

Community psychology is consistent with behavioural and ecological approaches. Traditional psychiatry individualises risk, locating it within the person. East Sussex Assertive Outreach Teams have adapted Clements' (1992) functional analysis approach, highlighting contextual factors in risk assessments:

Example:

By examining the settings, triggers and consequences in Steve's violence towards others, we noticed that his behaviour could be contextualised as happening around the anniversary of his mother's death; to people who had abused him, or who looked like people who had abused him in the past, and especially in places where he was disempowered, such as acute wards. This formulation enabled both the team and Steve to move away from seeing him as a high risk, and instead to see him as someone struggling with issues of oppression.

Community psychology is influenced by liberation social psychology from Central and South America, which acknowledges situations of social, economic and political domination and supports people to develop awareness, to have a voice, and promote change through collective action (e.g. Freire, 1970). Edge, Kagan and Stewart (2004) suggest that community psychology may learn from radical movements for social change and liberation to develop 'a practice of accompaniment'. They suggest that psychologists must listen to what people themselves say about their lives and consider the implications for psychology. This may include taking time to live in the communities we work with, to walk alongside, listen to and witness the realities of people's lives. Likewise, psychology and psychiatry must listen to other less dominant discourses, to the lives and meanings of people who live with mental disability and have not engaged with traditional mental health services.

Social inclusion and community development

Repper and Perkins (2003) describe the social exclusion experienced by many of the people who use assertive outreach services:

the local GP surgery refuses to register you because you make excessive demands on them; the general hospital does not take your physical health problems seriously; and employers will not consider your application. And, of course, the poverty that ensues from a life on state benefits means that you cannot afford to go to the pub, travel, go to the cinema, join a sports club, and too often means that you are living in a high crime area where you are afraid to go out.

(Repper and Perkins, 2003: 133)

Addressing social inclusion is a community endeavour. Psychological work may be carried out by peers, family, day centres and others, and not just psychologists and mental health teams. It may involve helping people to develop the confidence and social skills lost through mental health problems and institutionalisation; identify coping strategies and graded exposure to manage anxiety in new situations; information or systemic work with friendship or family groups; encouraging meaningful negotiation over what, if any, medication is useful, its effects and the impact of side effects. It might mean using a day centre to practise social skills in a safe place before attempting a supported community activity. Assertive Outreach Teams are often skilled at supporting people with this, for example providing transport and accompanying people in activities they enjoy, such as going to football matches, church or cafés. However, even with the tools and support to go out, people can only be socially included if stigma and discrimination are tackled.

Community psychologists can work with communities to reduce stigma and exclusion. Projects like 'Open Up', by Mental Health Media, train service users about their rights and to tackle discrimination. Psychologists can work with service users, co-delivering training for staff, other service users and the public. They can be more open about their own mental distress where appropriate, tackling misconceptions and mysteries about mental health problems and opening up conversations so that people are less afraid to say, 'Yes I have had mental health difficulties and yes I could do with support'.

Sayce (2000) concludes that the evidence for media campaigns and public education in reducing prejudice and discrimination is mixed, but improved when combined with grassroots approaches where survivors make contacts with communities. She describes user-run drop-ins which tackle discrimination by making links with local shops and cafés; which model anti-discriminatory practice by being accessible and non-discriminating themselves; that contribute to the local community and train employers in anti-discrimination law.

We must also tackle prejudice within mental health services as well as the wider community:

> 'When I was in hospital one of the nurses said that because I had schizo-phrenia, I would never be able to work or have a family – it made me want to kill myself.'
>
> (service user, Sussex, 2000)

A survey of a London borough found that 44 per cent of people with mental health problems who were in paid employment had previously been advised by their mental health professionals not to work (Rinaldi and Hill, 2000). Inclusion must be considered for a service to be recovery oriented, for example by supporting people to do the things they want to do; demonstrating hopeful and positive attitudes; clearly signposting services; having user-employment policies and not having 'staff only' toilets.

Repper and Perkins (2003) suggest it is more effective to promote inclusion of individuals rather than groups of people with mental health problems; to discuss strengths and difficulties as they are specifically relevant to that activity; to allow people to express their concerns and find solutions together, and to provide a person whom they can contact if there are any issues. We need to support people when and if they want us to do so, helping them to access such things as work, college, and leisure activities. And before engaging with local community resources we must first discuss with the person whether or not they want to 'come out' as having mental health problems.

Example:
Jane wanted to attend college. She was keen and bright but troubled by voices and felt anxious and paranoid on public transport. The local college were not confident about her joining mainstream classes, thinking it would be inappropriate for someone with 'schizophrenia'. We worked with Jane to develop ways of coping with the voices and anxiety. An assistant psychologist travelled with her on the bus and met her during break times, gradually withdrawing as she gained confidence. We organised a homework drop-in at the college for people experiencing mental distress. With her permission, we met with the lecturer and provided consultation and a point of contact in case difficulties arose. Jane succeeded in her studies and went on to work in a related field.

There is strong evidence for the effectiveness of social inclusion work, especially supported employment whereby people gain real jobs with real pay (Crowther *et al.*, 2000; NICE 2002). By working with people to support them to get jobs, go to college or make friends, we may find this helps with the psychosis itself, as well as achieving these other important goals.

Assertive outreach services and community psychology

This chapter has considered ways of engaging creatively with clients in assertive outreach services through a community psychology framework. We have shown that, by acknowledging aspects of power, discrimination and inequality, it is possible to offer support to clients in a way that is different from that found in the practice of conventional mental health services. The emphasis of community psychology is to look beyond the individual person to wider social, historical and political contexts. This chapter suggests that a change of attitudes is required across mental health services. Assertive outreach may be needed, not only by clients, but by services which need to learn to work together in order to develop. It is important to turn the gaze of community psychology in on the very teams that provide the service.

The values of equality, justice, respect, participation and collaboration are as important in Assertive Outreach Teams as they are in any other service. Formulation should not be dominated by any one model. Psychologists can help teams to reflect and formulate in ways which include multiple perspectives, including social, economic and cultural factors. Transparency of power structures and decision making in teams is essential. All team members have valuable contributions to make. People need to be given information and all opinions should be equally valued. Similarly, people who use services can be involved in all aspects of their care, service development and monitoring. Services should be influenced by user-led research and perspectives. Just as we have described how people can be supported to develop peer support and research, so properly resourced and supported service-user advisory groups may influence service development.

We have noted that a central consideration of community psychology is to become strengths-based, rather than focusing on diagnosis or limitations. This can also be applied to staff groups and teams. Assertive outreach services need to find a balance between risk management and promoting therapeutic risk taking. Staff need to be supported themselves so that they can nurture and support clients to take appropriate risks and link up with the various recovery opportunities described earlier in this chapter.

We have emphasised the importance of collaboration in the process of creatively engaging with clients. But how can assertive outreach services collaborate meaningfully with other services? There may be confusion, where other mental health teams consider assertive outreach teams to be something separate, or even as working in isolation from other services. In reality, all mental health teams have a responsibility to develop joined-up services. The communication between inpatient mental health wards and assertive outreach services is as crucial as any other inter-team relationship, yet it sometimes appears less consistent and co-ordinated. Whilst it is important to define the core business and what is specific to assertive outreach, this may contribute to a false sense of difference between assertive outreach and other community-based mental health teams. Therefore, in the same way that we have called for greater clarity in communication and action between workers and clients, similar improvements are required across the various teams that comprise mental health services.

Conclusions

We have tried to define community psychology through use of examples, suggested principles of practice and how these could form the backbone of a recovery-oriented service which assertive outreach could provide. We have emphasised the importance of listening to experts by experience and support-ing people who use services to organise themselves and to encourage discourse which takes account of social and material factors.

Traditionally, assertive outreach clients have been seen as difficult people who don't engage with services. Alternatively, it may be argued that they are people who highlight difficulties with services; people who need help but choose not to be labelled, controlled or treated in coercive ways. Instead of this, they want a needs-led, recovery-oriented and accessible service.

Assertive outreach is in a good position to promote ideas and practices across all services, to work in collaborative, needs-led ways, listening to people using services and working together to find solutions. Community psychology offers a framework of values and practice to guide such developments.

Acknowledgement

With thanks to Dave Shaw who created the cartoon for this chapter.

References

Anthony, W.A. (1993) 'Recovery from mental illness: the guiding vision of the mental health system in the 1990s', *Innovations and Research*, 2: 17–24.

Beeforth, M., Conlan, E. and Graley, R. (1994) *Have We Got Views For You? User evaluation of case management*, London: Sainsbury Centre for Mental Health.

Bostock, J. (2004) 'Addressing poverty and exploitation: challenges for psychology', *Clinical Psychology*, 38: 23–27.

Browne, D. (1995) 'Sectioning: the black experience', in S. Fernando (ed.) *Mental Health in a Multi-Ethnic Society*, London: Routledge.

Cantor-Graae, E. and Selton, J.-P. (2005) 'Schizophrenia and migration: a meta-analysis and review', *American Journal of Psychiatry*, 162: 12–24.

Clements, J. (1992) 'I can't explain ... "challenging behaviour": towards a shared conceptual framework', *Clinical Psychology Forum*, 39: 29–37.

Cochrane, R. (1983) *The Social Creation of Mental Illness*, London: Longman.

Commission for Audit and Healthcare Inspection (2007) *Count Me In 2007*, Healthcare Commission and Care Services Improvement Partnership.

Cromby, J. and Harper, D. (2009) 'Paranoia: a social account', *Theory and Psychology*, 19: 335–361.

Crowther, R., Marshall, M., Bond, G. and Huxley, P. (2000) *Vocational Rehabilitation for People with Severe Mental Disorders*, Cochrane Review.

Deegan, P. (1988) 'Recovery: the lived experience of rehabilitation', *Psychosocial Rehabilitation Journal*, 11: 11–19.

Diamond, B., Parkin, G., Morris, K., Betinis, J. and Bettesworth, C. (2003) 'User involvement: substance or spin?', *Journal of Mental Health*, 12: 613–626.

Downs, J. (ed.) (2001) *Starting and Supporting Hearing Voices Groups: a guide to starting and facilitating hearing-voices groups*, Manchester: Hearing Voices Network.

Edge, I., Kagan, C. and Stewart, A. (2004) 'Living poverty in the UK: surviving on the edge', *Clinical Psychology Forum*, 38: 28–31.

Epstein, W.M. (2006) *Psychotherapy as Religion: the civil divine in America*, Reno: University of Nevada Press.

Freire, P. (1970) *Pedagogy of the Oppressed*, New York: Continuum.

Fryer, D. (1990) 'The mental health consequences of unemployment. Towards a social psychological concept of poverty', *British Journal of Clinical and Social Psychiatry*, 7: 164–176.

Fryer, D. (1992) 'Signed on the "Beroo": mental health and unemployment in Scotland', *The Psychologist*, 5: 539–542.

Hagan, T. and Smail, D. (1997) 'Power-mapping: background and basic methodology', *Journal of Community and Applied Social Psychology*, 7: 257–267.

Harrison, G., Gunnell, D., Glazebrook, C., Page, K. and Kwiecinski, R. (2001) 'Association between schizophrenia and social inequality at birth: case-control study', *British Journal of Psychiatry*, 179: 346–350.

Hayward, M., Ockwell, C., Bird, T., Pearce, H., Parfoot, S. and Bates, T. (2004) 'How well are we doing?' *Mental Health Today*, October: 25–28.

226 *Meddings, Shaw and Diamond*

Healthcare Commission (2007) *Healthcare Commission Acute Inpatient Mental Health Service Review 2006/7*, London: Healthcare Commission.

Holland, S. (1992) 'From social abuse to social action: a neighbourhood psychotherapy and social action project for women', in J. Ussher and P. Nicholson (eds) *Gender Issues in Clinical Psychology*, London: Routledge.

Kagan, C. (2007) 'Working at the "edge": making use of psychological resources through collaboration', *The Psychologist*, 20: 224–227.

Kotecha, N., Fowler, C., Donskoy, A.-L., Johnson, P., Shaw, T. and Doherty, K. (2007) *A Guide to User-Focused Monitoring: setting up and running a project*, London: Sainsbury Centre for Mental Health.

Kretzmann, J.P. and McKnight, J.L. (1993) *Building Communities from the Inside Out: a path toward finding and mobilising a community's assets*, Evanston, Illinois: The Asset-based Community Development Institute, Institute for Policy Research, Northwestern University. Chapter one available online at http:// www.northwestern.edu/ipr/publications/community/buildingblurb.html [accessed 16 May 2008].

Leete, E. (1989) 'How I perceive and manage my illness', *Schizophrenia Bulletin*, 15: 197–200.

McFarlane, L. (1998) *Diagnosis: Homophobic. The experiences of lesbians, gay men and bisexuals in mental health services*, London: PACE.

Meddings, S. and Cupitt, C. (2000) 'Clinical psychologists and assertive outreach', *Clinical Psychology Forum*, 137: 47–31.

Meddings, S. and Perkins, R. (2002) 'What "getting better" means to staff and users of a rehabilitation service', *Journal of Mental Health*, 11: 319–325.

Meddings, S., Perkins, A., Wharne, S., Ley, P., Collins, T. and Wilson, J. (2007) 'Being assertive effectively – does assertive outreach work – and why?', *Mental Health Today*, May: 24–37.

Meddings, S., Robinson, M., Wharne, S., Ley, P. and Perkins, A. (2006) 'AOT Audit 2006: inpatient admissions pre and post AOT and demographics'. Available from the authors.

The Mental Health Foundation (1997) *Knowing Our Own Minds: a survey of how people in emotional distress take control of their lives*, London: The Mental Health Foundation.

Moloney, P. (2006). 'The trouble with psychotherapy', *Clinical Psychology Forum*, 162, 29–33.

National Institute for Clinical Excellence (2002) *Schizophrenia: core interventions in the treatment and management of schizophrenia in primary and secondary care*, London: NICE.

Orford, J. (1992) *Community Psychology Theory and Practice*, Chichester: Wiley.

Prilleltensky, I. and Nelson, G. (2002) *Doing Psychology Critically: making a difference in diverse settings*, Basingstoke: Palgrave Macmillan.

Read, J. (1996) 'What we want from mental health services', in J. Read and J. Reynolds (eds), *Speaking our Minds: an anthology*, Basingstoke: Macmillan.

Read, J., Mosher, L. and Bentall, R. (2005) *Models of Madness: psychological, social and biological approaches to schizophrenia*, Hove: Routledge.

Reed, J., van Os., J., Morrison, A.P. and Ross, C.A. (2005) 'Childhood trauma, psychosis and schizophrenia: a literature review with theoretical and clinical implications', *Acta-Psychiatrica-Scandinavica*, 112: 330–350.

Repper, J. and Perkins, R. (2003) *Social Inclusion and Recovery: a model for mental health practice*, London: Bailliere Tindall.

Rinaldi, M. and Hill, R. (2000) *Insufficient Concern: the experience, attitudes and perceptions of disabled people and employers towards open employment in one London borough*, London: Merton MIND.

Roberts, G. and Wolfson, P. (2004) 'The rediscovery of recovery: open to all', *Advances in Psychiatric Treatment*, 10: 37–49.

Romme, M. and Escher, S. (1993) *Accepting Voices*, London: MIND publications.

Roth, A. and Fonagy, P. (2005) *What Works For Whom? A critical review of psychotherapy research*, New York: Guilford Press.

Sayce, L. (2000) *From Psychiatric Patient to Citizen: overcoming discrimination and social exclusion*, London: Macmillan.

Seikkula, J. and Arnkil, T.E. (2006) *Dialogical Meetings in Social Networks*, London: Karnac Books.

Serrano-Garcia, I. (1990) 'Implementing research: putting our values to work', in P. Tolan, C. Keys, F. Chertok and L. Jason (eds) *Researching Community Psychology: issues of theory and methods*, New York: American Psychological Association.

Shepherd, G., Murray, A. and Muijen, M. (1995) 'Perspectives on schizophrenia: a survey of user, family carer and professional views regarding effective care', *Journal of Mental Health*, 4: 403–422.

Smail, D. (2005) *Power Interest and Psychology*, Ross-on-Wye: PCCS Books.

Smith, M. and Morris, M. (2003) 'Recovery teams', *Openmind*, 119: 22–23.

Social Exclusion Unit (2004) *Mental Health and Social Exclusion*, London: Office of the Deputy Prime Minister.

SURGE – Service User Research Group England (2005) 'Guidelines for good practice: service user involvement in the UK Mental Health Research Network'. Available online at http://www.mhrn.info/index/ppi/SUR/good-practice-guidance.html [accessed 1 December 2007].

Sussex Hearing Voices Groups (2007) 'The role of psychologists in developing Hearing Voices groups'. Available online at http://www.sussexvoice.org.uk [accessed 12 January 2008].

Thomas, C., Bartlett, A. and Mezey, G.C. (1995) 'The extent and effect of violence among psychiatric in-patients', *Psychiatric Bulletin*, 19: 600–604.

Van Os, J., Driessen, G., Gunther, N. and Delespaul, P. (2000) 'Neighbourhood variation in incidence of schizophrenia', *British Journal of Psychiatry*, 176: 243–248.

Wallcraft, J. and Michaelson, J. (2001) 'Developing a survivor discourse to replace the "psychopathology" of breakdown and crisis', in C. Newnes, G. Holmes and C. Dunn (eds) *This is Madness Too: critical perspectives on mental health services*. Ross-on-Wye: PCCS Books.

Warner, R. (1994) *Recovery from Schizophrenia: psychiatry and political economy*, 2nd edn, London: Routledge.

Wicks, S., Hjern, A., Gunnell, D., Lewis, G. and Dalman, C. (2005) 'Social adversity in childhood and the risk of developing psychosis: a national cohort study', *American Journal of Psychiatry*, 162: 1652–1657.

Williams, J. (1999) 'Social inequalities and mental health', in C. Newnes, G. Holmes and C. Dunn (eds), *This is Madness: a critical look at psychiatry and the future of mental health services*, Ross-on-Wye: PCCS Books.

Young, S.L. and Ensing, D.S. (1999) 'Exploring recovery from the perspective of people with psychiatric disabilities', *Psychiatric Rehabilitation Journal*, 22: 219–231.

Zubin, J. and Spring, B. (1977) 'Vulnerability: a new view of schizophrenia', *Journal of Abnormal Psychology*, 86: 103–126.

10 Ethics and professional issues: the universal and the particular

Abi Gray and Paul Johanson

> So far as the casuistic question goes, ethical science [is] just like phy-
> sical science, and instead of being deducible all at once from abstract
> principles, must simply bide its time, and be ready to revise its conclu-
> sions from day to day . . . For every real dilemma is in literal strictness a
> unique situation; and the exact combination of ideals realized and ideals
> disappointed which each decision creates is always a universe without a
> precedent, and for which no adequate previous rule exists.
>
> (William James, 1891: 349)

Ethics is normally defined as the theory of moral conduct: it is concerned
with philosophical inquiry and the discovery, or construction, of principles
for action and conduct. Ethics are so fundamental to practice in health and
social care that it is possible to characterise this whole area of work as
an articulation of ethical principles. Indeed, when the Beveridge report was
published in 1942, the then Archbishop of Canterbury, William Temple, said
it was 'the first time anyone had set out to embody the whole spirit of the
Christian ethic in an Act of Parliament' (Barnett, 1986: 29). Most, if not all,
health and social care professionals enter their chosen field out of a conscious
desire to do good, and there is probably a general public expectation that care
professionals act out of altruistic motivations, although some would suggest
that the unconscious reasons may be more complex. In the field of mental
health care, however, this wholesome ethical picture of altruistic carers doing
good is compromised by doctrines which conceive of mental ill health as a
social construction (e.g. Szasz, 1974; Foucault, 2006) that comes in handy for
policing deviancy and managing 'social junk' (Spitzer, 1975).

Mainstream mental health services, now admonished by NICE guidance
and validated by increasingly close partnerships with service user organisations, tend to suffer less from the 'social police' epithet. They offer services to
individuals who are inclined to cooperate and accept the different diagnostic
labels together with the various treatments and interventions – pharmacological, psychological, social and occupational.

In contrast, the clients of Assertive Outreach Teams have either rejected or
been rejected by the mainstream and have rarely had successful relationships

with services. One approach to this small group of 'hard to engage' individuals is to assume that they would accept standard mental health services, if only they would give us enough time to convince them of the value of what we are offering – support, sanity, social inclusion. This works for some, but there is a smaller sub-group of clients who do not succumb to this 'more of the same, only more assertively' approach. It is this group who most often require a psychologically informed approach to engagement and intervention. And it is often through attempting to provide services to this group of clients that the most challenging ethical dilemmas arise.

In addressing the question of the ethical application of psychology to assertive outreach we are rehearsing age-old debates. The default position popularly imputed to health and social care professionals, especially those working with people who hold non-mainstream viewpoints, is one of ethical relativism: the impossibility of making ethical or moral judgements about another's actions because moral absolutes do not exist. However, in any body of thought and practice there lie, at the base, fundamental propositions which must resist analysis. The British Psychological Society's (BPS) *Code of Ethics* (2006) cites two formulations of Kant's Categorical Imperative as the basis of the code. In so doing it appeals to modernist notions of reason and universality. Yet, further on, it acknowledges the singular nature of many ethical dilemmas and how unyielding these can be to the application of universal principles, which resonates with postmodernist ideas of particularity and contingency. This reflects the sentiments in the quotation from James at the head of the chapter: we may keep trying to discover universal rules for moral behaviour, but we always seem to come across particular situations which make us question our rules.

So, our approach here is to take as our starting point the pluralist notion of ethical practice as an ongoing discourse – a debate or dialogue – which encompasses fundamental, age-old debates of right/wrong and good/evil, as well as modern questions of rights and responsibilities, the individual and society. The conception of ethics as an ongoing dialogue or discourse with many different viewpoints seems particularly apposite for assertive outreach: the team approach can create the ideal setting for a dialogue about the ethics of our practice, about the universal and the particular.

In this chapter we will consider some of the ethical difficulties that often confront the psychological practitioner working in assertive outreach. Issues such as paternalism, consent to treatment, therapeutic boundaries and compulsory treatment will be discussed with regard to the unique challenges raised by the nature of Assertive Community Treatment.

Paternalism

The accusation of paternalism in assertive outreach work (e.g. Spindel and Nugent, 2000; Williamson, 2002) is an obvious one to make. As an American import, Assertive Community Treatment (ACT) arrived in the UK with its baggage laden not only with glowing reports of the efficacy of the model, but also images of uniformed workers in official vehicles tracking down reluctant patients, either to medicate or hospitalise them. Although the model has been indigenised in Britain without this SWAT team approach, early reviews of the how the model was functioning (e.g. Priebe *et al.*, 2003) strongly favoured medical interventions, such as Clozapine deliveries, over explicitly psychological interventions. This apparent emphasis on 'same treatment, different location' has made it easier to caricature assertive outreach as coercive and denying clients their right to autonomy and self-determination.

In fact the original architects of assertive outreach (e.g. Stein and Test, 1978) were very far from being biological in their approach to working with people suffering from serious mental health problems, and we too have found that the reality of assertive outreach work is much more complex than the simplistic, paternalistic picture which may be painted by critics. It is absolutely true that issues of paternalism and disempowerment pervade what we do, in the much same way that they do for every worker in health and social care (Townsend, 1998). However, because of the very fine line that divides 'assertive' from 'coercive' these issues are much more of an obvious problem for us. And because it is obvious, addressing these issues becomes a more urgent task.

The issue of paternalism has been controversial at least since Hobbes' *Leviathan* (1651), with its notion of a social contract: the sacrifice of a portion of one's individual liberty to the sovereign or the state in order to maintain social stability and minimise the risk of a war of 'all against all' over scarce resources. Such risk management by the state has now extended to many areas of our lives: laws to make sure your car is roadworthy; laws to stop you taking certain recreational drugs; forcing employers to have regard for their workers' health and safety, and so on. In this light the Mental Health Act can be seen as a series of measures to protect the individual and others from the consequences of serious mental ill health, rather than a way of policing aberrant, socially unacceptable behaviour.

Certainly the genesis of assertive outreach in the UK took its cue from Stein's (op. cit.) original psycho-social approach in wishing to offer much needed help to a small group of the most vulnerable people in the country. In *Keys to Engagement* (1998) the Sainsbury Centre for Mental Health (SCMH) had this to say about the assertive outreach client group:

> There is a small but significant group of severely mentally ill people who have multiple, long-term needs and who cannot or do not wish to engage with services. Unless engagement is achieved and people in the group are provided with safe and effective services, they will continue to face social exclusion.
>
> (SCMH, 1998: 7)

And they said this about assertive outreach staff:

> The style of working by staff is key to engagement – they must be able to go out and meet people on their terms, in their normal environment. They must also be able to persist in this approach over considerable periods of time.
>
> (SCMH, 1998: 4)

Here paternalism is seen in its benevolent form – a service that focuses on engagement and building relationships and, moreover, explicitly takes account of clients' preferences. However, the report goes on to say that, although engagement is absolutely essential, 'unless [it] leads to acceptance and receipt of services, care and interventions, little will have been achieved' (op. cit.: 57). The document also lists the type of treatments and services that should be provided, with medication and medication concordance leading the list, and cognitive/behavioural interventions bringing up the rear.

So, while services should be patient-led, there still seems to be a lack of anything particularly new in the way of choices. This 'same treatment, different packaging' stance seems to be based on certain assumptions: that social inclusion is better than isolation; that the attempted achievement of mental wellness (i.e. an absence of psychotic/affective symptoms and attendant behaviours) through medication, as the main treatment, is better than accepting mental illness. Broadly speaking, the ethical subtext of the report is saying that nobody would choose madness and social exclusion and therefore benevolent paternalism is justified. From the perspective of someone who values sanity and inclusion, which includes the vast majority of the population, you have to broaden your mind considerably to think otherwise.

Example:
Steve lived rough, eschewing benefits, housing and support. He had previously been a client of the homelessness team, who had collectively decided that his lifestyle was freely chosen and had not attempted to interfere in this choice. When he was referred to the Assertive Outreach Team there was a protracted debate about whether Steve was mentally well enough to make this choice. As a team we decided to test the hypothesis that if Steve was mentally well he would not choose to live the life he was leading. Accordingly, we began to attempt a more assertive approach to working with him and began daily visits, eventually offering Olanzapine to Steve on a daily basis, which he freely took, as well as providing him with small amounts of money, food and a new, much warmer sleeping bag and tent. Over time we built relationships with Steve and he seemed to appreciate contact with the team, especially with his care co-ordinator.

We learned to respect the ways in which he put limits on our contact, but persisted with our intervention. He rarely exhibited any positive symptoms of schizophrenia, which was his diagnosis, apart from a certain guardedness, which could also be interpreted as a desire for privacy. Eventually Steve agreed to consider the possibility of temporary accommodation at the YMCA and shortly afterwards took up an offer of a room. This was the first roof that Steve had had over his head for many years. It emerged that he had family in another part of the country and he was eventually reunited with them. His family had assumed Steve was dead and they were very pleased to resume contact with him. Tragically Steve died soon after re-establishing contact with his family. He had begun to spend his newly acquired benefit money on vodka and seemed to have a fixed idea that he had to drink ¾ of a litre bottle in ¾ of an hour. He was admitted to A & E twice in the space of a few weeks after doing this, and shortly afterwards was found dead in a bus shelter from alcohol poisoning.

It could be argued that had we not intervened – or interfered – in Steve's life he might still be alive because when he was living rough he had no access to money to afford large quantities of alcohol. It could equally be argued that the last few months of his life were more positive, more comfortable, less lonely and more optimistic for him than they would have been without intervention.

In assertive outreach the team approach provides the ideal situation for generating dialogue about ethical practice as well as providing checks and balances against unsafe and unethical interventions (see chapter two). In the case of Steve we had many whole team discussions about the ethics of our intervention. The team members who were most involved with Steve really wrestled with the issues of choice, empowerment and the relative benefits of social inclusion and exclusion for people who find relationships very difficult to cope with. It was extremely important in this piece of work that we were open about our practice and the different ways in which we gently persuaded Steve to gradually move towards greater participation in society.

We consider that this whole team involvement in debates and decisions about ethical practice makes it much more likely that our approach to working with Steve was well thought through and contained the right balance between respect for autonomy and gentle, respectful persuasion. We think that we helped to bring Steve to a point where he was better able to make choices about his way of life. If at this point he had chosen to remain living rough we would have fully respected this decision. Indeed, if we had not respected his freedom to choose we would not have had such a positive working relationship with him. The risk of not doing anything, the risk of leaving people 'to rot', who may choose otherwise given a change in their circumstances, seems to be a much less ethical option.

So, while for the majority of our clients better health and social circumstances may be desirable outcomes, it is also important to acknowledge that for some people the treatments that are offered and/or the results of that treatment do not seem attractive enough for them to engage with services. It is in these instances where either paternalism in its malevolent form is apparent, as enforced and sometimes quite aggressive treatment against their will, or a psychological approach is considered. Given the BPS (2006) ethical diktat that all psychological treatment should be preceded by informed consent from the client, how is it then possible to practise ethically? The General Social Care Council (2002) and the Nursing and Midwifery Council (2004) codes of practice, for social care workers and nurses respectively, both balance the duty to respect the client's right to self-determination with the duty to protect the client and public from harm. It would be ironic indeed if, in the cases where they are most needed, psychological interventions were the only forms of treatment to be officially considered unethical.

Consent to treatment

> Informed consent is a process of sharing information with patients that is essential to their ability to make rational choices among multiple options in their perceived best interest.
>
> (Beahrs and Gutheil, 2001: 4)

The issue of consent to psychological treatment may seem at first glance to be relatively straightforward. In traditional adult services clients would be referred to a psychological practitioner who would offer them an appointment, explain their approach and reach an agreement with the client on those areas of their life that they would like to think about changing. Consent to treatment might then be inferred from the client's continued attendance or may be requested formally by the signing of a written consent form.

However, even with this apparently simple procedure there are issues that are not easily answered: does the client really know what they are consenting to? To what extent does the therapist know how the therapy will proceed and what the outcome will be?

> Within nearly any psychotherapeutic process, neither party knows at the outset in what directions the therapy might evolve, what information or understanding might unexpectedly emerge, what roadblocks the therapy will need to surmount, or what the final outcome will be.
>
> (op. cit.: 6)

For the assertive outreach client and practitioner these issues become ever more complex. Initially the work involves simply creating a relationship between the client and the team. Perkins and Repper (1996: 42) describe the process of establishing relationships with people with severe mental health difficulties as 'a delicate "wooing" of the client, ensuring that they can see some value in developing the relationship'. Hemming, Morgan and O'Halloran (1999) emphasise the development of trusting working relationships as a critical characteristic of assertive outreach work. Gray and Lavender (2001) describe how the development of this relationship is facilitated by the provision of practical help, holistic understanding, building rapport, responsiveness and the empowerment of clients through the provision of information.

At this early stage what is it that the client is consenting to? Superficially they are consenting to being given practical help and receiving contact from assertive outreach workers. This is not what would be traditionally conceived as 'psychological work'. However, a psychological understanding may be informing this process (see chapter four). For example, a formulation using attachment theory as a framework may guide the worker in the way that they attempt to engage with the client. Arguably, at this stage the client is not giving informed consent for a psychologist to be involved in their treatment.

An interesting perspective on this issue is provided by Nelson (1997) when considering the ethics of providing Cognitive Behaviour Therapy to someone who has a firmly held 'delusional' belief system. She argues that they will be unable to provide consent for their beliefs system to be modified, as they cannot conceive of another way of understanding the world other than their own. However, she also suggests that if their beliefs are causing them to suffer, or causing others to suffer, and the client will experience no disadvantage from a change to those beliefs, the psychologist is ethically justified in pursuing the treatment. Using this perspective one could argue that if the client is experiencing unwanted symptoms, or is behaving in such a way that they are being repeatedly readmitted to hospital against their will, using a psychological approach to inform an intervention aimed at improving their circumstances is justified.

It might also be argued that the social isolation endured by many people with severe mental health difficulties is arrived at as a result of fear, rather than an 'ability to make rational choices among multiple options'. Someone who is crippled by unusual experiences and unmanageable feelings probably does not perceive multiple options to choose from.

Psychotherapy by stealth?

There is also the issue of psychological therapists conducting generic work with clients as part of a team approach. This raises the potential problem of conducting 'therapy by stealth'; for example, is it possible for a psychologist to help someone do their shopping without being a psychologist or interacting with the client in a psychologically informed way? If 'being a psychologist' means offering explicitly psychological advice, interpretations and interventions, we would suggest that it's not possible and, therefore, it seems important for practitioners to be open and honest about their professional roles, to allow the client to decide whether this is a relationship that they wish to develop. However, consider the following:

Example:

I am standing with Adam, a client I know very well, outside a café. On the way to the café he tells me that he drank a bottle of whisky yesterday (he is a fairly serious binge drinker) and is feeling a bit 'delicate'. At the café doorway he vomits onto the pavement. 'Are you alright? Do you want to go back home?' I ask, concerned not only about Adam's physical state, but also the prospect of him being sick again in the café. 'Naah' he says, wiping his mouth. Then, by way of explanation he spits, 'F***ing Satan', and I know he means that Satan is inside his body, causing him to vomit. I smile slightly and ask, rather archly, whether he thinks there may be other explanations for him being sick? Adam grins at me, eyes watering, and says 'Open your mind, Paul' and I retort, laughing, 'Open yours, Adam!'

Adam is a man who made it very clear from the outset of our contact that he didn't want to talk about mental illness, and he is generally quite disparaging about all mental health professionals. By the time of the scene described, he had been informed of the roles of each of the team members who regularly visited him, and he had shared a lot of his quite unusual beliefs and mental experiences with me. However, although he appreciated the contact with our team, we were very cautious when offering or discussing more formal interventions, such as appointments with the psychiatrist or medication, because his worldview tended to make him suspicious of people, particularly professionals.

It is possible to describe my input here as a basic cognitive challenge, and I certainly spoke with the purpose of highlighting the absurdity of Adam's attributing his vomiting to the action of Satan, rather than making the quite obvious link to the large amount of alcohol he had consumed the day before. So, is this 'psychological treatment' and has he consented? We would suggest that in instances such as these, where the client has consented to contact and relationships are sufficiently developed, it is possible to apply the logic of Nelson (ibid.) and interact with clients according to our role as workers.

Direct psychological interventions

Alternatively, once the client has established a working relationship with other members of the team, it may be appropriate to discuss with them the option of direct psychological intervention. The psychological therapist might then be introduced to the client and offer an explanation of the types of input they could offer. Often this can be a useful conversation, as it allows the client to identify certain problems they experience, but might have difficulty raising. For example, the therapist may explain that one area therapists commonly work with involves helping people who have unusual experiences, such as hearing voices, that they find disturbing. Some clients may respond enthusiastically and with apparent relief, on discovering that these are experiences they can talk to someone about. Others might feel unable to talk about this with someone they hardly know, and will need to wait until a relationship is more established before they feel safe enough to share some of their worrying experiences. Issues of abuse or other past traumas can take much longer to surface. As Beahrs and Gutheil (2001) argue, how can either client or therapist really know what they are embarking upon at the outset of therapy and, therefore, can consent ever be truly informed?

In a sense, assertive outreach clients are already a part of a system that is involved with their lives regardless of their consent. The safety of the client and the public as protected by the Mental Health Act means that most clients have already received mental health services without consent. Assertive Outreach Teams are at least endeavouring to encourage a more two-way process of engagement, and one which empowers the client. But is it acceptable for us to be paternalistic and to override the problem of informed consent, or at least to enter into a relationship whose main aim is to change the client in some sort of predetermined way, because we think that whatever we are offering is better than what clients currently have? This is a tough question for people who are attracted to working with this client group and who may be able to empathise with the client's rejection of inclusion and socially defined 'sanity'. Nevertheless, it is an important question to address, as the assumption underlies the foundations of this type of service.

However, where specific interventions are concerned it is important to remain mindful that the client is not simply a passive recipient of treatment; they can, and often do, choose to vote with their feet and avoid contact.

It seems that the process of engagement involves repeated negotiation of consent at each stage, with an injunction upon the psychological practitioner to be as transparent and open about their motives and methods as possible. With assertive outreach clients' consent may simply mean permission to have a conversation or to permit a relationship; for some this may be the most frightening step of all.

Therapeutic relationships and boundaries

The relationship between assertive outreach workers and clients often unfolds in unlikely settings and can be unusual in terms of the time spent, and the tasks undertaken. People might be seen at home, in their local café, launderette, snooker hall, in a park or any number of other settings. The visit may consist of a very brief medication delivery or it could involve the worker spending a whole day or more with a client. One example of the latter was a worker accompanying a client to another county to visit the client's daughter. This involved an overnight stay and two long car journeys. The issue of therapeutic boundaries, therefore, becomes both vital and complex.

In relation to the issue of boundaries, the BPS *Code of Conduct* (2006) only speaks about 'refraining from engaging in any form of sexual or romantic relationship' with clients. The Nursing and Midwifery Council (NMC) and

General Social Care Council (GSCC) codes of practice go into more detail, stating that therapeutic relationships should 'focus exclusively on the needs of the patient or client' (NMC, 2004: 5) and that workers should responsibly recognise and use 'the power that comes from your work with service users and carers' (GSCC, 2002: item 4.4).

Self-disclosure

Different models of therapy have very different approaches to personal boundaries and self-disclosure. At the one extreme is the psychoanalytic 'blank screen' of the therapist about whom the client knows very little; at the other the more open relationship encouraged by the CBT practitioner, particularly in rehabilitation work. In therapeutic relationships the guiding rule involves consideration of whether personal information is being disclosed for the sake of the client or the worker. In assertive outreach the additional consideration is whether to disclose for the sake of the relationship, which is arguably for the sake of the client in the longer term.

The development of the relationship with people with severe mental health difficulties, the 'wooing', means that personal disclosure is often at a far greater level than that in other areas of work. Workers have described how their clients often require this as a prerequisite to developing a relationship (Gray and Lavender, 2001) and they explain how providing some personal information can have a hugely beneficial effect on the relationship.

> ... as long as I feel comfortable ... things that others may consider taboos I'd be quite happy to talk about ... as a student I used to smoke the odd bit of dope so that's actually quite under-rated, people knowing you've had that kind of experience in the past.
>
> (Gray and Lavender, 2001: 57)

However, the increased level of disclosure, combined with the lack of office-based appointments, means that attention to the boundaries of the relationship becomes, arguably, even more important than in other types of mental health work. The use of the whole team working can help protect against the relationship between individual workers and clients becoming too involved (see chapter two). However, the reality of the work often means that a client will prefer, and develop, a closer relationship to one or two workers. This can have benefits in terms of establishing what attachment theorists would call a secure base (Bowlby, 1969) which provides the client with a sense of safety and stability from which to take risks and explore other relationships. However, there are fine lines between disclosing enough personal information to the client to facilitate a helpful relationship, whilst not disclosing so much that the relationship becomes about meeting the worker's needs, or disclosing information that subsequently makes the worker feel uncomfortable.

The way in which the relationship is defined can also be somewhat different from that of more traditional forms of mental health work. Gray and Lavender (2001: 58) describe interviews with assertive outreach staff, in which they express the belief that, whilst the clients knew the relationship was a professional one, they often preferred to think of workers as being like friends or relatives, or as one worker put it, '. . . she likes to see me in terms of being her personal assistant'.

Because of the type of relationship that assertive outreach staff have with their clients, there is clearly a risk that boundaries can become blurred and relationships too intense, as they start to lose their professional nature. This is an issue that must be examined in supervision, with both supervisor and supervisee remembering that often the clients who get discussed most are those with whom relationships are difficult and tenuous, or who present the highest levels of risk. It could be easy, given the level of complexity and anxiety being worked with, to allow those relationships that are easier to go unexamined for too long. For some clients assertive outreach workers may be the only people with whom they have a current relationship. It can be easy to underestimate the importance of the relationship to the client, or perhaps to the worker, or even to miss the way in which the relationship is being construed, until it is too late to renegotiate the boundaries without harm being done.

Dependency, intimacy and loss

Even within a relationship that retains its professional boundaries, the issue of dependence is important and difficult to address. In the early stages of engagement, the workers do everything they can, respecting professional boundaries, to make themselves useful to clients. As time passes the clients often develop strong attachments to the workers, and vice versa. For some clients, in the absence of relationships with family or friends, or where these relationships are often fraught with tension and are not perceived as secure and supportive, the relationship with one or more workers in the team can become something of a lifeline. In this sense, to an extent, there is a period during the development of the engagement where we actively encourage a degree of dependence on the team.

One of the aims of the team approach is to minimise the tendency for clients to become overly dependent upon one worker (see chapter two). However, our experience is that clients can, and do, develop very strong attachments to individual workers, which are not the same as the dependence that they may feel towards the team as a whole. Inevitably, those clients have been severely affected when one or more of those workers have left the job. This may be considered an unavoidable part of the work, but the emotional impact can at least be buffered by taking certain steps. Firstly, to ensure that the client is visited every week by two or three workers so that even if they have a preference for one, they become equally familiar with several others. Secondly, if a worker knows that they will either be leaving the job or taking extended leave, how and when this is explained to the client is thought about at length by the team. In our experience it is not as simple as applying the normal rules of ending within psychotherapy practice, i.e. explaining the ending at the earliest opportunity and returning often to explore the person's feelings about this. Whilst this will be appropriate with some people, for others the intense emotions aroused might be too much to tolerate and could trigger a crisis. We need to expect at these times for some people to use 'unhelpful' coping strategies such as increased alcohol or drug use and care needs to be taken as to how this is addressed. Each individual needs to be considered within supervision and a uniquely tailored approach must be devised, taking into account all that is known about the client, in an attempt to make the loss more manageable.

We have had continued debates within our team about the ethics of allowing relationships to develop in such a way that a high level of closeness and intimacy is inevitable, in a context where someone perhaps has little hope of developing other intimate or romantic relationships in the near future. One side of this argument is that what we are doing is somewhat cruel, by showing our clients what they haven't got in their own world. The counter argument is that if the desire for a close relationship without professional boundaries comes to exist this may be the spur to action to make life changes in order to achieve this. However, these issues make it even clearer why the provision of strong and clear professional boundaries is vital to help keep clients safe within their relationships to team members.

In practice we have found that certain structures can help with maintaining a professional frame around the relationship, for example clients know our working hours and we never arrange to meet them outside those times unless sanctioned by the team in exceptional circumstances, such as overnight working; if the team is lending money to a client we ask the client to sign a receipt; when spending money on clients we always ask for receipts.

Confidentiality

Generally Assertive Outreach Teams offer team, not individual, confidentiality. In practice this can be more difficult than it might at first sound. When working psychologically with someone, I would not always share very sensitive information with the wider team if I didn't feel it was necessary for them to know. However, risk issues are always shared and this is explained to the client, both at the start of any work and as the need arises. As the therapeutic relationship develops it seems that clients can forget that certain information gets shared with the team and when this becomes clear it can be awkward for the practitioner and upsetting for the client. In addition, if we think that a client may be becoming increasingly risky to either themselves or others, there can be a dilemma about how much to push the client to disclose.

Example:
My client Jane is attending a psychology session; this is the tenth time that we have met and she has become more comfortable in the sessions and with the relationship. Everyone who sees Jane, including the psychiatrist, believes that the voices she used to hear have subsided since she began taking medication. This is important, as three years ago, whilst experiencing command hallucinations, Jane jumped in front of a car narrowly avoiding injury to herself but causing the car to crash and the driver to sustain minor injuries. In the session she confides in me that the voices have not gone away but she feels that they have less power over her; she would like to talk to me about them, but worries that if I share this information with the team that she will be hospitalised again.

The dilemma here is that speaking about the voices in the context of a trusting relationship would most likely be very therapeutic for Jane. It could assist in the development of strategies that might, in the long term, help Jane to manage her relationship with the voices and reduce the future risk to both herself and others. If confidentiality is breached and the information shared, Jane may never again feel able to share her thoughts and experiences in this way. The damage could be minimised if others involved in Jane's care felt able to tolerate the situation and show Jane that she would not be immediately detained under these circumstances; indeed such a response could help Jane to develop an increased sense of trust in the team as a whole. However, it is impossible to know for sure what the response of other team members will be and the danger is that, in the long term, Jane's risk could be increased as she learns to keep her experiences to herself, so missing out on potential help.

The difficulty in deciding how much to share, and with whom, is reflected within note keeping, where practitioners need to consider how much information they record in shared notes. It can be helpful to share any reports with the client and ask their opinion before incorporating them into files, encouraging clients to add their own perspectives, especially if there is an area they disagree with. Whilst this should be possible within a well-developed relationship, in the fragile early stages of a relationship there are times when such openness may not seem possible. All these dilemmas need to be given careful thought and should be shared within clinical supervision.

Further problems with confidentiality involve balancing the needs and rights of the clients with the concerns and, sometimes, frustrations of their family, friends and neighbours. At times the team can be on the receiving end of much anger and resentment from the wider community as we help clients to stay in their accommodation during episodes of crisis. Previously, family and neighbours would have seen someone being admitted to hospital, often under section, and it can seem as though the assertive outreach approach is uncaring. It can also be considerably less convenient to relatives to have someone supported at home during a crisis than have them removed to hospital.

At such times the team can be put under pressure to share information, which the client is not willing to share, about why a Mental Health Act assessment is not being undertaken, or why it has not resulted in someone being detained. The lack of information can be frustrating for concerned parties and in these situations we have found that a standard letter of response, explaining the laws surrounding the Mental Health Act and confidentiality, can be helpful.

There is also the need to be sensitive to client confidentiality when you are meeting in public places. Difficulties can arise if a conversation becomes more personal and emotional in a very public space, such as a busy café. In such circumstances, whenever possible, our practice is to suggest to the client that it might be better for us to move to a quieter setting, since other people might overhear our conversation.

Medication, detaining people and compulsory treatment

The use of medication to treat mental distress is perhaps the most controversial area of mental health care. On the one hand, the power and influence of pharmaceutical companies in setting the mental health agenda is a source of serious ethical discomfort (Shooter, 2005; Sharfstein, 2005). There is also significant doubt about the mechanism and efficacy of medications (Valenstein, 1998; Hopper and Wanderling, 2000) and, perhaps most controversially, people diagnosed with a mental illness risk having pharmacological treatments forced upon them against their will:

> Involuntary treatment is extremely rare outside the psychiatric system, allowable only in such cases as unconsciousness or the inability to communicate. People with psychiatric disabilities, on the other hand, even when they vigorously protest treatments they do not want, are routinely subjected to them anyway, on the justification that they 'lack insight' or are unable to recognize their need for treatment because of their 'mental illness'. In practice, 'lack of insight' becomes disagreement with the treating professional, and people who disagree are labeled 'non-compliant' or 'uncooperative with treatment'. After years of contact with a system that routinely does not recognize their preferences or desires, many people with psychiatric disabilities become resigned to their fate and cease to protest openly. Although this is described in the psychiatric literature as 'compliance', it is actually learned helplessness (also known as 'internalized oppression') that is incompatible with hope and with the possibility of recovery.
>
> (National Council on Disability, 2000: 11)

On the other hand, many people with serious mental illness obtain significant symptom reduction from medication, leading to a less marginalised existence. Burns and Firn (2002) consider that the more effective and beneficial assertive outreach interventions are those which bring about better medication compliance. There is increasing evidence that early medical treatment for psychosis can minimise the risk of chronicity (Birchwood *et al.*, 1998). Such early interventions can be seen as 'humane' and 'ethical' (Singh and Fisher, 2005: 72). However, this is contradicted by some of the cross-cultural evidence reviewed by Warner (1994) and Hopper and Wanderling (2000) which suggests that in some pre-industrial societies, people who have experiences that would be diagnosed as schizophrenia in the West have a better long-term prognosis without any medication or input from mental health services.

Clinicians need to consider how to approach the issue of medication and whether to take a position which encourages adherence. Our experience is that it only becomes possible for us to express an opinion regarding medication adherence once we have known a client during periods when they have been taking medication and when they have not. I know some people to whom I can honestly say that my experience of them is that they appear much better able to manage the demands of life when they are taking medication and I can give them examples of this. There are others for whom I have seen no such benefit and should they ask my opinion I would give it, both to them and to the doctors involved in their care. The psychological practitioner may therefore at times act as an advocate in negotiations with the prescribing physician if the client wishes to reduce or stop taking the medication.

Many clients of Assertive Outreach Teams are said to have chronic, 'treatment resistant' mental disorders, which tends to indicate that medications have not achieved significant symptom reduction, although they are still asked to take them. Psychologists are not the only professionals to feel compromised when pharmacological treatments are emphasised, especially in situations where they don't seem to be having a beneficial effect. Social workers, occupational therapists, and community support workers as well as many medically trained professionals may consider that other approaches need to be given greater consideration where biological interventions have been so thoroughly rejected by particular clients.

In assertive outreach this issue becomes more pressing as the team approach, and the focus on engagement, place far more emphasis on generic working. A psychological practitioner may be asked to make medication deliveries as part of their generic role. Different practitioners need to make their own decision about how they choose to approach this issue. Some choose to retain a distance from medication whilst others are more willing to contend with the issue. It may be that taking medication to a client, without adopting an opinion about whether or not they should take it, allows for a conversation about their feelings towards medication that otherwise does not arise.

The revised Mental Health Act (Department of Health, 2007) has implications for both Assertive Outreach Teams and those who work in them: the introduction of Community Treatment Orders allows clients to be discharged from hospital on certain conditions, such as the continued use of medication. There is also a new provision for practitioners other than approved social workers to be involved in Mental Health Act Assessments, a task that could be undertaken by psychological therapists.

There has been vigorous debate about the role of psychologists (e.g. Pilgrim, 2005; Johnstone, 2006; Harper, 2006) in the compulsory detention of people with acute mental distress. Psychology does not easily fit into the current social and biological framework that shapes debate over compulsory detention. Social work has an explicitly social or societal view and therefore protecting society, as well as the individual, is part and parcel of the job. For a medically trained professional, someone who has become so unwell that they are unable to make sound decisions about their own and others' welfare needs to be treated, in order that they may regain their capacity to make autonomous decisions. Psychology has tended to steer clear of the social and biological aspects of mental illness, but it could prove to be very valuable for psychologists to step more fully into the arena of compulsory detention and widen the parameters of the debate.

It is always worth remembering that once a client is discharged from hospital, Community Treatment Order notwithstanding, they can simply disappear from view should they choose. Morgan (2000) cautions against the use of more coercive powers by arguing that they simply increase the levels of risk that Assertive Outreach Teams were designed to try to reduce. If our agenda is perceived as being about enforcing medication, clients may once again disengage from services and risk becoming socially isolated, resulting in increased distress. With no one to observe the deterioration in their mental state, the risk to themselves and others once again increases. Therefore, it may become increasingly incumbent on psychological practitioners to use their formulation skills to present arguments to the team as to why enforced medication may do more harm than good. Such arguments may be perceived as more powerful if psychological practitioners take more of a central role in formal admissions to hospital.

Our experience suggests that many clients do become so mentally disturbed that they present a serious risk of harm to themselves or other people. In such instances we are often left with only one option which is hospital, and only one method of achieving this: formal admission under the Mental Health Act. Compulsory admission and treatment run so counter to ethical principles of personal autonomy, liberty and consent that this commonplace occurrence in assertive outreach work often feels like failure.

However, this may not always be the case: we are reminded of a client we worked with who continued to have repeated admissions under section three in spite of considerable, whole-team, wholehearted efforts to prevent this. In the course of a team discussion the senior social worker suggested that perhaps compulsory admission was the client's way of managing mental disturbance – a way of ensuring containment – and that maybe we should cease to see admission as defeat and adjust our input to facilitate this, rather than fight against it. That the team could embrace this suggestion demonstrates how assertive outreach work can present opportunities to fully engage with each situation and create unique approaches for unique problems.

Conclusions

Clearly, the ethical considerations surrounding the provision of psychological treatment to assertive outreach clients can be highly complex. Whilst we are not providing answers, we are explaining the position from which we feel able to undertake the work; perhaps for others the ethical concerns would prove too problematic. It seems important to examine our underlying assumptions about mental health, social inclusion, social control, suffering and unhappiness. We work from a position of believing that human relationships are important; that social inclusion is necessary, or at least for an individual to be in a position from which to make a choice about whether to engage with wider society rather than to be marginalised from it, owing to forces beyond their control. We acknowledge that we live in a society with certain constraints and demands and whilst one way to address this is to engage politically with that society to try and change it, another concurrent way is to acknowledge those constraints and try to help people work within them or, at least, recognise them for what they are.

We accept that sometimes we will find ourselves working without the client's express consent, but that our aim is to bring those clients to a position of greater clarity, where their basic needs of shelter, food, clothing and money are met, sometimes using a psychological approach to enable this to happen. At this point we suggest that they can make an informed choice. We have had clients who, at this point, have chosen not to continue working with us, and others who have been grateful for the help and have chosen to embrace a life within the confines of societal norms, and many who fall somewhere in between. At times our work, and our underlying beliefs about it, bring us into conflict with our clients, with wider society and with each other. However, working from within a well-functioning team, which can tolerate and even enjoy discussion and conflict, provides a forum within which we can explore these 'universes without a precedent'. Reflecting on these struggles as they take place within an Assertive Outreach Team illuminates the way that these questions can, at times, be ignored or marginalised within mainstream services. It is, to some extent, the ethical basis of traditional services that our clients have rejected; the ethics of professional boundaries which result in a straightforward dynamic of helper to helped, professional to client; the ethics of defining reality and discussing whether another person has 'insight' into it; and the ethics of the power that resides with us, as mental health professionals, over the lives of others. The challenge which our clients pose to us embraces both the theoretical and the personal and can greatly enrich our practice, expanding our professional and ethical world views.

References

Barnett, C. (1986) *The Audit of War: the illusion and reality of Britain as a Great Nation*, London: Macmillan.

Beahrs, J.O. and Gutheil, T.G. (2001) 'Informed consent in psychotherapy', *American Journal of Psychiatry*, 158: 4–10.

Birchwood, M., Todd, P. and Jackson, C. (1998) 'Early intervention in psychosis. The critical period hypothesis', *British Journal of Psychiatry Supplement*, 172: 53–59.

Bowlby, J (1969) *Attachment and Loss: Vol. 1 Attachment*, New York: Basic Books.

British Psychological Society (2006) *Code of Ethics and Conduct*, Leicester: BPS.

Burns, T. and Firn, M. (2002) *Assertive Outreach in Mental Health: a manual for practitioners*, Oxford: Oxford University Press.

Department of Health (2007) *Mental Health Act*, London: Department of Health.

Foucault, M. (2006) *History of Madness*, trans. J. Murphy and J. Khalfa, London: Routledge.

General Social Care Council (2002) *Code of Practice for Social Care Workers*, London: GSCC.

Gray, A.S. and Lavender, A. (2001) 'Relationships with clients who find it difficult to engage', unpublished paper.

Harper, D. (2006) 'Some problems with the case for psychologists becoming clinical supervisors: a response to Pilgrim and others', *Clinical Psychology Forum*, 168: 7–12.

Hemming, M., Morgan, S. and O'Halloran, P. (1999) 'Assertive outreach: implications for the development of the model in the United Kingdom', *Journal of Mental Health*, 18: 141–147.

Hobbes, T. (1651; OUP edition 1998) *Leviathan*, Oxford: Oxford University Press.

Hopper, K. and Wanderling, J. (2000) 'Revisiting the developed versus developing country distinction in course and outcome in schizophrenia: results from ISOS, the WHO collaborative follow-up project', *Schizophrenia Bulletin*, 26: 835–846.

James, W. (1891) 'The moral philosopher and the moral life', *International Journal of Ethics*, 1: 330–354.

Johnstone, L. (2006) 'Clinical psychologists as supervisors', *Clinical Psychology Forum* (correspondence), 157: 1.

Morgan, S. (2000) 'Risk-making or risk-taking?', *Openmind*, 101: 16–17.

National Council on Disability (2000) *From Privileges to Rights: people labeled with psychiatric disabilities speak for themselves*, Washington, DC: NCD.

Nelson, H. (1997) *Cognitive Therapy with Schizophrenia*, Cheltenham: Stanley Thornes Ltd.

Nursing and Midwifery Council (2004) *NMC Code of Professional Conduct: standards for conduct, performance and ethics*, London: NMC.

Perkins, R. and Repper, J.M. (1996) *Working Alongside People with Long Term Mental Health Problems*, Gloucester: Stanley Thornes.

Pilgrim, D. (2005) 'A case for psychologists becoming clinical supervisors', *Clinical Psychology Forum*, 155: 4–7.

Priebe, S., Fakoury, W., Watts, J., Bebbington, P., Burns, T., Johnson, S., Muijen, M., Ryrie, I., White, I. and Wright, C. (2003) 'Assertive outreach teams in London: patient characteristics and outcomes: Pan-London Assertive Outreach Study, part 3', *The British Journal of Psychiatry*, 183: 148–154.

Sainsbury Centre for Mental Health (1998) *Keys to Engagement*, London: SCMH.

Sharfstein, S. (2005) 'Big pharma and American psychiatry: the good, the bad and the ugly', *Psychiatric News*, 40: 3.

Shooter, M. (2005) 'Dancing with the Devil? A personal view of psychiatry's relationships with the pharmaceutical industry', *Psychiatric Bulletin*, 29: 81–83.

Singh, S.P. and Fisher, H.L. (2005) 'Early intervention in psychosis: obstacles and opportunities', *Advances in Psychiatric Treatment*, 11: 71–78.

Spindel, T. and Nugent, J. (2000) 'Polar opposites: empowerment philosophy and assertive community treatment (ACT)', *Ethical Human Sciences and Services*, 2: 93–101.

Spitzer, S. (1975) 'Toward a Marxian theory of deviance', *Social Problems*, 22: 638–651.

Stein, L. I. and Test, M. A. (eds) (1978) *Alternatives to Mental Hospital Treatment*, New York: Plenum Press.

Szasz, T. (1974) *The Myth of Mental Illness: foundations of a theory of personal conduct*, New York: Harper and Row.

Townsend, E. (1998) *Good Intentions Overruled: a critique of empowerment in the routine organisation of mental health services*, Toronto: University of Toronto Press.

Valenstein, E. (1998) *Blaming the Brain*, New York: The Free Press.

Warner, R. (1994) *Recovery from Schizophrenia: psychiatry and political economy*, 2nd edn, London: Routledge.

Williamson, T. (2002) 'Ethics of assertive outreach', *Current Opinion in Psychiatry*, 15: 543–547.

Yalom, I. (1989) *Love's Executioner and Other Tales of Psychotherapy*, London: Penguin Books.

Conclusions

Caroline Cupitt

The aim of this book was to convince the reader of the need for a psychological approach to assertive outreach. All too often services for people with psychosis and complex mental health difficulties are dominated by medical approaches imposing biological accounts of illness. Although assertive outreach originally grew out of a critique of such medical dominance, ironically in recent years assertive outreach has gained a reputation for promoting it. We hope that this book goes some small way towards correcting this drift, and returning assertive outreach to its psychosocial roots.

At the centre of the task of assertive outreach is the concept of engagement. At its best this can be seen as a helpful extension of the related concept of therapeutic alliance, which places the relationship between staff and service users at the centre of all mental health interventions. However, when the term 'difficult to engage' comes to be used like a diagnosis, locating the difficulty within the person, it fails to capture the need for services to change. Most difficulties in engagement arise because of the failure of services to understand and provide for the particular needs of individuals. Good assertive outreach must therefore place a high emphasis on psychological assessment and formulation so that a service can be both individualised and sensitive. In addition the use of a team approach recognises the need for reliable human relationships to form the bedrock of the service, in all their diverse forms.

For staff who work in assertive outreach, part of the motivation for this particular model is the possibility of working very closely with people on the practical, emotional and social realities of their lives. The closeness of the relationships that can develop between staff and service users can be both the strength of the model and also the greatest challenge. For in getting close to the realities of people's lives, staff can become overwhelmed, lose hope or find that emotional issues from their own past are triggered. A psychological approach therefore seeks not only to offer those who use the services of assertive outreach a high quality of care, but also to support the staff whose long-term commitment is needed.

In trying to summarise the contribution that psychological approaches make to assertive outreach, one theme in particular emerges. Over and over again in each chapter the authors have suggested that for these teams to be effective they need to be able to stop and think; to resist the rush to react to their clients' distress, and instead to reflect on the person's history, relationships, family and social context. They also need to create spaces for team members to identify and process their own emotional reactions. The majority of people referred to Assertive Outreach Teams have already experienced the well-intended crisis interventions of many services, but they are unlikely to have experienced the careful reflections of a whole team who both know them and care about their long-term future. It is this capacity to stay still in a storm, and understand the complexities of people's lives, that can really make assertive outreach effective when other services have failed. The chapters of this book have demonstrated how much psychologists can contribute to developing this reflective capacity.

No account of assertive outreach is complete without reflection on the ethical aspects of delivering a service to people who have not overtly requested it. For some even the idea of offering psychological interventions in these circumstances remains unthinkable. However, whilst the users of assertive outreach may have rejected mainstream mental health services, this does not necessarily mean that they do not wish to access emotional support. If assertive outreach is viewed as a genuine response to people's needs and wants, not only must the service as a whole be psychologically sophisticated, but psychological therapies must form a large part of the service provided.

Finally, it is our hope that in the future research into assertive outreach will pay more attention to psychological factors. Rather than judge a service by the numbers of hospital admissions in its first year of operation, it may be more meaningful to look at whether teams foster hope and positive long-term relationships, as defined by people using the service.

Index